INDEPENDENT
JUSTICE

INDEPENDENT
JUSTICE

THE FEDERAL
SPECIAL PROSECUTOR
IN AMERICAN POLITICS

Katy J. Harriger

University Press of Kansas

© 1992 by the University Press of Kansas
All rights reserved

Published by the University Press of Kansas (Lawrence, Kansas
66049), which was organized by the Kansas Board of Regents and is
operated and funded by Emporia State University, Fort Hays State
University, Kansas State University, Pittsburg State University,
the University of Kansas, and Wichita State University

Library of Congress Cataloging-in-Publication Data

Harriger, Katy Jean.
Independent justice : the federal special prosecutor in American
politics / Katy Jean Harriger.
p.   cm.
Includes bibliographical references (p.   ) and index.
ISBN 0-7006-0535-5 (hardcover)
1. Special prosecutors—United States.   2. Misconduct in office—
United States.   3. Conflict of interests—United States.
4. Separation of powers—United States.   5. United States—Politics
and government—20th century.   I. Title.
KF4568.H37   1992
345.73'01—dc20
[347.3051]   91-39258

British Library Cataloguing in Publication Data is available.

Printed in the United States of America
10 9 8 7 6 5 4 3 2 1

FOR AARON AND BOB

CONTENTS

PREFACE

Archibald Cox and Richard Nixon. These two men represented the potential for good and evil in a political world I, a teenager during the summer of 1973, understood only slightly. Cox stood for the rule of law, Nixon for the abuse of power. When Nixon fired Cox that October my unquestioning faith in the constitutional system faltered. When Nixon was forced to resign the next year it was restored. My interest in the Constitution began that summer, and Watergate became, as it did for so many, a transforming event in my political socialization. My faith in the system is not so unquestioning anymore nor my view of good and evil so simplistic. But my desire to understand the American constitutional system continues. This desire drew me to specialize in public law in graduate school and sustained my interest in this project. The use of special prosecutors in American politics reveals much about the importance of the rule of law and the suspicion of those in power that are a part of our national psyche. It also teaches us about the separation of powers and the checks and balances around which our system is structured.

In this book I examine the use of special prosecutors within the framework of the separation of powers. I seek to understand the way in which that office has interacted with the other actors in the American political and legal system and the extent to which these relationships enhance or inhibit the ability of special prosecutors to conduct the investigation assigned to them. In pursuing these questions, I adopted two primary methods of research. One was to seek out all of the documentary evidence available from special prosecutor investigations. The other was to interview the various actors involved in the process.

As with any research design, the choices one makes about the questions to ask both enlighten and obscure. By choosing the institutional approach I lost something of the people involved. With the exception of Theodore Olson, I did not interview any of the targets of the investigations; I chose rather to interview their defense attorneys. I decided that this would enhance the understanding I sought of legal actors while still giving some voice to the position of the target. These attorneys provided insight into the legal questions I wanted answered, and they acted as empassioned advocates for their clients. They were certainly more detached from the case than their clients no doubt would have been, but they nonetheless urged me to consider the effect that these investigations had on their clients' personal lives.

As this book was being completed, the story of the Iran-Contra scandal continued to unfold. During the summer of 1991 the investigation was rejuvenated by the guilty plea of former CIA official Alan Fiers. The new hearings on whether Oliver North's convictions were based on any of his immunized testimony had not yet been held. Consequently, my coverage of the Iran-Contra scandal is based almost completely on secondary sources. The story of Iran-Contra is not over. But a better understanding of both the strengths and weaknesses of independent investigation and prosecution can only add to the assessment of that investigation at its conclusion.

I am grateful for the intellectual, financial, and personal help that I have received from so many while working on this book. The many people involved in the special prosecutor process who gave me their time for interviews and the benefits of their experience are listed in the bibliography. Many of them will not agree with my conclusions, but I appreciate the time they took from very busy schedules and their candid responses to my questions. I have also benefited from the comments and criticisms made by colleagues at professional meetings, anonymous reviewers of an early draft, and Louis Fisher and Richard Pious, who reviewed the book for the University Press of Kansas.

At different stages of this project I have received financial help from the Richard D. Irwin Foundation and the Archie Fund for Faculty Excellence at Wake Forest University. I could not have completed this book without the research leave I received from Wake Forest in the fall of 1989.

Elide Vargas, Patrick Auld, Kristin Terchek, and Anne Jones provided me with substantial help in library research and in the preparation of the manuscript. I am grateful also to Mike Briggs at the University Press of Kansas for his support, encouragement, and advice. I thank my colleagues in the Department of Politics at Wake Forest for giving me the time to finish this, and especially Jack Fleer, for always believing that I would finish it. Of course, I owe the most to my husband and son, who bore the costs of the time and attention that had to be directed to research and writing. It is to them that I dedicate this book.

ONE

THE SPECIAL PROSECUTOR AND
THE SEPARATION OF POWERS

The problem of ensuring that officials act with integrity in serving the public is an enduring one. Official misconduct is particularly troublesome in a democratic republic. In a government dependent upon citizen support and confidence, it seems essential that citizens perceive their officials to be honest and concerned with the public good. In a system that rests on accountability to the public, it is equally important that there be means to ensure that public trust, once granted, is not abused. James Madison identified this concern when he wrote: "If men were angels, no government would be necessary. If angels were to govern men, neither external nor internal controls on government would be necessary. In framing a government which is to be administered by men over men, the great difficulty lies in this: you must first enable the government to control the governed, and in the next, oblige it to control itself."[1] Madison's solution for controlling the governors was to structure a government of separation of powers, of checks and balances. "A dependence on the people is, no doubt, the primary control on the government;" he wrote, "but experience has taught mankind the necessity of auxiliary precautions."[2]

Recognizing the importance of citizen confidence in the resolution of public corruption cases, three twentieth-century American presidents have responded by providing for special prosecutors to pursue independent investigations into major national political scandals. After the Watergate scandal of the early seventies Congress used Madison's argument for "auxiliary precautions" to create a statutory arrangement that provided for judicial appointment of a temporary special prosecutor to investigate allegations against high level executive branch officials.[3] Between 1978 and 1990 independent counsel were publicly[4] appointed in nine cases under this arrangement.

The use of an independent special prosecutor is rooted in the ongoing problem of political influence, leading to possible corruption, in the administration of justice. The institution of special prosecutor has had several formulations, varying in jurisdiction, appointment method, and degree of independence from the executive. The common characteristic has been its removal from the established law enforcement chain of command in order to make an impartial investigation more likely.

THE PROBLEM OF POLITICIZED JUSTICE

How is it that justice becomes politicized? In discussing the problem of political influence in the distribution of justice it is essential that we first acknowledge the necessary, inevitable, and desirable connections between the legal and political processes. The laws of a society are written, interpreted, and enforced within a political system by political actors. Some of these actors—judges, for example—may be less overtly political than others. Nonetheless, we have long understood that the legal system is a subsystem of the political system. In fact, it has been suggested that "one cannot comprehend American law without understanding its roots in American politics."[5] This general political control of the legal process is desirable to the extent that it ensures accountability on the part of legal actors and brings the popular will to bear on the distribution of justice. The connections between politics and law should be viewed as natural and beneficial in a democracy.

The idea that politics shapes law becomes more problematic as we move away from "politics as system" explanations to "politics as power and influence" explanations. In this context politics and law frequently seem to be opposites instead of natural partners: "Law seems dignified whereas politics seems seamy. Law appears predictable whereas politics seems typified by the unexpected. Law seems to search for justice while politics seems to seek the expedient."[6] Beyond these popular conceptions, the idea of justice being driven by politics conflicts with values deeply rooted in constitutionalism. If justice is "political," then those with the ability to be successful politically are more likely to find "justice" than those without political influence, a notion in clear conflict with "an image of justice in which the rule of law prevails and equal treatment is accorded each person."[7]

If we look at the federal criminal justice system in operation we can see both the positive, inevitable connections and the more problematic ones between the American political and legal systems. Federal criminal investigation and prosecution do not occur in a political vacuum, however much we might wish that they did. The criminal justice system is political because "it is engaged in the formulation and administration of public policies in which choices must be made among . . . competing values."[8] The federal criminal law, written for the most part by Congress, is a reflection of the nation's desire to consider some behaviors as affronts to societal norms. The officers charged with the enforcement of these laws (the president, the attorney general, his subordinates, and various others) are political actors in that they are answerable, either directly or indirectly, to the electorate. In theory this electoral check, as well as various others structured into the separation of powers system, holds the enforcers of the law accountable for the faithful execution of the laws.

In practice, the constitutionally structured checks on law enforcement do not make these actors immune to the "seamy" side of politics. The president and his subordinates have partisan and personal motivations that may be, or appear to be, in conflict with their duty to execute the law faithfully. Furthermore, laws are frequently ambiguous and permit alternative interpretations, some of which better match the "political" interests of the executive than others. The amount of discretion necessarily afforded the executive in the law enforcement arena makes it almost inevitable that some decisions will be perceived by political opponents (and by more objective observers in some instances) to have been guided by illegitimate "political" considerations.

Accusations of politicized law enforcement have haunted virtually every president,[10] suggesting that the tensions inherent in having political actors enforce the law are not easily overcome. Certainly in the twentieth century the Watergate scandal stands as the extreme example of this problem. The perception that Richard Nixon believed that he was above the law and could use his political power over law enforcement to serve his personal and political interests undoubtedly was at the center of his downfall. It was this kind of politicized justice that Congress sought to eliminate in its inclusion of the special prosecutor provisions in the Ethics in Government Act.

AD HOC USES OF
THE SPECIAL PROSECUTOR

The use of an independent special prosecutor was not new with the creation of the 1978 statutory arrangement. State courts have traditionally appointed special prosecutors when the regular government attorney was disqualified from a case, whether for incapacitation or interest.[11] For example, the state of New York has a long tradition of using special prosecutors in public corruption cases. In the early twentieth century, Thomas Dewey built his reputation for leadership on special investigations and prosecutions centered in New York City.[12] Gov. Nelson Rockefeller created a special prosecutor's office in 1972 to investigate allegations of widespread corruption in the New York City criminal justice system.[13] After the exposure of former governor Spiro Agnew's misconduct, the government of Maryland created a state office of special prosecutor to deal with charges of public corruption.[14]

Prior to 1978, federal special prosecutors had been appointed to investigate three major national scandals in American politics. In 1925 Congress urged President Coolidge to appoint special prosecutors to investigate the Teapot Dome scandal of the Harding administration. Attorney General Harry Daugherty was perceived to have dragged his feet on the investigation, presumably because friends were implicated in the affair. Two special prosecutors were chosen by the president and confirmed by the Senate to investigate the scandal.[15] During the Truman administration Attorney General J. Howard McGrath appointed a special prosecutor to investigate the tax scandals of 1951 where allegations of "tax fixing" implicated both the Internal Revenue Service and the Department of Justice Tax Division.[16]

In the recent past it is the Watergate scandal that is most closely associated with the institution of the special prosecutor. During the five years in which the scandal unfolded, four special prosecutors were appointed by the president after some consultation with Congress. The first, Harvard law professor Archibald Cox, was fired in the infamous "Saturday Night Massacre" of October 1973. Leon Jaworski, a Texas lawyer, served until after Richard Nixon's resignation and pardon. He was succeeded by former deputies Henry Ruth, and finally, Charles C. Ruff, who followed through on the pending court trials and appeals.

It was the Watergate experience that especially influenced the creation of the special prosecutor provisions of the Ethics in Government Act of 1978. But supporters of the provisions relied on the previous incidents as evidence of the need for an institution to deal with recurring misconduct by executive branch officials.

ETHICS ACT PROSECUTORS

During the first decade of the Ethics Act's existence, eight special prosecutors were publicly appointed in accordance with the provisions. In each of the first four investigations, the evidence proved insufficient to warrant prosecution. More recent investigations have led to several indictments and convictions.

During the Carter administration two special prosecutors were appointed to investigate allegations that Chief of Staff Hamilton Jordan and White House staff member Timothy Kraft had used cocaine on separate social occasions. Special prosecutors Arthur Christy (Jordan case) and Gerald Gallinghouse (Kraft case) both concluded after grand jury investigations that there was insufficient evidence to prosecute.[17]

All of the remaining Ethics Act appointments involved allegations of wrongdoing by officials in the two terms of the Reagan administration. In 1981 allegations of organized crime connections led to a special prosecutor investigation of Secretary of Labor Raymond Donovan. After an investigation that was closed, reopened, and closed again, special prosecutor Leon Silverman announced that there was insufficient credible evidence to warrant prosecution. Donovan was later indicted by a New York City grand jury on similar charges but was acquitted after a 1986 trial.[18]

Attorney General Edwin Meese was twice the target of investigations by special prosecutors. The first investigation took place in 1984 as the result of allegations of unethical conduct that were revealed during stormy confirmation hearings early that year. Meese's confirmation was delayed until independent counsel[19] Jacob Stein reported that his investigation revealed that the evidence did not warrant prosecution. Meese's nomination was resubmitted after the 1984 election, and Stein's report was used by his supporters as evidence of his fitness for office.[20] In 1987 Meese was implicated in the Wedtech scandal, an affair involving a New York City defense contractor under investigation by the United States attorney for the Southern District of New York. Meese was accused of using his influence to help the company gain defense contracts. Independent counsel James McKay uncovered other evidence that implicated Meese in a proposed oil pipeline deal that raised the possibility of violations of the Foreign Corrupt Practices Act. In the end McKay declined to prosecute Meese, although he concluded that the attorney general had probably violated the Ethics in Government Act and the Internal Revenue Code.[21]

A bumper crop of independent counsel investigations was reaped in 1986. In May an independent counsel was appointed to pursue an investigation into allegations that stemmed from a 1982 congressional investigation into misconduct in the Environmental Protection Agency. Theodore Olson, a Justice Department official in the Office of Legal Counsel, was accused of lying to Congress and of withholding evidence needed for the investigation.[22] Independent counsel Alexia Morrison took three years to reach the conclusion that there was insufficient evidence to indict Olson because the investigation was delayed by litigation over the independent counsel's jurisdiction and the constitutionality of the arrangement itself. In June of 1988 the United States Supreme Court, in *Morrison v. Olson*,[23] upheld the constitutionality of the independent counsel provisions, and Morrison completed her investigation shortly thereafter.[24]

In June 1986 Whitney North Seymour was appointed to investigate allegations that former White House aide and longtime Reagan friend Michael Deaver had violated the illegal lobbying provisions of the Ethics Act. Deaver was indicted and convicted for perjury before a congressional committee and a grand jury investigating the illegal lobbying charges. No indictment was sought for the Ethics Act allegations that had originally triggered the independent investigation.[25]

The Iran-Contra scandal, which broke in late 1986, led to the only investigation under the Ethics Act that could rival Watergate in its length, breadth, and significance. In December 1986 Lawrence Walsh was appointed to conduct an investigation into the scandal. President Reagan requested his appointment after it was revealed that money obtained from the sale of arms to the Iranians in a deal to gain the release of American hostages had been diverted for use in aiding the Nicaraguan Contras. These actions were contrary to congressional statutes restricting arms sales and aid to the Contras and to the administration's stated position that the United States would not negotiate with terrorists. Implicated in these actions were a number of officials in the Reagan administration including the director of the CIA, two National Security assistants, and the president himself. At the time, there was a great deal of concern that Attorney General Edwin Meese had not acted quickly enough to avoid the destruction of documents needed for the investigation.[26] A grand jury indicted John Poindexter (National Security assistant), Oliver North (member of the National Security Counsel staff), Richard Secord (retired Air Force officer), Albert Hakim (Secord's business partner), and Joseph Fernandez (CIA station chief in Costa Rica) on various charges related to the scandal. Walsh obtained guilty pleas from several other participants. North was convicted of several of the charges, Secord pled guilty to some of the charges against him prior to trial, and Poindexter was convicted of the charges against him in April 1990. Charges against Hakim and Fernandez apparently implicated national security secrets and required the dropping of charges.[27] The prosecution of these cases was hampered significantly by the congressional decision to grant North and Poindexter immunity in 1987 in order to get their testimony in televised hearings. In July 1990 North's convictions were set aside by a federal appeals court because of the possibility that the prosecution had been tainted by exposure to the immunized testimony.[28]

The last two investigations by independent counsel during the Reagan administration resulted from scandals involving the Wedtech Corporation and the Department of Housing and Urban Development. Early in 1987 Independent Counsel James McKay was appointed to investigate the role of former White House aide Lynn Nofziger in the Wedtech scandal. Nofziger was accused of illegal lobbying on behalf of the defense contractor. He was convicted in 1988, but the appeals court overturned that conviction in 1989, citing flaws in the language of the Ethics Act lobbying provisions.[29] Finally, a congressional investigation into allegations of fraud and favoritism in the awarding of HUD contracts led to the 1990 appointment of an independent counsel to investigate former HUD Secretary Samuel Pierce, Jr.[30]

Implementation of the special prosecutor provisions has not been without controversy. Until the Supreme Court's 1988 decision in *Morrison v. Olson*, the key issue in dispute was the constitutionality of the arrangement. That dispute will be discussed in detail in Chapter 4. For now, it is sufficient to say that the controversy concerned whether Congress could remove the power of law enforcement from the executive branch in the manner it did in the special prosecutor provisions. Opponents suggested that the independent counsel arrangement violated the separation of powers doctrine.[31] Proponents contended that Congress's appointment authority under Article II, section 2, of the Constitution ensures the act's constitutionality.[32]

Critics have also expressed concern about the damaging effect upon the accused's reputation of the publicity surrounding the triggering of the mechanism and the issuing of a public report;[33] the dual standard of justice for public officials created by the charging of crimes not prosecuted for ordinary citizens (i.e. minimal cocaine use);[34] the waste of public funds resulting from special investigations of charges that the Justice Department could do routinely;[35] the lack of checks on the independent counsel's power;[36] the lack of attention in the provisions to ethical, as opposed to criminal, questions;[37] and the amount of discretion granted the attorney general in triggering the act.[38] Supporters of the mechanism argue that it is the only practical response to the conflict of interest problem; it is necessary for the appearance of impartial justice and for the maintenance of public confidence in the justice system;[39] its use has demonstrated that there are adequate checks on the independent counsel;[40] and it serves the interests of the accused because, if cleared, their exoneration is not "tainted" by questions of conflict of interest.[41]

What has been lacking in the debate about the special prosecutor has been any effort to study the implementation of the provisions to test whether or not the arguments of the opponents or supporters are correct.

Perhaps because it took a decade before the Supreme Court addressed the constitutional dispute at the root of the debate, the arguments have tended to focus on issues of constitutional theory as opposed to practice. The arguments about how it operates in practice generally depend upon the particular theoretical perspective one adopts. For example, advocates of a strong executive tend to argue that there are no restraints on the independent counsel. The criticism flows naturally from their beginning assumptions about the scope of executive power. If the separation of powers system is viewed as one where the executive, legislative, and judicial powers are neatly parceled between the three branches in an exclusive and exhaustive way, then an officer such as the independent counsel, who does not fit neatly into any category, must be one outside of the system and, therefore, unrestrained. The theory, and not actual evidence, drives the conclusion. Similarly, advocates of the legislative provisions have a tendency to equate constitutionality with good policy. That is, they seem to assume that if Congress has the constitutional authority to create an independent counsel, then it is a given that the policy will result in the desired outcomes of eliminating conflict of interest and restoring public confidence. Again, these arguments for the independent counsel are taken on faith as opposed to evidence.

The validity of these arguments can be tested by a study of how the offices of independent counsel operated in the first decade of their existence. The purpose of this book is to assess the practical political consequences of creating an independent prosecutorial body separate from established law enforcement arrangements. In 1992 Congress will decide whether to reauthorize the independent counsel provisions for the third time. At that time, the arrangement's practical consequences for the constitutional order should be considered.

A SEPARATION OF POWERS FRAMEWORK

Has accountability, so essential to democratic government, been sacrificed for independence, so critical to the appearance of impartiality? Does an independent officer lack the constraints on power imposed on regular actors in the separation of powers scheme? What kinds of relationships does an independent prosecutor develop with the other actors in the system? How do these relationships influence the way in which independent prosecutors carry out their responsibilities?

This analysis offers answers to these questions by studying how federal special prosecutors have actually operated within the system of separation of powers. A separation of powers framework is a useful way to study special prosecutors because the strengths and weaknesses of the arrangement are best revealed through an understanding of the boundaries and constraints imposed by the governmental structure within which it operates. Further, it allows a closer look at how the separation of powers system functions in practice. The use of special prosecutors is, at its core, an issue concerning the separation of powers. The study of the use of special prosecutors is the study of the separation of powers writ small. It allows us to examine several important questions about the larger system that are implicated in the use of special prosecutors. To what extent do the competing theories of separation of powers underlying the debate reflect or conflict with the way the system operates in practice? How well does the system of checks and balances work? What is the best way to prevent, expose, and respond to the problem of official misconduct in a constitutional democracy? What "auxiliary precautions" can best reassure the people that their governors are not corrupted by the power granted them?

The Federalist provides an initial guide to understanding the American system of separated powers. The separation of powers and checks and balances were viewed by Madison as the internal instruments for checking the human propensities for the aggrandizement of power and abuse of the public trust. The goal of this dispersion of power was to ensure that no one group or individual could gain control of the government and act against the public good. The public good was to be protected by competition among the separate parts of government, each checking the other while protecting itself.[42]

But competition alone would insure only deadlock. The system also required the cooperation of the branches to achieve the ends of government. Given the competition and separate interests inherent in the system, cooperative efforts by the legislative and executive branches that did result could only produce public-spirited outcomes. Madison wrote that such an arrangement insured that "a coalition of a majority of the whole society could seldom take place on any other principles than those of justice and the general good."[43]

The Federalist provides us with several key principles that guide our present understanding of the purposes of the structure of American government. Its vision assumes the flaws in human nature will always pose a threat to democratic government but that structural arrangements can correct for these flaws. In this view, the arrangements created in 1787 provide the essential "auxiliary precautions" against abuse of power. Further, Madison posits the central importance of accountability in democratic government. Public officials must be made responsible not only to the electorate, which is an ultimate but inadequate external check, but also to each other. Republican government is safer and more effective than "true" democracy, but measures of accountability (both electoral and structural) preserve its essential democratic character.

Finally, *The Federalist* encourages us to view the separation of powers doctrine as a flexible one, one that permits, and expects, cooperation among the branches in pursuit of the public good. Thus the checks and balances flesh out the rather austere separation of powers among the legislative, executive, and judicial branches by providing for the sharing of powers.[44] These mechanisms provide the means by which democratic government may be effective and insure liberty.[45] Checks were added to the separation of powers structure "to maintain the separation by keeping the branches independent, to work against hastily passed, badly considered laws, and ultimately, to remove from office those who abused their public trust—all the while preventing governmental deadlock."[46]

While still rooted in the understanding found in *The Federalist*, our modern understanding of the separation of powers has been shaped further by two hundred years of practice. While a formalistic and overly rigid view of the doctrine has been given some credence of late,[47] the more widely accepted and enduring view of the arrangement is one that emphasizes the flexibility of the doctrine. This interpretation has been demonstrated in most of the opinions of the Supreme Court dealing with the distribution of power in government[48] and in scholarly work on the doctrine.[49] At the heart of this flexible view is the belief expressed by John Marshall in 1819 that the Constitution

was intended to endure for ages to come, and consequently, to be adapted to the various crises of human affairs. To have prescribed the means by which government should, in all future time, execute its powers, would have been to change, entirely, the character of the instrument, and give it the properties of a legal code. It would have been an unwise attempt to provide, by immutable rules, for exigencies which, if foreseen at all, must have been seen dimly, and which can be best provided for as they occur.[50]

The separation of powers doctrine today allows for the ebb and flow of power between president and Congress, depending on the particular issue, the individuals holding office, and the political environment generally.[51] We understand that while it is generally the case that the legislature makes the law, the executive executes it, and the judiciary interprets it, this idealized image of the system, if it ever existed, has been fundamentally changed by events of the twentieth century.[52] The operation of the separation of powers system must be understood as far more complex than the simple "three branches with separate functions" model. Louis Fisher reminds us that "Congress and the presidency function within a political environment that consists of the judiciary, the bureaucracy, independent regulatory commissions, political parties, state and local governments, interest groups, and foreign nations."[53]

In Fisher's view, an understanding of the theory requires a recognition of the interaction between the abstract principles and actual practice; the realization that while the theory provides constraints on actions, that "executive-legislative actions shape theory."[54] A separation of powers framework, then, requires the examination of the complex set of relationships that make up modern American politics. It is essential that the bureaucracy, interest groups, and the media be examined in addition to a consideration of the roles of Congress, the president, and the judiciary.

In trying to understand the politics of special prosecutors, a study of the constitutionality of the arrangement is only a first step.[55] A flexible view of the separation of powers doctrine permits many actions that may be acceptable constitutionally but that may not necessarily be good ideas in practice. They might meet the letter of the law but violate its spirit in the way they operate. They may work at cross purposes to the goals set for them. Finding out whether legitimate constitutional actions are in fact good political actions requires us to study their actual operation in the political process.

Within this framework of the separation of powers, we will set out to answer several sets of questions raised by the use of independent counsels, each of which will be answered in a chapter of the book. Chapter 2 asks how different, in practice, is the statutory special prosecutor from ad hoc special prosecutors used in the past? What are the cost and benefits of relying on ad hoc as opposed to statutory independent prosecutions? Chapters 3 and 4 pose the questions what did Congress hope to achieve in creating a statutory special prosecutor arrangement and why did it choose the particular arrangement that it did? Chapter 5, is the special prosecutor arrangement constitutional? How can it be justified within the separation of powers system? Chapter 6, what role does the attorney general play in the independent counsel process? Has the arrangement adequately addressed the problem of conflict of interest when the executive investigates itself? Chapter 7 asks the questions, how accountable are the special prosecutors? What checks, or constraints, are there on the use of their power? Has their independence from the executive made them accountable to no one? Chapter 8, how well does the independent counsel arrangement work in reassuring the public that officials accused of misconduct are being impartially investigated? What is the symbolic importance of the arrangement to the public? To elites? Chapter 9 raises the issues: Is the independent counsel arrangement of the Ethics in Government Act a necessary "auxiliary precaution?" Measured against the concerns of *The Federalist* and of our current understanding of the separation of powers system, how does the arrangement stand up? What does it contribute to the resolution of the problem of official misconduct by public officials? What are the alternatives? What does it teach us about the effectiveness of the system of separation of powers?

The answers to each set of questions require the examination of the complex interrelationships of the various actors in the political system with the independent counsel. Throughout this book the reader will detect an ambivalence about the independent counsel provisions. This study finds that, in practice, the independent counsel is neither so bad as its critics paint it nor so good as its supporters believe it to be. Its flaws derive from the realities of the process that created it and within which it must operate, its strengths from the same. The politics of special prosecutors is a reflection of the larger politics of the American system. Any choices we make about addressing the problems of official misconduct will inevitably reflect this reality.

TWO

AD HOC APPOINTMENT OF SPECIAL PROSECUTORS: THE TAX, TEAPOT DOME, AND WATERGATE SCANDALS

Public corruption as a problem in American politics did not suddenly appear with Watergate. It is a problem that the framers wrestled with,[1] and one that every president since Washington has been forced to confront.[2] Despite regular efforts at reform, the American system has been unable to escape what political philosophers since the ancients have identified as a problem endemic to politics: the relationship between political power and public corruption.[3]

Since the turn of the century there have been three official corruption cases in which allegations of wrongdoing by members of the executive branch led to the ad hoc appointment of special prosecutors: the Teapot Dome scandal of the 1920s, the tax scandals of the 1950s, and the Watergate scandal of the 1970s. Each of these cases involved a decision to appoint independent prosecutors despite the lack of a statutory requirement to do so.[4]

THE TEAPOT DOME SCANDAL

The Teapot Dome scandal arose during the Harding administration, when powerful conservationists challenged the implementation (or lack thereof) of conservation policy by Secretary of Interior Albert Fall. By 1922, investigation into those policies "had begun to slip from the hands of conservationists into those of the United States Senate and the public press."[5] In April of that year the Senate voted overwhelmingly to pursue an investigation into Fall's handling of the U.S. government's leasing of the Teapot Dome naval oil reserves. The Senate Committee on Public Lands and Survey was given responsibility for the investigation, but it was eighteen months before the committee's hearings finally got under way. In part, the delay can be explained by the Republicans' desire to postpone the hearings until after the 1922 congressional elections.[6]

Early in 1923 Secretary Fall's resignation was announced. Washington was filled with rumors of corruption in the Teapot Dome leases and throughout the Department of Justice, but it was not until after President Harding's death in August 1923 that the rumors became "tangible charges and confessions." Finally, in October of that year the hearings began and "shortly thereafter, Teapot Dome began to engross the nation's attention."[7] As press and public attention mounted and the hearings and investigation began to uncover evidence that the leasing of the oil reserves had involved corruption, President Coolidge began to feel the pressure to respond and to demonstrate his concern about the charges. He directed Attorney General Harry Daugherty to send a Department of Justice employee to all the hearings and to be ready to act to protect the interests of the government. However, the committee and its conservationist supporters feared a whitewash and began to consider requesting a special counsel to carry out any litigation necessary to reclaim the reserves by canceling the illegal contracts.[8]

Republican members of the committee warned Coolidge of the committee's plan to request a special prosecutor. To preempt congressional action he announced the next day his intention to "employ special counsel of high rank drawn from both political parties" to handle the litigation arising out of the case. Coolidge's announcement was followed shortly thereafter by another Senate resolution, which directed the president to hire special counsel to begin a suit to cancel the oil leases. After the president submitted and withdrew his first two choices for special counsel, he nominated former Democratic senator Atlee Pomerene of Ohio and Owen Roberts, a Republican lawyer from Philadelphia. After a bitter battle in the Senate over the confirmation of the two nominees, they were finally accepted and were given their commissions on February 19, 1924.[9]

For the next four years the two prosecutors and their small staff litigated the cases arising from the scandal. Throughout that time, their papers suggest, they had regular contact with the White House, the Senate committee investigating the scandal, the Department of Justice, local United States attorneys' offices (several of which aided them in their suits), United States marshals throughout the country, and the Navy Department. The record suggests that in most cases these relationships were congenial and characterized by cooperation. In the meantime, the Senate committee continued its hearings. A special committee to investigate the Department of Justice, particularly Attorney General Daugherty's foot-dragging on the Teapot Dome case, began its work. The attorney general resigned shortly thereafter. Having been found guilty of accepting a bribe for the oil leases, Albert Fall entered federal prison in July 1931. Ironically, the men alleged to have offered the bribe were acquitted.[10]

The Teapot Dome case resembles the Watergate case in several ways. The early exposure of wrongdoing and the way in which committee investigations brought the scandal to the public's attention are very similar. The president appointed special counsel in the Teapot Dome case in response to congressional pressure and in order to try to preempt congressional action. The Senate's role in confirming the appointees was important in the choice of individuals and in eliciting promises of independence. The possibility of Senate rejection of the nominees was quite real, forcing the president to choose men of different parties and with reputations for integrity. The attorney general and Department of Justice were implicated in the allegations, and the attorney general was ultimately forced to resign. Finally, the case involved extensive and time-consuming litigation requiring the special counsel to continue to operate for a number of years. (A key difference between the two scandals lies in the fact that the special counsel were not required to investigate a sitting president and that the president who had been implicated was no longer alive.) The record suggests that despite the fact that the special counsel were appointed by the president, they had sufficient independence to carry out an investigation that was not found wanting by other elites in the process.

THE TAX SCANDALS

The tax scandals of 1951 and 1952 also bear some similarities to the Watergate scandal. Again, allegations of wrongdoing by members of the executive branch (the Bureau of Internal Revenue and the Tax Division of the Department of Justice) led to investigations into the charges by a congressional committee. The hearings revealed widespread tax fixing by the bureau with complicity by the Tax Division.[11] During 1951 sixty-six internal revenue officers were forced to resign. The next year the former commissioner of Internal Revenue and his assistant were convicted of tax fraud. President Truman ordered his attorney general, Howard McGrath, to fire the assistant attorney general in charge of the Tax Division. The assistant eventually was convicted of conspiracy to fix a tax case. Despite what appeared to be a wholesale housecleaning and the demonstrated ability to prosecute those involved, Congress continued its investigations.[12]

In response to the urging of his aides, Truman decided to set up a commission to investigate the tax-fixing allegations. When he could not get his first choice to head the commission, he chose Newbold Morris, a Republican lawyer from New York who had a reputation as a corruption fighter but "who possessed no political instincts whatsoever."[13] What followed was "an episode that was as preposterous as anything Washington had ever witnessed."[14] The Bureau of the Budget helped Morris to design a questionnaire, which it believed was to be used only for the attorneys implicated in the case. The questions sought to determine not just a person's income but how much he was spending, the presumption being that information on spending would indicate whether attorneys were living beyond their reported income. Morris decided that all United States government employees should fill out the questionnaire, including the president and beginning with the attorney general. McGrath balked at this suggestion and others complained of the intrusiveness of the questions. No one seems to have anticipated the zeal with which Morris would attack his job. In an early meeting with Truman, Morris told the president that he realized that it would be impossible to investigate every federal employee but that he believed it would be feasible to look into the net worth of the top ten thousand in order to set an example among the ranks.[15] Truman apparently suggested to McGrath that the new special prosecutor was reaching beyond his assignment. Without telling Truman of his plan, McGrath fired Morris, "whereupon Truman picked up the telephone and fired McGrath."[16] Truman garnered much negative publicity over the incident, and the Republicans used corruption as one of their key campaign issues in 1952.

The tax scandals demonstrate again the way in which public and congressional pressure can force a president to take action when charges of corruption are leveled against his administration. The case provides an important contrast to Watergate in terms of the consequences of firing a special prosecutor. Morris's firing was sensational and brought short-lived cries of protest from some quarters, but Truman weathered the storm because Morris was perceived by officials both inside and outside the executive branch as having reached beyond his authority. His approach had alienated more supporters than it had gained him and so he had no one to turn to when the president turned on him. In addition, while Truman was held politically responsible for the scandal, he was not himself implicated in it. The case demonstrates the potential for abuse of power that exists when an independent prosecutor is created and that presidential appointment can serve two important and interrelated functions. It forces the president to take responsibility for the conduct of the case, and it allows for the ultimate check—removal—if the independent prosecutor abuses his authority.

WATERGATE

Watergate is the premier political scandal of the twentieth century. No other scandal in American history has forced the resignation of the president. In addition, the fallout of the scandal included the criminal convictions of a former attorney general, a number of top White House aides, many more lower level executive employees, and a large number of private individuals and corporations.[17]

Given its importance in American political history, it is not surprising that the literature on Watergate is vast. Both participants[18] and observers[19] have deemed the scandal worthy of their attention, and there is considerable information about it in the public record. Watergate's importance to this study also lies in its role in shaping the 1978 special prosecutor provisions of the Ethics in Government Act. Certainly, in identifying "heroes" of Watergate one cannot overlook Special Prosecutors Cox and Jaworski. The Watergate scandal was one in which the appointment of a special prosecutor was both necessary and fortuitous. A closer look at the unfolding of the scandal and the operation of the Watergate Special Prosecution Force demonstrates both the dangers of presidential appointment and the advantages of placing the special prosecutor within the traditional separation of powers framework.

A Brief Chronology of Events[20]

On June 17, 1972, Washington police arrested five men who had broken into the Democratic National Committee headquarters, housed in the Watergate Office Building. In the months that followed, reporters for the *Washington Post* began to unravel a bizarre story of intrigue that implicated the Committee to Re-Elect the President (CRP), Nixon's 1972 campaign committee.[21]

Meanwhile, top officials of the Nixon administration and CRP were working furiously to keep the lid on the affair, engaging in a cover-up of their involvement in the break-in. Money was given to the Watergate defendants to keep them quiet and to encourage them to plead guilty, thus avoiding a trial. Evidence was destroyed and attempts were made to derail an FBI investigation into the incident. Despite the continued digging and uncovering of more evidence by the *Post* reporters, Watergate was a "non-issue" in the 1972 presidential campaign.[22] Nixon lost only Massachusetts and the District of Columbia to his Democratic opponent, George Mc-Govern.

In January 1973 the Watergate burglars, except for G. Gordon Liddy and James McCord, pleaded guilty to the charges against them and denied that they had been pressured to do so. The remaining conspirators provided no further evidence during their trial that implicated anyone higher than themselves. Nevertheless, by this time enough questions had been raised about the involvement of "higher-ups" that the Senate, on February 7, voted unanimously to establish a select committee to investigate the allegations.

While the committee, with Sen. Sam Ervin of North Carolina at the helm and Samuel Dash as its chief counsel, prepared for hearings, the Watergate burglars prepared for sentencing. At their sentencing in late March, James McCord revealed through a letter to Judge John Sirica that there had been pressure for the defendants to plead guilty, that perjury had occurred during the trial, and that there were others involved in the operation. McCord sought and obtained immunity from the Senate committee in exchange for his testimony at the upcoming hearings. John Dean, counsel to the president and a key actor in the cover-up, was not far behind. In addition, the two provided testimony to the grand jury that had been established by the Justice Department to investigate the case.

On April 30, 1973, President Nixon announced the resignation of his top two aides, H. R. Haldeman and John Erlichman, his attorney general, Richard Kleindienst, and the dismissal of John Dean. He granted his new attorney general-designate, Elliot Richardson, complete authority over the Watergate investigation and permission to appoint an independent prosecutor if he so desired. In response, the Senate voted to request that the president make such an appointment, and the Senate Judiciary Committee announced its intention to link Richardson's confirmation to the promise. During the confirmation hearings, Richardson agreed to appoint a special prosecutor and offered the Senate a chance to confirm his choice informally. He selected Harvard law professor Archibald Cox, who testified to his authority to pursue an independent investigation. Richardson was confirmed and the Watergate Special Prosecution Force was established.

In the meantime, the nationally televised Senate select committee hearings were keeping the scandal in the limelight. The hearings reached their zenith in late June, when John Dean began his testimony before the committee and implicated Richard Nixon in the cover-up. The key to unraveling the Watergate puzzle was revealed on July 16, 1973, when a White House aide testified that Nixon had a secret tape-recording system in the White House. Obtaining the tapes of conversations between Nixon and his aides was essential to the Senate committee and the special prosecutor. The tapes held the answer to the question of Dean's veracity.

An extended court battle ensued between Cox and Nixon over release of certain subpoenaed tapes. Cox emerged victorious. Judge Sirica ordered release of the tapes and his ruling was confirmed by the Court of Appeals. Cox's victory was to be a hollow one, however: the special prosecutor was fired, under Nixon's order, by Solicitor General Robert Bork. Attorney General Richardson and his deputy William Ruckelshaus had resigned first, rather than carry out the order. The events of that 1973 October weekend, which came to be known as the Saturday Night Massacre, provided a critical turning point in the Watergate scandal.[23] The public outrage that followed forced Nixon to release some of the tapes and to appoint another prosecutor. It also motivated the House Judiciary Committee to begin impeachment proceedings.

Leon Jaworski, a Texas Democrat, was appointed special prosecutor to continue the investigation. Before accepting the position, Jaworski received assurances that he would not be fired without consent of congressional leadership and that he was free to pursue the investigation wherever it might lead.[24] As we know now, it led to the Oval Office. Jaworski also became involved in litigation in an attempt to obtain more of the White House tapes.

As 1974 began, Nixon launched a counteroffensive. Contending that "one year of Watergate is enough," he announced his intention to release no further information to the Senate Watergate Committee. He also refused any further cooperation with Jaworski. The special prosecutor continued his legal battle for the tapes, successfully petitioning Judge Sirica for enforcement of a subpoena in April 1974. Nixon's lawyers appealed the decision and Jaworski, wishing no further delay, petitioned the Supreme Court for review of the case.

On July 24, 1974 the Supreme Court announced, in a unanimous decision, that Nixon must turn over the tapes for use in the upcoming trial of the Watergate conspirators.[25] Six days later the House Judiciary Committee approved three articles of impeachment, charging the president with obstruction of justice, abuse of presidential power, and defiance of congressional and special prosecutor subpoenas. The same day Nixon turned over some of the subpoenaed tapes, which revealed his early complicity in the cover-up. On August 8, 1974, Richard Nixon became the first United States president to resign from office.

On August 9, 1974, Vice President Gerald R. Ford was sworn in as the new president. Following weeks of speculation as to the likelihood of Nixon's criminal indictment for obstruction of justice, the new president pardoned his predecessor on September 8. Jaworski resigned shortly thereafter. The Watergate Special Prosecution Force continued to operate through 1975, successfully prosecuting the other Watergate conspirators and handling the appeals of the resulting convictions.[26] Finally, in 1976 the office closed its doors.

Independence and Accountability

What was the consequence of permitting presidential appointment of the Watergate special prosecutors? A closer look at the way in which the special prosecutors interacted with the other actors in the political and legal system illuminates what the Saturday Night Massacre obscured. Appointment by the president encouraged a healthy suspicion, and a resulting vigilance, by the other actors (Congress, the courts, the press, and the public) that served as a source of support for the special prosecutors and as a check on their power. It helped to insure an independence in reality that was tenuous on paper. If we can look beyond the events of Cox's firing to the subsequent resolution of the crisis, we can see that a special prosecutor appointed within the traditional separation of powers framework can be sufficiently independent to conduct an impartial criminal investigation and prosecution. This occurs because of the necessary relationships that the prosecutor must develop with the various actors in the system.

The Justice Department. The Watergate Special Prosecution Force was created by regulations of the attorney general[27] and was technically considered a part of the Department of Justice throughout its existence, despite its independent status. It maintained a fairly regular interaction with the department. The relationship was the result of both practical and personal factors.

Elliot Richardson selected Archibald Cox as special prosecutor after having been turned down by several other lawyers because of inadequate guarantees of independence.[28] Before accepting the position, Cox insisted that he be placed under no obligation to keep Richardson informed and that he be permitted to "go public" whenever he wished.[29] Nonetheless, Cox and Richardson had relatively frequent contact in the several months following the creation of the force. That contact was no doubt facilitated by the long-standing friendship between the two men. It also resulted from the ambiguous status of the force given its uniqueness in American history. Thus the early contact between the prosecutor, the attorney general, and their respective staffs was characterized as "part of a continuing process of clarifying questions about the scope of the Prosecutor's jurisdiction, discussing Government policy, especially sensitive matters, arranging for the exercise of powers which only the Attorney General could exercise, and developing mechanisms for accommodation and cooperation in areas of over-lapping interest between the Special Prosecutor and the regular operating divisions of the Department of Justice."[30]

For example, several situations arose in which Cox and Richardson had to negotiate solutions with regard to interpreting the charter of the force. After a newspaper article alleged that the prosecutors were investigating Nixon's expenses at his San Clemente home, Richardson expressed his view that an investigation of this topic was not within Cox's jurisdiction. While agreeing to announce publicly that the story was false, Cox disagreed with Richardson's interpretation. At another time the two met to discuss Richardson's suggestion that the department screen all allegations before referring them to the force, thus weeding out charges outside the jurisdiction of the office. Cox also objected to this attempt, believing that it was his function to screen the allegations. In August 1973 the jurisdictional question surfaced again with regard to Cox's authority to investigate allegations of illegal wiretapping and domestic surveillance. The attorney general wished to issue unpublished guidelines for narrowing the force's jurisdiction in this area for national security reasons. Cox again balked, arguing that if the guidelines were to be issued, they ought to be made public. In September 1973, after negotiations with Richardson, Cox agreed to "temporal boundaries" on his jurisdiction: that is, that he would not pursue allegations of activity that occurred after his May 1973 appointment, unless it involved an infringement upon his investigation, or before January of 1971, except with the permission of Richardson.[31]

In other instances, Cox was willing to compromise with Richardson. They met in the early months of the investigation to discuss the issue of executive privilege and how the force would approach its legal challenge to that claim. While wishing to challenge the claim in order to obtain evidence for a criminal trial, the special prosecutor also recognized that "he was an officer of the Department of Justice and that the Department of Justice had for years been asserting and defending claims of executive privilege."[32]

The two searched for a way to accommodate "their respective responsibilities with the least damage to the positions and responsibilities of the other."[33] Finally, they determined that Cox would make his narrowed claim against executive privilege in cases where information is needed as evidence in a criminal trial while the department maintained its interpretation that the claim should be upheld in civil litigation. In this way a confrontation was avoided. In addition, Cox worked out compromises with the department on the handling of sensitive national security matters and on the granting of immunity.[34]

Leon Jaworski also found it necessary to have contacts with the attorney general, first with Robert Bork and then with William Saxbe, although these contacts were less frequent, more formal, and more likely to have occurred during the transition. Jaworski negotiated with Bork and Saxbe over his initial charter before accepting the position, sought clarification of it at one point shortly after assuming his title, and informed the attorney general of the White House's lack of cooperation and of his intention to resign after the pardon.[35] After Cox's dismissal both the frequency and nature of the special prosecutor–attorney general contacts changed. Besides the fact that the new relationship was not preceded by a longstanding friendship between the parties and that most of the "structural issues" had been resolved before that time, the nature of Cox's dismissal militated against a friendly relationship. The 1975 report of the force points out that "the public and congressional reaction to the dismissal of Cox, and to the White House effort to override his independence and undercut his judgment, would have made it very difficult as a political and policy matter for subsequent Attorneys General to assume any significant role in directly questioning the Special Prosecutor's judgments or even raising issues about them."[36]

In addition to contact with the attorney general, it was necessary for the Watergate Special Prosecution Force to work with lower echelon department employees and field office personnel. The office had frequent contact with the criminal division, which had initial responsibility for the investigation and which resumed that responsibility during the interim between Cox's firing and Jaworski's appointment. The force also consulted with the civil division of the department on various aspects of the investigation.[37]

It was necessary for the newly created office to work closely with the U.S. Attorney's Office for the District of Columbia because it was this office that was engaged in conducting the initial trial of the Watergate burglars and that had established the sitting Watergate grand jury. Cox moved quickly to assure the attorneys on the case that he wished for them to continue working on it until his office was prepared to take over. However, he did expect them to consult with him before making any decisions and he assigned several staff members to work with the department attorneys. By July 1, the force took over completely but it continued to consult with the original attorneys throughout the next two years on various aspects of the cases. The U.S. Attorney's Office "provided valuable assistance" whenever asked.[38]

These few examples, and all of the other evidence available on the relationship between the Watergate Special Prosecution Force and the Department of Justice,[39] suggest that there was a significant amount of interaction between the two offices. Given the extent to which the department was implicated in the scandal, the mutual trust and respect between Cox and Richardson, the breadth and complexity of the investigation, and the repercussions of the Saturday Night Massacre, it is not surprising that such a relationship would exist. It was in the personal and organizational interests of all to engage in cooperation. Of course, this increased need to compromise worked two ways. On the one hand it acted as a check on the special prosecutor, increasing accountability, but on the other it interfered with his ability to make completely independent judgments, increasing the influence of the department in his decisionmaking.

The Judiciary. The number of legal questions that arose in the Watergate special prosecutor investigation was vast. The investigation also produced numerous criminal indictments.[40] Consequently, there was by necessity frequent interaction between the force and the judiciary, particularly with District of Columbia District Court Judge John Sirica, who was the primary judge responsible for most of the cases throughout the five years of legal action. Sirica played a critical role in ensuring that the truth of the Watergate cover-up was revealed. It was his unwillingness to accept the original stories of the Watergate burglars that put pressure on both the defendants and the initial prosecutors from the U.S. Attorney's Office. He imposed harsh but conditional sentences upon those who pleaded guilty, hoping to encourage cooperation. He believed that it was his probing questions during the trial that provoked James McCord finally to reveal the fact that the trial had involved perjury and political pressure.[41]

Sirica also provided invaluable support for the special prosecutor's office in upholding the subpoena of the tapes and issuing orders of enforcement to the White House for release of the tapes. Had he not believed that as a member of a coequal branch of government he had a responsibility to the rule of law that went beyond his deference to the presidency,[42] it is hard to imagine what the outcome of the Watergate case might have been. Sirica's decision was backed by the D.C. Court of Appeals in 1973[43] and ultimately by the Supreme Court in 1974.[44]

Following the Saturday Night Massacre, Judge Sirica again played an important role in keeping the investigation on track. On the Tuesday following the weekend's events, he called the two sitting grand juries into open court and advised them that they were still operative and would "continue to function and pursue their work. You are not dismissed and will not be dismissed except by this court as provided by law upon the completion of your work."[45]

Sirica felt that the attendance that day by the staff of the Special Prosecution Force was motivated by a need for reassurance. While he did not speak to them in court, he did call them into his chambers later for a discussion in which he told them, "The law can take care of this situation." He also "praised them for not issuing inflammatory statements . . . (and) . . . urged them to proceed with their work while I considered what more I could do. They seemed relieved to have that reassurance."[46]

Leon Jaworski also indicated the existence of this relationship between the force and Sirica. Jaworski visited the judge upon arriving in Washington. Sirica appeared happy to have another special prosecutor, and Jaworski "found him to be a man who you could get along with very well, providing you demeaned yourself properly and played the game fairly and did not undertake to overreach."[47] All available evidence of Sirica's involvement throughout the process suggests that relationships based on mutual interests evolved in the Watergate case between the judge and the force.

Congress. Several congressional committees played critical roles in the unfolding of the Watergate scandal and in its ultimate resolution. In doing so, they also acted both as supporters and as checks on the power of the prosecutors. The Senate Select Committee on Presidential Campaign Activities was a premier actor in the early exposure of the Watergate cover-up and of other misconduct in the Nixon administration. Its investigation and public hearings in the spring and summer of 1973 aided in capturing the public's attention to the Watergate case and thereby increased public concern about the affair.[48] The committee's work also provided a substantial and critically important body of information that was turned over to Special Prosecutor Cox upon his appointment.

The relationship between the WSPF and the Select Committee was by no means a unilateral one in which Cox and his office were dominant. One of the best examples of this fact is provided in an exchange that occurred shortly after Cox's appointment. Fearing that the televised congressional hearings and the committee's ability to immunize witnesses would damage his criminal investigation, Cox unsuccessfully attempted to have the hearings postponed. He sought a court order that permitted grants of immunity only for congressional witnesses who would testify in executive session. Judge Sirica refused to issue such an order. Sam Dash, chief counsel of the Senate Watergate Committee, met with Cox about the possibility of stopping the hearings and was angered by the suggestion that Cox take over the investigation alone. Dash later recalled that he left the meeting "feeling I had just witnessed an unparalleled display of arrogance. In effect, Cox had told me that now that he, Mr. Clean, had come to Washington, everybody else had to stop what he was doing and get out of Cox's way to let him attack the Watergate dirt all by himself."[49]

The committee resisted Cox's attempt because it believed it had a very different but equally important task: to expose wrongdoing in the presidential campaign of 1972, thereby informing the public and providing information for future legislation.[50] Despite its early efforts to stop the hearings, the WSPF later contended that the committee's hearings ultimately provided it with important public support at a critical time. The 1975 WSPF Report acknowledged: "In the end, the continuation of public hearings through the summer of 1973, among other benefits brought to public attention testimony relating to alleged White House involvement in the Watergate cover-up. Thereby it helped to create for the special prosecutor investigation a base of public and congressional support that did much to force re-establishment of the WSPF after the President tried to abolish it."[51]

Throughout their operation the WSPF and the Senate Select Committee had regular interaction based on their "mutual needs to share information and coordinate often parallel investigations."[52] Cox and Ervin established a procedure by which the exchange of information could take place between the two investigatory units. The committee's early requests to the Department of Justice were referred to Cox, who then turned over some of the information requested. Later, the WSPF was to seek and receive much information, both formally and informally, from the Select Committee.[53]

After the Select Committee concluded its hearings, it began work on its final report which was due in February of 1974. By this time, Leon Jaworski had become the special prosecutor and he expressed to Dash his concern that the report not be released before the indictments on the Watergate cover-up were issued in March 1974. Dash agreed to withhold the report.[54] The Final Report of the Select Committee was released in July of

1974.[55] Its files were turned over to the Senate Rules Committee and the WSPF continued to obtain documents that it needed from this committee.[56]

The record of relationships between the Senate Select Committee and the special prosecutor suggests exchanges based on mutual needs for information and support. In addition, that reciprocity was no doubt enhanced by the friendships that existed among the key actors on the committee and the force. For example, Cox had been Dash's labor law professor at Harvard and Dash knew Cox's assistant James Vorenberg from the National Crime Commission established during the Johnson administration. They had further frequent contact as the result of each being a director of a criminal justice research center at their respective schools. Dash also had developed a friendship with Leon Jaworski, which facilitated cooperation between the two. Jaworski later recalled, "The staff worked closely with the Ervin Committee. . . . I knew Sam Dash quite well. We had a fine rapport with them. We had to make sure that there wasn't any crossing of paths that embarrassed either one."[57]

The Watergate Special Prosecution Force also developed an important relationship with the Senate Committee on the Judiciary. Throughout the unfolding of the Watergate scandal this committee acted as a "protector" of the prosecutors and enabled each of them to maintain their independence from the White House. The Senate Judiciary Committee first became involved during Elliot Richardson's confirmation hearings in May 1973. The committee announced its intention to tie Richardson's confirmation to the appointment of an independent prosecutor. During the hearings it worked with Richardson in drawing up an acceptable charter for the new prosecutor, and Archibald Cox appeared before it to assure the committee of his independence.[58] It was in part these promises, elicited by the committee during his confirmation hearings, that led Richardson to his later refusal to fire Cox and to his resignation.[59]

Between the time that Richardson was confirmed and the Saturday Night Massacre, the committee had little or no contact with Cox. However, after Jaworski's appointment it played a more active role, assuming "a guardian posture over the WSPF's work."[60] When the committee was informed by ex-Prosecutor Cox of the lack of White House cooperation in turning over evidence, Chairman Eastland wrote to Acting Attorney General Bork requesting a list of all information sought and received from the White House by the WSPF. The letter was referred to Jaworski, who sent the committee a list of requests indicating those that had not been honored.[61]

The Senate Judiciary Committee became involved as a protector of the special prosecutor in another way as well. In the charter re-establishing the WSPF, a provision was included that required majority support of the committee before Jaworski could be removed. This connection became critical in the spring of 1974, when Jaworski ran into a stone wall in trying to obtain further tapes and documents from the White House. When Nixon's lawyer, James St. Clair, refused to turn over further evidence, Jaworski subpoenaed the requested documents and tapes. In the legal battle that ensued, St. Clair introduced a new argument to the dispute. He contended that the disagreement between the prosecutor and the White House was an intraexecutive one and that consequently Jaworski had no standing to sue. Jaworski was incensed by this turn of events, and after an unsuccessful attempt to get St. Clair to drop the argument,[62] he wrote to Eastland to inform him of this action. In the letter, Jaworski referred to his testimony before the committee at the time of his appointment and to the guarantee he had received of his right to bring action against the White House to obtain evidence. Jaworski stated that "any claim raised by the White House Counsel on behalf of the President that challenges my right to invoke the judicial process . . . would make a farce of the special prosecutor's charter."[63]

Although Sirica had by this time rejected St. Clair's argument, Eastland wrote a letter to Attorney General Saxbe on behalf of the Judiciary Committee, urging him to do whatever was possible to guarantee Jaworski's independence as required by the regulations issued at the time of his appointment. Enclosed with the letter was a copy of the resolution passed by the committee on May 21, 1974, which resolved that Jaworski was acting within his authority in seeking the tapes and commended him for his efforts.[64]

The House Judiciary Committee was also involved in an ongoing relationship with the WSPF. As it began to consider the possibility of impeachment, it became clear that it would need a great deal of information from the special prosecutor. Shortly after Cox's firing, committee attorneys met with WSPF staff and were assured of the force's cooperation. In February 1974 the committee obtained a list of documents and recordings the force had received from the White House and another list of denied requests. The chief counsel of the committee, John Doar, then requested this evidence from the White House.[65]

The impeachment process was facilitated by an important exchange between the House committee and the WSPF. While the House committee could not gain complete access to the information held by the force because much of it was grand jury testimony under seal of court, the WSPF was able to suggest witnesses and topics for interviews, provide the committee with leads, and allow Doar to review office memoranda outlining the case against the president. The special prosecutor also steered the committee away from unfruitful allegations that had already been abandoned in the criminal investigation. Most importantly, the WSPF drew up a "road map" of the evidence against the president which provided direction to the committee in preparing the articles of impeachment.[66]

Leon Jaworski later contended that the prosecution force's decision to turn over the information to the committee was central to the impeachment process. When the impeachment proceedings began, the committee "had nothing except a little stuff that it had gotten from the Senate Committee. . . . it really couldn't get started, didn't know how to get started."[67] There was some initial tension between the Committee and the Force over exchange of information, which inhered in the differing natures of the interests of each group: the committee's in obtaining information for impeachment, the force's in ensuring secrecy to protect its criminal cases. That tension was mediated by the press with each side making its interests known publicly. Jaworski explained that Chairman Peter Rodino's "way of covering his tracks was to tell the news media constantly that it was my responsibility to get these matters to him. . . . he was engaging in inferences as if I were holding out on him until finally I got on Issues and Answers; and I blasted Rodino, pointing out in very clear language that I was . . . under a rule of contempt . . . if I furnished any information [from the grand jury-]."[68] Jaworski further pointed out to the news media that Rodino had two lawyers working for him, "both of whom are good friends of mine; and I know that each of them knows the way to the courthouse. So all they need to do is go ahead and file their proper suit and ask me to turn it over. And if the court says: turn it over, then I've got that protection, and I can turn it over."[69]

The special prosecutor's friendship with John Doar and Bert Jenner, the committee's minority counsel, appears to have eased tensions and provided a groundwork for exchange between the two investigative units. Jaworski "hated to turn John down; he was such a good friend" and Jenner "had been a warm friend from the ACTL (American College of Trial Lawyers) days and the ABA days." Jaworski would assure them that he was "at work trying to get the stuff into your people's hands."[70] Much of the exchange between the force and the committee was carried out behind the scenes. "It wasn't very well known," Jaworski recalled, "but we just had John in our office night after night after night coaching him, as poor John didn't know which way was front. He walked into a situation that was in mid-stream so, . . . when we got this stuff turned over to us, we in turn coached John. Our group just stayed with him to educate him and bring him up to date. This was all done sub rosa."[71]

Finally, the Senate and House judiciary committees acted as important pressure groups on the White House and Leon Jaworski after the Saturday Night Massacre. After Cox was fired, both committees began actively considering legislation that would create a special prosecutor with independence guaranteed by statute. It appears that the White House decided to appoint Jaworski in order to preempt congressional action. In addition, Leon Jaworski felt pressured by the committees' continued consideration of legislation following his appointment. In his memoirs he wrote: "The debates and discussions in the House and Senate on proposals for a Special Prosecutor other than one appointed by the President weighed heavily on my mind. When committees presented both houses with separate bills for consideration, it sorely taxed my spirit."[72]

While Congress was considering special prosecutor legislation, Acting Attorney General Bork strengthened Jaworski's charter, Jaworski testified as to his independence at the confirmation hearings of Attorney General-designate William Saxbe, Saxbe promised that there would be no interference from the Department of Justice, and Deputy Special Prosecutor Henry Ruth assured the committees that the investigation was proceeding uninterrupted. In addition, several federal judges questioned the constitutionality of the proposals for judicial appointment and stated their lack of interest in having the appointment responsibility.[73]

Jaworski appears to have felt the need to prove his independence by pressing for the evidence that Cox had sought from the White House. He felt that many in Congress, on his staff, and in the press did not trust him because Nixon had appointed him and he had the image of an "establishment" man.[74] He recalled that "the sounds emanating from Congress and the studied prose of the editorial pages made it appear likely that my stay in Washington would be a short one." Not wanting to appear "slow of foot," he immediately began requesting the evidence needed from the White House. The uncertainty of his position was never far from his mind during the first month of his tenure. He later wrote: "Uncertainty gnawed at me, but I tried to hide it as I went about my work. My staff did not exactly rally around, but I sensed that most of them had at least accepted that my intentions were good."[75] Finally, in December 1973, Congress appeared satisfied that Jaworski intended to pursue the investigation with vigor and independence. Senate Majority Leader Mike Mansfield announced that the Senate had dropped consideration of the proposals for an independent prosecutor, and the House followed suit.[76]

Overall, Congress's actions were of great strategic importance in the intricate maneuvering among the various actors in the Watergate affair. While the force and Congress shared an interest in uncovering the truth in the Watergate case, their interests in the appropriate means to do that often conflicted. The record of congressional action during this period suggests that the legislative branch, as a whole and through its committees, both provided a base of support for the independent prosecutor and acted as a check on, or monitor of, the force's investigation. Likewise, the WSPF provided valuable information to the committees but also restrained them from fully disclosing all of the information uncovered by the investigations in order to protect their criminal prosecutions. Out of the tension that resulted from these conflicting and mutual interests, a working relationship was forged.

White House. The nature of the Watergate case required much contact between the WSPF and the White House. The force's interest in obtaining evidence from the president was counteracted by its deference to the presidency and its recognition that it could lose crucial public support if it appeared to be harassing Nixon.[77] Consequently, it moved slowly and with care in the early months of its operation. For example, Archibald Cox's personality appeared to impact upon the ability of the WSPF to obtain the information it needed. "Archie's background, his experience, and his personal view of the Presidency undoubtedly reinforced the institutional restraints holding us back from a full scale investigation of the President," two of his assistants later wrote. "He was steeped in an intellectual tradition that stressed achievement of a proper balance between competing governmental institutions."[78]

The WSPF Report chronicles the efforts of the force to obtain information from the White House in the months preceding the Saturday Night Massacre. During June 1973 Cox and Vorenberg met with White House lawyers Fred Buzhardt, Leonard Garment, and Charles Wright in order to discuss the availability of evidence. At that time the special prosecutor was informed of the president's intent to claim executive privilege for most of the evidence the force had requested. While some documents trickled in, the White House continued to stall the prosecutors on most of their requests. After the existence of the tapes was revealed in July, Cox and his staff selected the conversations most relevant to their criminal cases and requested them from the White House. After a refusal, Cox announced his intention to subpoena the tapes, and the first court battle over the tapes followed.[79]

Throughout the time preceding the standoff over the tapes, Cox moved with great care, seeking cooperation rather than conflict. One participant's account of the Watergate prosecution suggests that "Cox's patience, his desire to lean over backward to be fair, his deference to the White House, and his willingness to assume good faith on their part . . . combined to produce a drawn out, frustrating series of skirmishes over documentary evidence that by late summer had netted us little of consequence."[80]

Cox admits to his reluctance to appear to be overstepping his bounds: it was a reluctance based upon his recognition of the uncertainty and ambiguity of his position.

> I really didn't know for sure if I had the public support I needed. One of the most worrisome things all during this time . . . was what do you do if the President says "I won't comply with the court decree?" What do you do? What does the judge do? If the President doesn't comply, you are then faced with a confrontation. If the President gets away with non-compliance, what does that do to our system of constitutionalism? Churchill said one time something about never exposing the weaknesses of democracy. That you must never press what you can't enforce. So I thought maybe you musn't force a confrontation if you can't win. On the other hand, what good are constitutions and laws if you can't rely on them? That was a most agonizing question for me.[81]

Leon Jaworski's tenure as special prosecutor was characterized by less formal and more combative relationships with the White House. Although on somewhat insecure footing due to the lack of confidence that many had in him when he started, he appears to have been more certain of his independence and ability to confront the president if the need arose. Nevertheless, the new special prosecutor was also constrained somewhat by his deference to the institution of the presidency. Looking back on Nixon's complicity in the cover-up, Jaworski found it "very difficult . . . to believe that a President of the United States could be guilty of such as that . . . always [having] had a great regard and esteem for the Presidency."[82]

Despite this shared deference to the president, Jaworski was a different man than Cox with a different style and with much more evidence against the president available to him than Cox had had.[83] It was true that "Jaworski was consistently reluctant to move against the President," his assistants remember, "But when he had pondered his course . . . and made a decision, he was ready for bold action . . . The weighing and reweighing of the ultimate fairness of what he was about to do was not his style. For the greatest gut fight of his career, President Nixon made the mistake of choosing as an opponent a first-class gut fighter."[84]

It is apparent that the special prosecutors had conflicting pressures upon them in their dealings with the White House. They were not only responsible for getting to the truth in the Watergate case but they also had to accomplish that by taking on the president of the United States, a formidable opponent revered by the people and the prosecutors themselves. The White House also had conflicting interests that caused its relationship with the WSPF to be characterized both by cooperation and by conflict. It was necessary to appear cooperative in order not to appear as though the president had something to hide. On the other hand, the president did have something to hide.

The interaction between Jaworski and Alexander Haig, Nixon's chief of staff, appears to have been the primary contact between the WSPF and the White House. From the time of Jaworski's appointment until the resignation of Nixon, the two engaged in a tension filled but respectful relationship, one that Jaworski's staff was often uncomfortable with. The staff "knew that I had . . . confidence in Haig up to a certain point," Jaworski said. "I didn't swallow everything that Haig told me by any means, but I had to make allowances for the fact that this man was serving his Commander-in-Chief."[85]

Haig played a major role in convincing Jaworski to accept the special prosecutor position after the firing of Cox. Jaworski recalled in his memoirs that he found Haig to be "articulate and persuasive" but also believed that Haig was purposely trying to charm him, telling him of his great reputation and suggesting that Jaworski was a highly ranked candidate for the Supreme Court. Jaworski wrote, "The remark could have been part flattery, part fact, but I suspected that it was all bait."[86]

Jaworski also believed that he had been selected because the White House and Haig had concluded that he was "a political conservative and a member of the Establishment" and therefore, that he would be less dangerous than Cox as the special prosecutor. When he accepted the position, Haig told him, "You are a great American," and then reminded him that "the key words in any news conference are that you've got the right to take the President to court."[87] It appears that the White House believed that given Jaworski's political inclinations he would be unlikely to exercise that right. History reflects how seriously they misread Mr. Jaworski.

Jaworski realized fairly quickly that the "new" relationship with the White House was not much different from the old. After failing to obtain the information he sought in written requests, he met with Haig and Buzhardt in order to remind them of their promises of cooperation. "Haig was at his persuasive best" at this meeting, Jaworski said, "I could not help but admire the way he set about trying to channel my thinking." The special prosecutor stood his ground and ultimately obtained another promise that the evidence would be forthcoming. That exchange appears to have made it clear to Haig that Jaworski was not going to back away from the investigation. The new prosecutor left the meeting feeling that "Haig had become an adversary, not a supplicant. He would be one without hate and . . . a candid one, but he had drawn the battle line, however faintly."[88]

Despite this suggested cooling of their relationship, the special prosecutor and Haig continued to meet in attempts to work out, informally, disputes between the force and the White House. Jaworski's memoirs are full of references to these contacts.[89] As the WSPF got closer and closer to the Oval Office, and more and more of the participants pleaded guilty to involvement in the cover-up, the White House became increasingly worried about Jaworski's work. He recalled that during this time he was in "almost constant communication with Haig" either by telephone or in meetings at the Map Room in the White House.[90]

When it became clear to Jaworski that Nixon was implicated in the cover-up, he met with Haig to tell him that he had this evidence and that the president ought to get the best criminal lawyer he could find. Haig regularly attempted to disuade Jaworski from this position. An exchange that occurred just before the spring 1974 announcements of the Watergate cover-up indictments demonstrated Haig's efforts to pressure Jaworski and the special prosecutor's own ambivalence about his position. In describing the days before the bringing of the indictments, Jaworski recounted a conversation with Haig about what to expect in the indictments. In notes on the conversation he wrote: "Twice during the conversation he said that he really called to tell me that I was a 'great American'—the second time he mentioned it I said 'Alex—I really don't want any of the cheese—I just want out of this trap as soon as is reasonably possible.' "[91]

Another illustrative exchange occurred in late April 1974, when the second legal battle over the tapes was imminent. Haig and Jaworski met in the Map Room, and Haig "began immediately to try to sell his ideas and channel" Jaworski's. Haig attacked the reliability of the prosecution's witnesses, especially Dean, and implied that Cox and the force had mishandled the witnesses and committed other grievous wrongs against the president. Haig had sent a military plane to Texas to pick up Jaworski and bring him to the White House for the meeting. At it, he asked Jaworski to read a fifty-page summary of the tapes, which the president intended to release instead of the tapes Jaworski was seeking. Haig wanted the special prosecutor's comments on the transcripts and his agreement to accept them instead of the tapes. Haig also suggested that the White House's willingness to cooperate with the WSPF had ended and that the president's new counteroffensive would be "bloody."[92] Jaworski interpreted Haig's efforts as threats and was angered by them. Right after the meeting, he approved the plan to reveal the fact that Nixon had been named an unindicted coconspirator in the cover-up as part of the legal argument for enforcing the tapes subpoena. Aides recall; "Jaworski displayed no regret over this plan. Haig's 'threats' had obviously rankled him, and he wanted to make it clear to the President and everyone else that Leon Jaworski was not going to be deterred from seeing the work of the office through, come hell or highwater."[93]

After Nixon lost the tapes case in the Supreme Court and the House Judiciary Committee voted out the articles of impeachment, Jaworski and Haig had one more round of contacts in bringing their relationship to a close. On August 5, 1974, after Haig heard the "smoking gun" tape of June 23, 1973, that demonstrated Nixon's early knowledge of and participation in the cover-up, he called Jaworski at home, telling him, "I am particularly anxious that you believe me, Leon. I didn't know what was in those conversations."[94] On August 7, Haig called again to set up a meeting with Jaworski. The next day they met and Jaworski was informed of Nixon's intention to resign that night and of the arrangements being made for the president's speech and departure. Jaworski felt "a sadness in our parting. Both of us had been knee-deep in an unparalleled tragedy, and it had forged a strange kinship."[95] Later, Jaworski's regular contact with Haig, including this last meeting, were used by some critics of the pardon to imply that in those final days Jaworski may have struck a deal not to indict Nixon.[96] Jaworski denied that any deals were made.[97]

The record on the special prosecutor–White House relationship during Watergate suggests that the combination of conflict and cooperation explains the careful and deliberative pace by which the force went about this process. In each case, the participants were motivated by the desire to maintain or obtain public support for their position. The resulting tension in these interests may be credited, in part, for the ultimate resolution of the crisis.

The Press and Public Opinion. A later chapter will discuss in more detail the importance of the press in bringing Watergate before the public eye and the way in which "saturation" news coverage impacted upon public opinion. There is no dispute that the media played a critical role in the resolution of the Watergate crisis. Not only did they expose many of the allegations initially but they also acted as mediators among the various actors, providing a forum in which these actors could fight "the battle for public opinion."[98]

That the WSPF recognized the importance of the press in securing a base of public support is evidenced by Cox's early creation of a public affairs office to act as a liaison with the press. He appointed an experienced journalist, James Doyle,[99] to head the office. One of the office's early tasks was to prepare and disseminate a press kit that contained information on the special prosecutor's charter, the organization of the force, and resumés of the staff members.[100] Cox set up the office because he "was mindful of the national concern over Watergate and of the public's right to be kept as fully informed as possible about the work of his office."[101] The WSPF report noted the degree to which public attention to the case required regularized dealings with the press, "the notoriety of the cases brought by the office, the massive press and public interest in the outcome of the office's investigations, the amount of evidentiary material laid out on the public record by the [Select Committee] and others, and the President's possible personal involvement created intense pressures to find out what was going on behind the heavily guarded entrance to the Special Prosecutor's office."[102]

Press attention and its potential impact on public attitudes was seen by the WSPF as a valuable asset in fulfilling its ultimate goal. The force viewed its work in "symbolic terms, as a test of the criminal justice process." The force members believed that "the success or failure of our effort would . . . have a grave impact on the public's future respect for the legal system and its confidence in the rule of law."[103] This concern about public support acted as a constraint upon the force's actions:

The investigation could not succeed without continued public support. While directly accountable to no one in government, we were dependent on the credibility we maintained with the public—on the confidence we could instill that a thorough investigation could and would be carried out. . . . [We] anticipated that any investigation of someone who thought he was being unjustifiably pursued would quickly be publicized, and might arouse suspicion of our office if we could not defend our action.[104]

Archibald Cox found the press to be "both a help and a hindrance." He credits the media with keeping the investigation alive prior to his appointment but also with creating problems because of leaks and the ability of defense lawyers to manipulate press coverage to their advantage. "Generally speaking," however, Cox saw the press as "much more supportive than non-supportive of our work."[105]

Leon Jaworski was also sensitive to press attention. His distress over the lack of media enthusiasm for his appointment and his use of "Issues and Answers" to clarify his position vis-à-vis the House Judiciary Committee have already been mentioned. Jaworski also looked to Doyle for advice on how to interpret "certain things that were hovering in the press's mind." He had Doyle give him a daily press briefing which he considered to be very important because he "needed to know what others were saying . . . where the doubts were—what the White House was putting out . . . what the speculations were . . . [and] what leaks there might be that had some basis to them." He also conducted background briefings with some members of the press with the agreement that they would not use the information given them without his permission. He found this to be a useful way to ensure that the coverage of the force's investigation was accurate.[106]

Generally, Jaworski felt that his relations with members of the press were good because of their desire to cooperate in order to have access to further information. "They didn't want to fall out with me," he recalled, because "they were fearful that I would then exclude them from certain things that others might get. So they were all playing up to us pretty well."[107]

The press did not always cooperate with the WSPF. In one instance the *New York Times* published a "sensational story" after a background briefing with Jaworski, using material that he had given them off the record. The special prosecutor and Doyle were very angry and refused any further sessions with the newspaper. Jaworski felt that the news media generally were fair to him and that they were his allies but there were exceptions. "You have to find one so-and-so among every crowd; and this fellow Bill Safire from the *New York Times* was my fly in the ointment . . . because old Bill would come out . . . saying that we were covering up for John Dean, that he had committed all kinds of perjury. I told Haig that the next time [Safire] said this I would call him before the grand jury for evidence of perjury. And you never heard another chirp out of him."[108]

The media's need for information and recognition on the part of the prosecutor's office that the press had an important role in providing it with public support generated an atmosphere conducive to cooperation. However, the press was not solely dependent upon the WSPF for information; it also participated in relationships with congressional committees and the White House. In turn, the WSPF had a competing interest in keeping some of its information secret. In addition, it could impose sanctions in efforts to control the press, as the two Jaworski examples above demonstrate. This relationship too appears to have been characterized by the pursuit of sometimes conflicting, sometimes mutual interests.

The WSPF report points out:

> most of what WSPF personnel experienced . . . was dramatically atypical of criminal justice generally. The prosecutors had adequate resources; . . . the courts had time and resources to meet all the demands of Watergate litigation in a detached, unhurried atmosphere; private defense counsel brought all their skills to thorough pre-trial investigation, legal attack, trial strategy, and fully briefed appeals; . . . and constant press and public scrutiny provided a careful watchdog to make sure that Government investigations proceeded without abuse of power or undue leniency.[109]

Nevertheless, the relationships that developed between the WSPF and the other legal and political actors in the federal system appear to have been very similar to the relationships found to exist with regular prosecutors. Despite the extraordinary character of the Watergate case, the historical record paradoxically reveals rather ordinary relationships based on mutual and competing interests developing among the actors in the case.

An explanation for this paradox appears to lie in the method of appointment of the special prosecutor. When the special prosecutor was appointed by the president with approval by the Senate, the ambiguity over how independent the office was, or what its base of support was, served as a check on the office, encouraging it to move slowly and deliberatively. The press rallied to its defense, when necessary, but also acted as a check on the prosecutors' powers. Because the prosecutor was an executive creation, it was never to be fully trusted, and a healthy skepticism was maintained. When the guaranteed independence of the prosecutor was violated by the president's order to remove him, the outrage that followed not only insured the appointment of a prosecutor with more independence but it also placed responsibility for this unpopular act directly upon the president and his subordinates.

AD HOC PROSECUTORS AND
DEMOCRATIC ACCOUNTABILITY

The study of ad hoc uses of special prosecutors suggests that there are some advantages to presidential appointment of special prosecutors that would exist to a lesser extent under a statutory independent appointment mechanism. Executive appointment seems to have motivated Congress, the judiciary, and the press to play more active oversight roles in the investigations. These other actors provided potential bases for support for the prosecutors, which permitted them to maintain their independence from the executive while engaging in necessary and productive cooperative relationships with the various actors. This increased oversight activity also acted as a check upon the prosecutors, ensuring that they did not abuse their prosecutorial discretion.

Rather than permitting the nonexecutive actors to sit idly by while the independent prosecutor pursues the investigation, the tensions inherent in the ad hoc form of appointment require these other actors to play an active role in order to defend their institutional prerogatives. A special prosecutor, appointed by the president with some form of congressional approval, is placed in the maelstrom of competing institutional interests that underlies the American separation of powers scheme. Consequently, the accountability of the special prosecutor is ensured along with that of the other actors.

These findings suggest that the case against executive appointment has been overstated and is based more on appearances than on reality. They also demonstrate, however, two points in support of the argument for alternative appointment schemes. In the three cases prior to adoption of the statutory arrangement, two ad hoc special prosecutors were fired by the president. This fact makes compelling the argument that an executive appointed special prosecutor's independence is always in question, an inescapable cost of presidential appointment. A degree of independence is sacrificed for increased accountability. The second point is linked to the first. The doubt about independence can have a significant impact on the perceptions by attentive elites that an impartial investigation is taking place. In this sense, appearances may become more important than the reality. If the suspicion becomes great enough, it may undermine public confidence in the investigation and consequently defeat the purpose of appointing an independent prosecutor in the first place.

Presidents must weigh this cost of executive appointment with the benefits gained by maintaining appointment power before adopting a blanket position that they must have the power to appoint. If statutory independent counsel were completely unaccountable creatures, one could well argue that it was necessary to incur these costs. But as we shall see, accountability is not seriously lacking in the statutory arrangement. This chapter suggests that neither is independence seriously threatened in ad hoc appointments. In the post-Watergate period, as Congress attempted to address issues raised by the scandal, the assumption that presidentially appointed prosecutors could not act independently was taken for granted. This review of ad hoc appointments demonstrates that this assumption was not fully accurate. Nonetheless, it was this assumption that drove the five-year effort to create a statutory independent prosecutor and that lies at the root of the 1978 provisions.

THREE

A WATERGATE LEGACY:
THE INDEPENDENT COUNSEL PROVISIONS
OF THE ETHICS IN GOVERNMENT ACT

What did Congress hope to achieve in creating a statutory independent counsel arrangement? Why did it choose the particular arrangement that it did? In order to answer these questions we must understand the environment within which Congress deliberated and the institutional forces that structured its decisionmaking process. The Watergate scandal, and in particular the Saturday Night Massacre, was the "focusing event"[1] that placed the issue of independent counsel on the agenda, that shaped the possible alternatives considered, that "selected" the individual members of Congress who would lead the way on this issue, and that determined the final structure of the arrangement that was adopted. There were also other forces at work. For example, the decline in public confidence in government that appeared to motivate some of the actors had been going on throughout the decade preceding Watergate.[2] And the congressional–executive struggle and congressional resurgence that also were at work were driven by far more than Watergate.[3] But Watergate is critical to the creation of this statutory arrangement because the arrangement would not exist had the scandal not occurred and because the scandal channeled these other forces toward the adoption of this particular response.

Given the political environment, there were many possible responses that might address the problem posed. The likelihood of certain alternatives being chosen over others was determined by these institutional characteristics that structure legislative action.[4] In addition to these institutional factors, there are also the more general constitutional constraints on how any institution in American politics may act. These constitutional constraints proved crucial to the structure of the final legislative outcome. The possible alternatives can be grouped into three broad categories falling along a continuum of the amount of change from the current situation that would be implied by such a move.

The first option was to do nothing. Perhaps no legislative response was needed. This position was based on the argument that "the system worked" in the resolution of the Watergate crisis and that no inherent systemic flaw was revealed that required a statutory remedy. There were resources already constitutionally available for controlling the executive in such cases, not the least of which were the Senate's power to confirm the attorney general and

Congress's oversight capabilities. Further, a vigilant press and an aroused public could provide an ultimate check on the abuse of presidential power. A second option was to institute reforms within the executive branch. This alternative would require action, not necessarily legislative, to create new arrangements or alter old ones to reduce the likelihood of politically motivated influence in public corruption cases. It might include permitting more independence on the part of the Criminal Division of the Department of Justice, instituting reporting requirements for cases of this type, creating a new division in the department with responsibility for official misconduct cases, or requiring the appointment of special prosecutors who were appointed by the president and confirmed by the Senate for these cases. Finally, new independent institutions could be created. The greatest move from the existing situation would have been to create new institutions, independent from the established executive law enforcement mechanisms. These could include permanent or temporary special prosecutors appointed outside the executive branch or a completely independent justice agency (an idea proposed by Sen. Sam Ervin in 1974).

Congress ultimately passed new legislation that fell into the third category of alternatives. Conventional wisdom suggests that choosing the legislative path that requires this amount of change is an unusual occurrence. More incremental change is far more likely. Why is it that Congress did not choose either to do nothing or to impose internal reforms on the Department of Justice? A study of the legislative history of the independent counsel arrangement aids in answering this question.

THE POLITICAL ENVIRONMENT: WATERGATE, PUBLIC CONFIDENCE, AND CONGRESSIONAL RESURGENCE

The Ethics in Government Act is firmly rooted in the Watergate experience. Special prosecutors had been employed in the Teapot Dome and tax scandals, but it was the central role played by the Watergate Special Prosecution Force (WSPF) in the resolution of that scandal that laid the groundwork for the creation of a statutory arrangement.

The Saturday Night Massacre

The firing of Archibald Cox, the first Watergate special prosecutor, on October 20, 1973, was a turning point in the resolution of the Watergate crisis.

The events surrounding that firing and the resignations of Elliot Richardson and William Ruckelshaus have been well chronicled elsewhere.[5] It is sufficient here to outline the chain of events leading to the dismissal and their impact on the creation of a statutory special prosecutor by Congress.

As the Watergate cover-up began to unravel early in 1973, Nixon announced the resignations of Attorney General Richard Kleindienst and White House staff members H. R. Haldeman, John Ehrlichman, and John Dean. In nominating Elliot Richardson to replace Kleindienst, Nixon announced that he had given Richardson the option of appointing a special prosecutor to handle the Watergate cases.[6] The Senate responded by requesting that the president appoint such a prosecutor. In addition, the Senate Judiciary Committee announced its intention of linking Richardson's confirmation to a promise to make the appointment.[7]

During his confirmation hearings, Richardson offered the Senate the chance to confirm his choice informally. Following a nationwide search and some bargaining over guarantees of independence, the attorney general-designate chose Harvard Law professor Archibald Cox. Cox testified about his authority to pursue an independent investigation, and Richardson was confirmed.[8] The Watergate Special Prosecution Force was established through the promulgation of regulations that codified Richardson's assurances to the Senate.[9] The force set to work.

Soon, Cox and Nixon's lawyers became embroiled in a legal dispute over the release of certain presidential tape recordings and other materials sought by the special prosecutor. Cox won the legal battle[10] and refused to settle for a political compromise offered by Nixon.[11] He was fired, under Nixon's orders, by Acting Attorney General Robert Bork on October 20, 1973. Richardson and his deputy, William Ruckelshaus, had previously resigned rather than carry out the order.[12] This Saturday Night Massacre, as it came to be known, was the most direct cause of Congress's subsequent move toward creating an independent special prosecutor. The firestorm of public outrage that followed the events of October 20, 1973, overwhelmed all involved. According to Western Union, the number of telegrams that arrived in Washington following Cox's dismissal was "the heaviest volume on record." Over the weekend 150,000 telegrams from around the country arrived in the District. Ten thousand went to the White House and the rest to Capitol Hill and the prosecution force. Within ten days that number had increased to 450,000 telegrams.[13] There is little wonder that Congress was compelled to act quickly and decisively in establishing a new and more independent special prosecutor.

Within days of the firing, both the House and Senate held hearings on the establishment of an office of special prosecutor with legislative guarantees of independence.[14] On October 23, Congressman John Culver introduced a plan drawn up by the Democratic study group, which provided for a judicially appointed prosecutor. The bill boasted 105 sponsors.[15] Culver's defense of the bill exemplifies the concerns held by most in Congress at the time. "Congress as a whole will find a wide consensus which will help to renew public confidence in the process of justice and in the fabric of our governmental system," he said, "Precisely because we are responding to an unmistakable and deeply felt public determination to restore full rule of law, we have a special responsibility to act with all possible dispatch."[16]

The concern over restoring public confidence was a predominant theme throughout the hearings. Action in the Senate centered on a bill introduced October 26, 1973, by Birch Bayh and fifty-two other senators. This bill also provided for judicial appointment of an independent prosecutor. In encouraging the Senate to act, Bayh began by arguing that "our system of government is facing a crisis of unprecedented proportions. . . . Congress must set out as its first order of business, the difficult, but . . . essential goal of reestablishing the public faith and confidence from which all else proceeds in a democracy."[17]

On November 1, 1973, in response to the overwhelming public reaction to the firing of Cox and in the hope of preempting congressional action, the White House announced the appointment of Leon Jaworski to head the prosecution force.[18] Initially suspicious of this executive appointment, Congress continued its hearings. The Senate Judiciary Committee finally brought them to a close on November 20. It first heard testimony from Jaworski regarding his independence and received his assurances that he was satisfied with his status. New regulations by the attorney general required the consent of a majority of the Senate committee before Jaworski could be fired.[19] These assurances diminished Congress's enthusiasm for creating a statutory independent prosecutor for the Watergate investigation.

Congressional interest in designing a special prosecutor arrangement for future use continued. Over the next few months 35 different bills with 165 sponsors were introduced in Congress, each attempting to insulate the Department of Justice from political influence and most proposing some sort of independent special prosecutor.[20] Thus, the impact of the Saturday Night Massacre was to survive beyond the resolution of the Watergate scandal. But the memory of Cox's firing was not the only force at work that contributed to keeping the issue on the public agenda. The decline in public confidence in government and Congress's resistance to domination on the part of the executive motivated the long-term legislative process.

The Problem of Public Confidence

Public opinion polls in the 1970s reflected a steady decline in confidence in government. That decline became marked during and following the Watergate crisis.[21] Chapter 8 examines more closely the issue of public confidence. Here it is most important to point out the broad trends in public opinion that contributed to the desire of many in Congress to formulate a legislative response to Watergate.

Two studies examining faith in government over time are particularly telling of this decline in public confidence. Data from the Center for Political Studies reveal that from 1958 to 1980 the percentage of respondents who felt that government could not be regularly trusted to do what was right rose from 25 percent in 1958 to 71 percent in 1980. The sharpest increase (of 14 percent) occurred between 1972 and 1974, the years that the Watergate scandal was unfolding. Between 1972 and 1978, the period during which Congress considered Watergate reform legislation, this lack of trust in government grew from 46 percent to 68 percent.[22]

The Harris survey has also tracked long-term trends of public confidence in government. In the decade between 1966 and 1976 the survey found that those having a "great deal of confidence" in the executive branch and in Congress dropped dramatically. Confidence in the president dropped from 41 percent in 1966 to 11 percent in 1976. Similarly, and probably more alarming to Congress, during that same time confidence in Congress dropped from 42 percent to 9 percent. After the 1976 election the same survey recorded some increase in confidence in both institutions, but those levels remained low.[23]

Public opinion on the Watergate scandal produced what many in Congress perceived as further evidence that it must act to clean up government and to restore public confidence. In January 1974 the Harris survey found the public dissatisfied with the way both Nixon and Congress were handling Watergate. Nixon's general disapproval rate on this topic was 82 percent, Congress's, 72 percent. On the issue of which branch was performing better at inspiring confidence in government, neither received anything approaching a public endorsement. But in this category, Congress received lower ratings than Nixon. He received a positive rating of 17 percent while Congress garnered only a 10 percent approval rating. Whatever the issue, "roughly 3 of every 4 adult Americans came up with a negative assessment of the job being done by Congress and the President."[24]

In August 1974, shortly after Nixon's resignation, Congress enjoyed a brief upswing in support. A Gallup poll revealed an approval rating of 48 percent, largely attributed to the televised impeachment hearings held by the House Judiciary Committee that summer.[25] The increase in support was short-lived. An early 1975 Gallup poll found another downturn in approval for Congress. Only 32 percent of Gallup's respondents approved of Congress's performance, a rating seven percentage points below that given President Ford.[26]

Finally, in 1976, a Harris poll focusing on priorities for the new Congress found very strong indications of public support for government reform. Of the respondents, 88 percent identified cleaning up corruption in government as a very important goal for the Congress. Making certain "no more Watergates take place" was considered "very important" by 78 percent of the respondents. In addition, 76 percent supported making government more open and less secret, and 57 percent agreed that Congress should act to "curb the power excesses of the White House."[27]

During the period that Congress considered Watergate reform legislation, public opinion polls were sending two messages. The first was that the public's confidence in its government had been shaken badly by the Watergate scandal. Second, there seemed to be a strong desire for a "cleaner" government, one less corrupt and more responsive to the public. These messages were interpreted by many in Congress to mean that the people expected them to lead the way in legislating government reform. In terms of specific policy proposals, these concerns translated into stricter regulation of elections, comprehensive financial disclosure for public officials, increased oversight of executive agencies (especially the Justice Department), and a special prosecutor arrangement, independent of the executive branch, to investigate allegations of criminal conduct by members of that branch.

Congressional Resurgence

The support for a special prosecutor also reflected increasing congressional resistance to executive domination. James Sundquist has identified the 1970s as a period of "resurgence" in Congress—a time when Congress sought to reassert its constitutional role in the national government.[28]

Sundquist documents what had been a long-term decline in congressional power prior to the re-election of Richard Nixon in 1972. After a landslide victory in that election, Nixon began consolidating his powers, "pushing those powers to the limit, in defiance of the sentiment of his political enemies who controlled the Democratic Congress. In doing so, he finally . . . spurred it to organize and fight back against the presidency."[29]

During this time Congress did not place all of the blame for its diminished power on Mr. Nixon. This period was also "a remarkable period of congressional introspection." Members were aware of the lack of confidence that the public had in them and felt the need to correct this problem.[30] A reassertion of power seemed the solution. Consider, for example, Congressman John Anderson's statement before the House in June 1974:

> Mr. Speaker, while one might expect the Congress to at least temporarily fill the power vacuum created by Watergate, the polls clearly indicate the contrary. Congress too is on the skids with the American people, and I think it fair to characterize this as a "crisis of confidence in Congress." I think it therefore behooves us at this critical juncture in our Nation's political history to conduct a serious self-evaluation of why the people's branch has lost the confidence of the people.[31]

Congressional resurgence over the next few years was marked by far-reaching attempts to regain power through the legislative and oversight processes. It began with the War Powers Resolution of 1973, was further evidenced in the Congressional Budget and Impoundment Control Act of 1974, and was the force behind increased scrutiny in requests for foreign aid, operation of the intelligence agencies, and other foreign policy issues. In domestic policy, Congress included extensive oversight provisions in its new legislation. In addition to increased use of "sunset" requirements, there was a dramatic upswing in the use of the legislative veto. Between 1972 and 1979, sixty-two legislative veto provisions were included in congressional legislation. Prior to 1972 only fifty-one such provisions had been included since the device was first employed in 1932.[32] Given this mood of resurgence, which was enhanced by the desire to restore its public image and spurred on by the unfolding of the Watergate story, it is not surprising that members of Congress persisted in their attempts at post-Watergate reform.

INTERNAL AND EXTERNAL INFLUENCES

What is it about members of Congress that would cause them to respond to the environmental forces in the way that they did? Why did they select the particular response of a judicially appointed, temporary independent prosecutor? The political environment does have an influence on Congress, but there remains much room for choice. Ripley contends that "a principal internal variable" influencing congressional behavior is "the wishes and preferences of the collection of individuals happening to serve in it at any particular time."[33] The reason members of Congress adopt one set of policy alternatives over another is determined by a set of institutional forces that cause members to behave in predictable ways and that make it more likely that some actions will be taken than others.

Constitutional Constraints

In the very broadest sense, congressional behavior is shaped by the constraints imposed by the Constitution itself. There are powers that belong exclusively to each of the branches and many others that are shared. The lines between executive and legislative power are not clearly drawn. There is a gray area within which periodic skirmishes between the branches will occur.[34] Members of Congress must consider their own powers, and the limitations on those powers, in choosing particular courses of action. This is particularly true when the policy issue at its root concerns separation of powers.

Just as constitutional issues were central to the discussions of war powers, impoundment, and impeachment, they were at the core of the congressional debate over an independent special prosecutor. The central issue was whether Congress could establish a prosecutor whose independence was assured through judicial, rather than executive, appointment. Secondary, but nonetheless constitutionally important, issues involved the length of term of the prosecutors and conditions for their removal.

Because the institution of the federal special prosecutor is rooted in the events of Watergate, the executive branch was not viewed as the most trustworthy agent for appointment. The Saturday Night Massacre was the driving force behind congressional efforts to insure future prosecutors' independence from the executive. In addition, District Court Judge John Sirica's role in the crisis caused many in Congress to look to the judiciary for appointment.[35] Finally, judicial appointment was the only constitutional alternative to allowing executive selection of the prosecutor.

The arguments for judicial appointment were based on several provisions in the Constitution, as well as on a body of supporting case law.[36] Proponents of the congressional establishment of an independent special prosecutor began by calling upon Article I, section 8, the "necessary and proper clause," to justify their action. Establishment of an independent special prosecutor was considered necessary and proper because under the rule of law, no one should be judge or prosecutor in his own case. Since there are times when high-level executive branch officials might be involved in a criminal act, it was important to the concept of impartial justice that someone outside of the executive branch investigate and prosecute the case.[37] This broad interpretation of Article I, section 8, was buttressed by Article II, section 2, which grants Congress the power to vest appointment of "such inferior officers, as they think proper, in the President alone, in the Courts of Law, or in the Heads of Departments." Proponents cited this constitutional grant as the most conclusive proof that they could create a judicially appointed special prosecutor.[38] The summation of their constitutional argument was that given the conflict of interest that arises in the executive investigating itself, it is necessary and proper to vest the appointment of a special prosecutor, an inferior officer, in the courts. In no instance where Congress has granted appointment power to the courts has such an act been found unconstitutional.[39]

Article II, section 1, states that the executive power is vested in the president. Just what the "executive power" includes is not altogether clear. The presumption that it includes law enforcement is based on Article II, section 3, which requires that the president "take care that the laws are faithfully executed." Opponents of a judicially appointed special prosecutor concluded that these two sections compel two conclusions: first, that enforcing the laws is an "inherently executive function," and second, that the executive branch has sole constitutional authority for law enforcement.[40] Executive authority over law enforcement has been affirmed fairly consistently by the courts. However, in the 1880 case of *Ex parte Siebold* the court upheld judicial appointment of election supervisors despite the fact that these officers were carrying out law enforcement activities.[41]

Proponents of executive appointment further argued that another aspect of the doctrine of separation of powers was violated by judicial appointment, that is, the blending of the "traditionally separate roles of the prosecution and judiciary." The proposals for court appointment, which allowed the judiciary to appoint and remove the special prosecutor and review his decisions, appeared to permit the court to supervise the prosecutor. Such supervision of the discretionary powers of a prosecutor had been forbidden as an infringement of the doctrine of separation of powers.[42]

There were further disputes over the ideal term of service for the prosecutor. Even among those who accepted the idea of creating an independent office, there were differences over whether the office should be a permanent or a temporary one. A number of legislative proposals called for the creation of a permanent office of special prosecutor: one where the prosecutor served a fixed term and had protection from summary dismissal by the president.[43] The underlying assumption of each of these proposals was that the problem of public corruption and conflict of interest was an enduring one, not unique to Watergate. Consequently, it was necessary to have a permanent mechanism in place, both to handle future situations similar to Watergate and to deter potential wrongdoers.[44]

There was much opposition to the creation of a permanent office. Many who agreed on the need for some sort of arrangement rejected the idea that such an arrangement be permanent. Arguments for a temporary arrangement were based on the following contentions: that a permanent independent office would create an unaccountable prosecutor; that the infringement on the constitutional power of the executive would be greater with such an arrangement; that high-quality lawyers would be less attracted to a permanent position; and that there would be insufficient work for a permanent office, given the aberrational nature of the Watergate scandal.[45]

Supporters of an independent arrangement who had reservations about its being permanent encouraged a temporary appointment that could be triggered when the need arose. After investigating and prosecuting specific allegations, the appointment would terminate. The American Bar Association takes credit for being the first to propose a workable triggering mechanism for temporary appointments, an idea incorporated into the final legislative product.[46]

Positions on the issue of removal of the special prosecutor were dependent on the broader position one took on the relative strength of the legislative and executive powers on this issue. The Saturday Night Massacre made it clear that some sort of protection from arbitrary dismissal would be an important ingredient in insuring independence. There was case law to support the insulation of independent officers from arbitrary dismissal by the executive.[47] But permitting dismissal by the judicial panel responsible for appointment would be troublesome since it would imply that the judiciary had an unconstitutional amount of control over the prosecutor. Supporters of the executive power argument felt that no removal restrictions were acceptable on officers carrying out what they considered to be the essentially executive function of law enforcement. Case law suggested that the executive should be able to remove purely executive officers at will.[48]

Members of Congress were faced, then, with conflicting provisions of the Constitution, each of which had a substantial body of precedent to support it. To some extent, this may have given them more maneuvering room since none of the proposals receiving serious consideration were clearly unconstitutional. But the constitutional ambiguities on this issue did create a degree of uncertainty about the constitutionality of certain proposals that had the effect of encouraging compromise, delaying action, and providing opponents with a theoretical explanation for their opposition to a plan that was, for political reasons, difficult to oppose.

The Electoral Connection

It is an article of faith in legislative studies that members of Congress behave in ways that will enhance their prospects for re-election. Mayhew contends that this electoral connection is what drives the internal structuring of the institution and the decisions and actions of its members. Members devote their energy to activities that enhance their re-election chances. They are unlikely to expend much energy on work they do not perceive as having electoral payoff.[49] On policy issues where there is at least a perception by the members that their constituencies are aroused and watching what they do, they are more likely to be mobilized into pursuing legislative action than on less visible issues.[50] The most likely activity to be pursued in the policymaking arena will be position taking, a behavior Mayhew defines as "public enunciation of a judgmental statement on anything likely to be of interest to political actors." Position taking may not actually lead to policy outcomes, for it is the "position itself" that "is the political commodity."[51] Members of Congress believe that taking positions makes a difference electorally, and in the search for electorally significant positions, they watch election returns closely. Mayhew argues that "nothing is more important in Capitol Hill politics than the shared conviction that election returns have proven a point."[52]

The first test of the electoral fallout from the Watergate scandal came early in the consideration of legislative responses. The midterm election of 1974 was a devastating one for congressional Republicans. The public response to the Saturday Night Massacre had already demonstrated that the public had been aroused by the Watergate scandal and that it was paying attention to what was happening in national government. The 1974 elections were a powerful indication that, a year later, the public was still watching. The Democrats gained forty-three seats in the House and three in the Senate. They won many of what had been solidly Republican seats.[53] By the start of the 94th Congress in 1975 there were ninety-two freshmen representatives, only seventeen of whom were Republicans. Among the Republicans in Congress there was an ideological shift to the left as a result of this election. Republican moderates fared far better than conservatives. The majority of Republican incumbents defeated were from the conservative wing of the party.[54]

The election of 1976 continued the trend. In addition to the election of a Democrat to the White House, the "retaliation of the electorate against the Nixon loyalists . . . continued to conclusion."[55] Of the six Republican senators first elected in 1970, four were defeated. The two who survived were moderate Republicans with no ties to Nixon. In fact, one of them, Lowell Weicker of Connecticut, had been a member of the Senate Watergate Committee and an outspoken critic of Nixon.[56]

For members motivated primarily by their re-election concerns, what better mobilizing force can there be than a set of elections like those of 1974 and 1976? The election returns had made clear that support for post-Watergate reform was an electorally significant position to take. Public hearings on reform efforts were full of statements demanding a legislative response to the problems exposed in the scandal, and these statements refer repeatedly to the public demand for such action.

On December 11, 1974, as the 93d Congress ended, Sen. Sam Ervin introduced a bill that proposed widespread reforms in response to Watergate.[57] The bill was based primarily on recommendations made in the final report of the Senate Select Committee on Presidential Campaign Activities (also known as the Senate Watergate Committee) which Ervin had chaired.[58] No action was taken before the session ended.

At the start of the 94th Congress, Sen. Abraham Ribicoff introduced the same bill, the Watergate Reorganization and Reform Act of 1975 (S. 495), and it was referred to the Committee on Government Operations, which he chaired. S. 495 recommended the establishment of a permanent office of public attorney, appointed by a panel of three retired Court of Appeals judges, with the advice and consent of the Senate. It stipulated a five-year term of office, with one reappointment possible. The public attorney's jurisdiction was to include "(1) allegations of corruption in the administration of the laws by the executive branch . . . ; (2) cases referred by the Attorney General because of actual or potential conflicts of interest; (3) criminal cases referred to him by the Federal Election Commission; and (4) allegations of violation of Federal laws relating to campaigns and elections for elective office."[59]

The bill also called for the establishment of a Congressional Legal Service to represent Congress in legal disputes with the executive. In addition, it contained provisions requiring financial disclosure by the president and vice president, limitations on political activity by government employees, a grant of jurisdiction to the District Court for the District of Columbia to hear civil actions brought by Congress, and restrictions on campaign contributions.[60]

Hearings began on the Watergate Reorganization and Reform Act of 1975 in late July of that year and concluded in March of 1976. During that time the Senate Government Operations Committee amassed an extensive record of comment on the legislation. Included in that record were the views of distinguished scholars, the ABA, Common Cause, the Department of Justice, the CIA, the Civil Service Commission, and many members of Congress. The frequency of testimony by fellow members demonstrates the value perceived in taking a position on this issue.

Sen. Lowell Weicker of Connecticut, a member of the Watergate Committee and a Republican who had escaped the retaliation at the polls, was the driving force behind the 1975 hearings. He had urged his fellow Connecticut colleague Abraham Ribicoff to call the hearings on the bill. Weicker's opening statement at the hearings reflected frustration with the slow pace with which Congress was responding to Watergate. He pointed out that ninety-eight bills related to the scandal had been introduced in Congress but that only fourteen had had hearings and none had become law. Weicker feared that Congress was willing to let Watergate die without a response. He berated the Congress, "which with visibility high labored mightily to ascertain the truth, and with television lights low failed to act on the truth."[61] Senator Weicker concluded his remarks with an argument based on the need to restore public confidence in government and to do it soon.[62]

Response to the proposal for a permanent office of public attorney was mixed. Supporters within Congress who testified in favor of the arrangement included Senators Lowell Weicker and Walter Mondale and Congressman Fred B. Rooney. Rooney urged adoption of the entire reform package. The symbolic theme predominated in his comments. He argued that passage of the bill would "not only . . . safeguard the proper functioning of our Nation's government . . . but also . . . help rebuild public confidence in its integrity."[63] Even opponents of S. 495 saw merit in this broader goal: their argument was over the means to achieve it.

Senators Ribicoff, Percy, Baker, Javits, and Glenn were equally committed to the broader goal of restoring public confidence in government but had serious concerns about the constitutionality of the permanent office.[64] Percy said, "I want to prevent future Watergate abuses, as we all do, but I want to be sure that we do not just react to Watergate and create new institutions or procedures that might not serve us well in the long run."[65]

Because of their reservations about the permanent special prosecutor, Senators Percy and Baker introduced an amendment to S. 495 that called for establishing a division of government crimes within the Department of Justice instead of within the Office of Public Attorney. The assistant attorney general heading the division was to be appointed with advice and consent of the Senate. The division's jurisdiction would encompass the same kind of allegations as those of the proposed public attorney.[66] The sponsors argued that this proposal would meet the need for increased attention to public corruption cases without encountering constitutional problems.[67]

Senator Glenn's testimony represented yet another view in congressional opposition to the permanent arrangement. This argument questioned the need for wide-scale reform because Watergate had demonstrated that the system worked. Nevertheless, even Glenn was concerned about the issue of public confidence. That argument clearly was a difficult one to escape, as evidenced by Glenn's ambivalence over the lessons of Watergate. In a classic example of Mayhew's position taking, Glenn said: "Some of the institutions of government were strained and public faith shaken. Even so, most functioned well and it was because of this, the country weathered Watergate and its attendant events. The experience also showed some weaknesses which we hope to correct. . . . one of the most important things Congress must do is to make every effort to restore public confidence in our institutions of government."[68]

The Senate eventually passed a version of the Watergate Reorganization and Reform Act, but it died in the House. The electoral connection was an important influence on the final outcome primarily because it kept the issue of post-Watergate reform on the congressional agenda. It is therefore part of the story of the eventual adoption of reform legislation. However, it does not tell us why a particular set of provisions was passed over others. To understand that we must look at the influence of particular actors in the process of making policy, including congressional colleagues and committees, interest groups, influential private individuals, and the executive branch. The electoral connection made it likely that some reform could be implemented. The constitutional constraints limited the options available. But the actors in the process made the choices among the options available that determined the final outcome.

Colleagues and Committees

Constituent influence alone does not explain why members of Congress make certain choices over others. Also important are the views of congressional colleagues and the positions taken by relevant committees. Congressional colleagues are among the most influential sets of actors in determining voting decisions. Much of this can be explained by the fact that members are likely to seek advice from colleagues with whom they share substantive agreement. Nonetheless, a reputation for being well informed and for having expertise on the issue because of committee specialization enhances the credibility of particular colleagues over others.[69]

The role of the members in committees is important as well. Congressional committees behave differently from one another, and those differences can be explained, in part, by the goals of the individual committee members. What do they hope to accomplish by being on any specific committee? Policy committees are dominated by members who place importance on pursuing particular policy goals; power committees by members who value influence within the institution; and constituency committees by members whose chief priority is constituency service.[70] It follows then that the extent to which a particular committee remains active in the policy process will be dependent upon the extent to which its members value the pursuit of policy goals.

The most influential members of Congress on the issue of post-Watergate reform were members who had played roles in the resolution of the Watergate scandal. In the Senate the primary movers were Sam Ervin (until his retirement in 1975), Lowell Weicker, and Howard Baker (who had been the Republican vice-chairman of the Watergate Committee). In the House it was members of the Judiciary Committee, most of whom had participated in the impeachment hearings of 1974. The Watergate experience of these members had two important impacts. On the one hand it made them particularly interested in the issue of post-Watergate reform. On the Senate side the interest sprung from the fact that the recommendations encompassed in the Watergate Reorganization and Reform Act were based on the final report of the Senate's Watergate Committee. Ervin, Baker, and

Weicker had an understandably heightened interest in the future of these recommendations. For House Judiciary Committee members, who had had the opportunity to study in depth the charges against Mr. Nixon and the responsibility to make the profoundly important initial determination about his impeachment, the experience had a lasting effect. It heightened their perception of the importance of the problems and convinced many of them of the need for a legislative response.

The Watergate experience also gave these particular actors heightened credibility among their colleagues on reform issues. They knew firsthand the problems that Watergate had revealed and had spent more time thinking about appropriate responses to those problems than had other members of Congress. Their interest in reform and their credibility among colleagues on the issue gave them the opportunity to shape the specifics of the final legislative outcome. The electoral concerns of all members made it likely that whatever emerged from the committees would be passed.

The public interest in reform led to a general consensus that some response was needed but there was not general agreement on the most appropriate response. Several moderate Republicans played key roles in shaping a consensus in the Senate on what should be done. They did this by playing the role of compromisers between those who advocated extensive reform and those who believed that none was needed and/or that the extensive reform proposals were unconstitutional. The concerns about constitutionality caused more problems in the Senate. Perhaps this was the case for reasons that demonstrate the differences between the two houses of Congress. The Senate has closer ties to the executive than does the House because of its powers to confirm executive appointments and to approve treaties. Further, it has among its members a number of presidential aspirants who, by the nature of their ambitions, may be less likely to be receptive to efforts to rein in the executive. The Senate is also a more collegial body than the House, more likely to seek bipartisanship, less likely (and less able) to ignore the concerns of its minority members. These characteristics contributed to the influence of senators who had doubts about the constitutionality of the independent special prosecutor.

By the end of the hearings on the Watergate Reorganization and Reform Act in March of 1976, there was a general consensus to reject the idea of a permanent office of public attorney. The vast majority of witnesses had concluded that a permanent office was undesirable, and that conclusion, coupled with the uncertainty of key members of the Senate Government Operations Committee (Ribicoff, Chiles, Glenn, Percy, and Javits), meant that a temporary mechanism would be seen as the more desirable arrangement among those who felt some action was needed. By the March hearings, this change had become readily apparent. "It is striking that the calls for the establishment of a permanent office of special prosecutor, once heard so loudly, have now become almost completely muted," noted one hearing witness. "Few individuals who have examined the problem from a legal and policy point of view now conclude that such a permanent office is the answer."[71]

In markup on S. 495 the Senate committee amended the bill to provide for a temporary special prosecutor in accordance with the American Bar Association's proposal. It also provided for a Division of Government Crimes in the Justice Department. Early in the summer of 1976 it reported the amended bill out of committee and the Senate prepared to debate it in mid-July. The Senate sponsors had not anticipated the strong opposition they encountered from Attorney General Edward Levi and the Department of Justice. Levi argued that the judicial role in the appointment of the special prosecutor was unconstitutional. In early July the department mounted an intensive lobbying effort against the bill in the Senate.[72]

During the week of July 12, department representatives met with the Senate Government Operations Committee in the hopes of finding a compromise. Supporters of the bill suggested that the department's decision to compromise was based on Republican fears about the 1976 campaign and the supporters' determination to follow through with the legislation.[73] Finally, the Ford administration offered a substitute proposal calling for a permanent independent prosecutor within the Department of Justice who would be appointed to a three-year term by the president. S. 495 was amended to reflect these changes during floor debate on July 19.

On July 20 the Senate committee met in special session to consider the Ford proposal. It supported the substitute and included Congress in the special prosecutor's jurisdiction to insure that the permanent office would have sufficient work. On July 21, 1976, the Senate passed the amended Watergate Reorganization and Reform Act by a vote of 91 to 5.[74]

The last-minute move by the Ford administration caused a great deal of confusion in Congress and has been blamed for the failure of Congress to pass a Watergate reform bill in 1976. But the Senate's willingness to compromise with the department on this issue should not have come as a surprise, given the constitutional concerns held by influential actors such as Ribicoff, Baker, Javits, and Percy. The department's position on the constitutional problems met a receptive audience. Once it saw the inevitability of some kind of reform legislation, the department wisely played its constitutional card to ensure that the least threatening of the reform proposals would be adopted. The audience in the House, however, was less receptive.

The Subcommittee on Criminal Justice of the House Committee on the Judiciary began hearings on a temporary special prosecutor bill (H.R. 14476) on July 23, 1976, just two days after the Senate had approved the amended S. 495. H.R. 14476 proposed the appointment of temporary special prosecutors by the attorney general subject to review by a panel of judges.[75] Senator Ribicoff was the first witness before the subcommittee, and he began with an explanation of the Senate's recent actions on S. 495. He explained that three factors led to the decision to make the special prosecutor a permanent one: (1) the Justice Department's estimate that there were sufficient cases available for a permanent office to handle, (2) the department's view that the triggering mechanism was too complicated and cumbersome, and (3) President Ford's willingness to accept a permanent office within the department.[76]

Senators Javits, Kennedy, Percy, and Weicker also testified before the subcommittee, urging it to act and arguing that the administration's changes, while not ideal, were acceptable and insured its support for the final bill. Weicker asked that the House get on with "the job of hammering the last nail in the coffin of Watergate."[77] Kennedy pointed to the practical problems inherent in the triggering device and assured the House that the Senate Judiciary Committee would exercise rigorous advice and consent in confirming the president's nominee for special prosecutor.[78] Percy testified to the amount of conflicting testimony received by the Government Operations Committee and explained its decision to adopt the department's proposal as one that "came down to our final judgment that we wanted legislation that the Justice Department believed in because they would have to carry it out."[79]

The House subcommittee was not ready to jump on the bandwagon. Members had many concerns about the permanent arrangement supported by the department. Elizabeth Holtzman was concerned that the permanent office's jurisdiction was too narrow.[80] Charles Wiggins had serious reservations about placing restrictions on the president's appointment and removal power.[81] The question of workload for a permanent office continued to be troublesome. Henry Hyde raised the specter of McCarthyism, suggesting such behavior was more likely to happen with a permanent office.[82] On the part of the subcommittee there was a general sense of suspicion and lack of support for the measure.

Attorney General Edward Levi also appeared before the House subcommittee, something he had not deemed necessary during Senate hearings. He argued that the temporary special prosecutor provisions in H.R. 14476 were of "highly questionable constitutionality," in addition to being impractical and undesirable. He pointed to the damage to reputation that could occur due to the lack of safeguards for confidentiality of the attorney general's report and to the possibility of multiple special prosecutors at any given time. Levi suggested that the proliferation of special prosecutors, each with only one case and independent of the department, would enhance rather than reduce "the likelihood of unequal justice."[83]In light of these constitutional and practical difficulties inherent in H.R. 14476, the attorney general urged adoption of the president's alternative proposal.

Within the House committee there were several conflicting forces, each of which worked against the likelihood of support for the Senate's version of the bill. On the one hand, Democrats, whose suspicion of a Republican Department of Justice was heightened by the Watergate experience, believed that a special prosecutor within the department would lack sufficient independence. Backing them up were the American Bar Association and influential individuals such as Sam Dash, chief counsel of the Senate Watergate Committee. For example, Dash argued that the appearance of conflict of interest was not removed under S. 495 and that this could only be accomplished by making the prosecutor independent of the department. Urging prompt action on the creation of a temporary arrangement with judicial appointment, Dash suggested that the Senate would be willing to accept such an office if it were adopted by the House. He pointed out that originally the Senate Government Operations Committee had approved a similar temporary mechanism and that despite the last minute changes, there would continue to be majority support in the Senate for the House arrangement. In addition, he suggested that Ford would not veto the bill for political reasons and that, if Jimmy Carter were elected president, they could be certain of support since he was said to favor the temporary appointment scheme.[84] Dash's assurances would prove prophetic.

Also working against passage of the Senate version were conservative Republicans who believed that even this arrangement was an unacceptable intrusion on executive power over law enforcement. While these members were unable to influence which arrangement the House would pass, they were able to contribute to the stalling of congressional action by joining with the opponents of the Senate version who thought it did not go far enough. Despite the urgency that many witnesses expressed, these conflicting forces at work in the House consideration caused a slower reaction. Representatives Wiggins and Hyde, both Republican members of the sub-committee, counseled caution. They worried that the Congress was overreacting to Watergate, that it was desperate to look like it was doing something, so it was not taking sufficient care in evaluating the proposals. Both representatives tended to believe that the Department of Justice could be trusted generally to deal with public corruption cases, and Wiggins was particularly concerned about infringing upon the president's law enforcement powers. Hyde suspected that many members feared that if they failed to act it would appear that they favored covering up corruption, when in fact their concerns were with "due process and the orderly processes of government."[85] He worried about "the need to legislate that all of us feel now that the election is approaching and we must prove ourselves to be purer than Caesar's wife."[86]

Ultimately, Congress did not pass a special prosecutor bill in 1976. The combination of the Ford administration's sudden effort to change the Senate bill and the upcoming election in November of that year effectively delayed any coherent congressional action on the bills before it. For while the Senate had passed the Watergate Reorganization and Reform Act with provisions for a permanent special prosecutor, the weight of evidence before the Congress favored a temporary prosecutor and those most active in reform efforts favored appointment by the judiciary instead of by the president. The House was less inclined to bow to the wishes of the executive or to its Republican members. Confusion ensued, the election approached, and the effort died. But the desire among the key actors for some reform legislation did not die. The issue remained alive within the Senate Government Operations Committee and the House Judiciary Committee because key members of these policy-oriented committees remained committed to reform.[87]

In the election of 1976 the Democrats regained control of the White House and enlarged their majority in Congress. On February 1, 1977, Senator Ribicoff introduced the Public Officials Integrity Act (S. 555), which provided for a Congressional Legal Counsel, an Office of Government Crimes, and a temporary special prosecutor mechanism designed in accordance with recommendations by a special committee of the American Bar Association. Hearings on S. 555 opened on May 3, 1977, before the Senate Committee on Governmental Affairs (formerly Government Operations). In opening the hearings, Senator Percy expressed his hope that the reform legislation would be enacted that year with the "vigorous support" of the Carter administration.[88]

The need to restore public confidence continued to be an overriding theme in these hearings. For example, in urging support for the legislation, Senator Chiles said "we have to have it. We must restore confidence in the Government."[89] His statement reflected the concerns of many in Congress that public distrust included their institution as well as the executive branch. Chiles went on to say, "All of us, to a greater or lesser degree, are under suspicion of misconduct. . . . Read the papers, talk to the people: More and more they speak less and less of a few rotten apples. Now they look with skepticism at the entire barrel."[90]

Senator Weicker, "at times a voice in the wilderness for this legislation," continued his campaign for reform. He reiterated his concern that if action were not taken soon, none would occur. His opening statement is a perfect reflection of the symbolic goal of the legislation, a goal that drove the supporters to continue their efforts despite the ongoing debate about the form the arrangement should take. Weicker said: "It is important that the American people be guaranteed that there is one standard of justice, and it will be applied to all Americans regardless of their station in life. . . . That is what the temporary Special Prosecutor provision establishes, and the image that it establishes is far more important than the specifics called for in this particular title of the legislation."[91]

On the first day of the hearings, President Carter made his support for the Public Officials Integrity Act clear. That morning he announced that he was sending a message to Congress requesting legislation that required financial disclosure by public officials and that created an Office of Government Ethics to oversee the disclosure process. In addition, he assured Congress of his support for the legislation creating a temporary special prosecutor.[92] Carter's bill, S. 1446, was introduced in the Senate by Ribicoff that day. The hearings that followed addressed the previously discussed issues involving arrangements for a special prosecutor but focused primarily on the financial disclosure law. Most of what could be said about the special prosecutor had already been said. The major difference in the debate over the bill this time was that the Department of Justice supported the proposed temporary mechanism. While it had some quibbles with the details, it conceded that the judicial appointment and restrictions on removal were constitutional in special cases.[93]

The Senate moved quickly. On May 15, 1977, just ten days after hearings were concluded, the Governmental Affairs Committee reported out the

Public Officials Integrity Act of 1977. One month later it was reported out of the Senate Committee on the Judiciary without changes. On June 27, 1977, it was considered and passed in the Senate by a vote of 74 to 5.[94]

The House bill (H.R. 9705) also called for a temporary special prosecutor arrangement but did not include Congress in its jurisdiction. This omission was the basis for further delay in House action. The Congress, with House members particularly implicated, was embroiled in a scandal of its own involving allegations of bribes by the South Korean government. Elizabeth Holtzman was highly critical of the Department of Justice's handling of the scandal. In the subcommittee's markup of the bill she urged that Congress be included in the jurisdiction of the special prosecutor. Holtzman's proposal was rejected by the subcommittee, but she threatened to bring it up again before the whole committee and in the floor debate. Supporters of the bill feared that the whole committee would hold up the reporting of the bill until the issue had been resolved. There was little support for Holtzman's proposal, but few congressmen wanted to be on record for voting against it.[95]

House action was also delayed because other ethics proposals, which were companion bills to the special prosecutor proposal, had been referred to other committees. In the House there were four committees with jurisdiction over the financial disclosure aspects of the bill.[96] The committees' efforts lacked coordination. Although Speaker of the House Tip O'Neill urged the various committee chairmen to complete their review of the proposals in time for House action in 1977, none of the bills reached the House floor that year.[97] The House Judiciary Committee did not report H.R. 9705 until June 19, 1978. The report revealed a still divided Committee on the issue of the special prosecutor. Holtzman continued to argue that the act should apply to Congress as well. Five Republican committee members filed dissenting views, arguing that a statutory special prosecutor was not needed because Watergate had demonstrated that the system worked without one.[98]

On September 27, 1978, the House finally passed the post-Watergate reform bill. As passed, H.R. 9705 did not contain provisions for a temporary special prosecutor nor did it establish an Office of Government Crimes. On October 6, House and Senate conferees met to iron out their differences. They agreed to a final version of the bill that adopted the Senate provisions for a special prosecutor and deleted the Office of Government Crimes. The conference report was adopted by voice vote in the Senate on October 7, 1978. In the House the same bill was approved on October 12 by a vote of

370 to 23, after an unsuccessful last-ditch effort by Representative Wiggins to delete the special prosecutor provisions.[99]

It had been five years, to the month, since Watergate Special Prosecutor Cox had been fired and Congress had begun consideration of creating a statutory special prosecutor arrangement. Within each house of Congress, key individuals used their Watergate experience and their committee assignments to continue the push for reform. While almost all members felt the need to support some kind of reform for electoral reasons, these individuals had other policy concerns that determined the final provisions of the arrangement. These policy concerns and their legislative solutions to them were shaped not only by their own experience but also by influential actors outside of Congress.

The Influence of External Actors

The influence of various interest groups on congressional behavior varies from issue to issue and over time. The number of issues in which interest groups take competing positions is actually quite small.[100] Interest group positions are most likely to be sought by committee members in order to present a particular point of view already held by the member or to provide background information on an issue affecting the group.[101] To the extent that an interest group is perceived as being able to mobilize the members' constituency, its influence increases.[102]

Two interest groups played an important role in shaping the specifics of special prosecutor legislation. The American Bar Association was influential because of its credibility on legal issues. Its most important contribution was proposing a triggering mechanism for the appointment of a special prosecutor that seemed likely to withstand constitutional challenge.[103] The other group, Common Cause, had influence because as a powerful public interest group in the seventies,[104] it was perceived as reflecting constituency concerns about "good government" and reform.

In response to the Watergate investigations, in June 1973 the ABA formed the Special Committee to Study Federal Law Enforcement Agencies. Its purpose was "to explore ways to make the law enforcement agencies professionally independent legal arms of the government by insulating them from partisan influences."[105] In October 1975 it issued a preliminary report of findings and suggestions for reform of the justice system. The final report was released in January 1976, and these recommendations were discussed with ABA representatives during the last hearings on S. 495 held in March 1976.[106]

William B. Spann, Jr., chairman of the special committee, testified that it had rejected the concept of a permanent office but agreed that some mechanism should be in place for the future. The committee concluded that an ad hoc approach to the problem was inadequate and determined that a "triggering mechanism" should be devised to ensure appointment of special prosecutors should the need arise. Its support for outside appointment reflected "the legal profession's constant concern with whether or not justice is administered with complete impartiality and, equally important, whether or not there is an appearance of impartiality. The public must be assured that crimes involving government officials at the highest levels can be prosecuted with complete impartiality."[107]

The ABA committee's proposal recommended a special court appointment procedure that would be initiated by the attorney general when he determined that he had a conflict of interest in handling a certain case. The temporary appointment could be made by either the attorney general or by a special court comprised of three senior or retired federal circuit court judges appointed by the chief justice to two-year terms. The attorney general could either appoint the special prosecutor, determine that one was needed, or ask the court panel to appoint one. In any case, he would be required to explain his decision in a memorandum to the court panel. The panel could then take whatever action it deemed necessary, including the appointment of a different prosecutor who would supercede the attorney general's choice, or the appointment of a special prosecutor even when the attorney general had decided that one was not needed. The attorney general could remove the temporary prosecutor for "extraordinary improprieties."[108] This proposal was the primary basis for the special prosecutor mechanism finally established in 1978. Clearly, the ABA special committee played a critical role in influencing the legislative outcome. The ABA continued to press for adoption of an independent temporary special prosecutor throughout the congressional deliberations. Spann testified again at House hearings on the Watergate Reorganization and Reform Act, urging the House to adopt a temporary arrangement rather than the plan proposed by the Ford administration that had been adopted in the Senate.[109]

The other group with an ongoing role in the formation of a legislative response to Watergate was the public interest group Common Cause. While its attention seemed to be focused primarily on the corresponding efforts of campaign finance reform and financial disclosure requirements, it also continuously urged the passage of some sort of independent prosecutor arrangement. During the December 1975 hearings, David Cohen, the president of Common Cause, expressed his organization's support for the ABA proposal for a temporary special prosecutor. In addition, he urged prompt action on the part of the committee. "We are in this fight all the way," he assured Ribicoff, "and we are ready to work with you, and the members of your committee, in developing workable, effective legislation, so that we can begin to reverse the tide, and people can say, this is a Government I am proud of, I respect its decisions, I know they are being made honestly and fairly."[110]

These two interest groups were important to the legislative outcome for three main reasons. First, they were the only groups attempting to influence the legislation and they were in agreement on the appropriate response. Second, they had a high level of credibility with members of Congress on the issues involved. Finally, their proposals provided support for the views of those members already inclined toward the creation of an independent prosecutor, and in the case of the ABA proposal, provided a means around the key constitutional stumbling block to such an office.

There are also a number of influential individuals outside of government who help to shape the national policy agenda. While unlikely to determine the actual decision made by a member of Congress, these elites can play an important role in structuring the alternatives considered as viable by the decisionmakers. When these "senior oracles . . . unite on a public question, their influence upon the atmosphere within which alternatives are generated and chosen by the government is very significant."[111]

With special prosecutor legislation there were a number of influential elites who helped to shape the alternatives taken seriously by members of Congress. Prior to the start of hearings on the Watergate Reorganization and Reform Act of 1975, the Senate Committee on Government Operations sought extensive outside advice and comment. In response to a letter from Chairman Ribicoff and Senator Percy, the committee received many letters from distinguished lawyers and academics commenting on the bill. Many of those in the academic and legal communities who responded by letter opposed the permanent office of special prosecutor, usually on the grounds that it encroached upon the power of the executive to an unacceptable degree.[112] Beyond the question of constitutionality, opposition to the creation of the office was based on practical questions of accountability and responsibility. Erwin Griswold, a former solicitor general, asked, "Is it not better to put the responsibility squarely on the Executive Branch, and then hold the Executive Branch responsible?"[113] Clark Clifford warned against creating "institutions which are both unnecessary and potentially harmful."[114] A former member of the Watergate Special Prosecution Force argued that "abuses of public office will not be cured by giving unbridled power to an ombudsman with a roving commission to do justice as he sees it."[115] Finally, Professor Harold Seidman wrote, "I want the President to be held responsible and accountable for maintaining the honesty and integrity of the executive branch, and I don't want this responsibility to be shared, even in a small way, with the Office of Public Attorney."[116]

Only Raoul Berger, Harvard law professor, and James Sundquist of the Brookings Institution gave the proposal for a permanent public attorney their whole-hearted support. Berger wrote, "Emphatically I am in favor of a permanent special prosecutor's office, completely independent of the Department of Justice."[117] Sundquist penned, "I cannot judge the constitutionality of the proposed method of appointment, but it appeals to me as an ingenious way to go about assuring that the prosecutor would be independent."[118]

A middle ground position was taken by a number of others who responded to the Ribicoff-Percy request. Several of these legal scholars argued that while some sort of arrangement was desirable, a permanent special prosecutor was not. Peter Dingman believed that there was "an incontestable need to establish a mechanism in which the public can have confidence" but felt that an ad hoc judicial appointment triggered when allegations arose was the best solution.[119] The other "compromise" position, held by Lloyd Cutler, James McGregor Burns, and Frederick Mosher, was that a permanent arrangement was desirable but that appointment should be by the president rather than the judiciary, thus avoiding the constitutional questions mentioned earlier.[120]

Perhaps the two most influential private individuals in the legislative history of the special prosecutor provisions were Lloyd Cutler, a Washington, D.C., lawyer, and Samuel Dash, former chief counsel to the Senate Watergate Committee and Georgetown University law professor. These two men worked for the creation of some kind of independent prosecutor arrangement throughout the five years of congressional consideration. Lloyd Cutler became involved early in the process, shortly after members of the Justice Department began to be implicated in the Watergate scandal. He was concerned about the number of lawyers involved in the affair. He became convinced that the conflict of interest inherent in the executive investigating itself was the core of the problem and that this problem could be solved through an independent investigatory apparatus for these types of cases.[121] A letter to the committee from Cutler noted the resemblance of S. 495 to a draft bill he had submitted to Senator Ervin in 1974.[122] He also enclosed a copy of a speech he had made the previous year proposing a continuing public prosecutor. In the speech, he had laid out the arguments for a permanent arrangement: "We should not be content with a system that requires massive purgatives once a generation. An ongoing institution devoted to the investigation and prosecution of such offenses would increase the likelihood of bringing offenders to justice, . . . and deter the commission of offenses that would be committed in its absence. Most important, a continuing public prosecutor might go a long way to restore public confidence in our institutions."[123]

When the committee hearings in the Senate continued on S. 495 in December 1975, Cutler appeared in person to urge passage of his proposal. In that testimony he referred to himself as the "principal draftsman" of the antecedent bill to S. 495.[124] Cutler preferred presidential appointment of the special prosecutor but other than that, agreed that a permanent office was necessary and desirable.[125]

Samuel Dash was an ardent proponent for the creation of a permanent public attorney. Dash pointed out that if the Senate Select Committee had only one recommendation to make it was that an independent office was needed. However, he felt S. 495 gave the public attorney too much discretion and too broad a jurisdiction. Dash envisioned the permanent office as one that would first receive complaints from people who had been wronged by the executive branch and then investigate these complaints. If the allegations constituted a prima facie case, the attorney would notify the attorney general, who would then be expected to proceed with the case. If the attorney general failed to do so, the public attorney could take the proceedings before a federal district court and request an order making the attorney general show why the public attorney should not become the special prosecutor in the case. This "accountability feature" would ensure that in most cases the public attorney would be simply an ombudsman. He would become a special prosecutor only when the attorney general refused a valid case.[126]

Former members of the Watergate Special Prosecution Force also provided valuable input in the debate over S. 495. On the whole, they opposed the creation of a permanent office and tended to support an ad hoc arrangement similar to their own: that is, one with presidential appointment and no statutory basis. During the July 1975 hearings former Special Prosecutor Leon Jaworski and the current Special Prosecutor Henry Ruth spoke against the proposal for public attorney in S. 495.[127]

The 1975 Report of the Watergate Special Prosecution Force was issued in October, and its recommendations for reform became part of the hearing record on S. 495. The report urged reforms in the Department of Justice and increased congressional oversight rather than the establishment of a permanent special prosecutor. In particular, it urged greater allocation of department resources to public corruption cases and closer Senate scrutiny of department nominees in the confirmation process. It agreed that in extreme cases such as Watergate, a special prosecutor would be needed and should be appointed but asserted that a permanent one was not only unnecessary but also undesirable. The report stated:

> Much of the Watergate and preceding abuses resulted from the public's delegation of public responsibilities to powerful men whose judgments were trusted and whose claimed need for secrecy was always accepted. Men with unchecked power and unchallenged trust too often come to believe that their own perceptions of priorities and the common good coincide with the national interest. There is no reason to believe that, in the long run, an independent special prosecutor's office would avoid this status.[128]

The consensus that emerged among elites interested in this issue was that the constitutional concerns about an independent prosecutor were soundly based and must be considered in the final legislative response. There was also broad agreement that a permanent office of special prosecutor was undesirable both for constitutional and for practical reasons. Beyond that, these elites varied in their response to what should be done. Their influence lay primarily in helping to set the constitutional boundaries of Congress's consideration.

We have already seen to some extent how the executive influenced congressional action. Its role merits some further explanation here. The influence of the executive branch on congressional decisionmaking depends upon the relationship between Congress and the particular individual in the White House,[129] the nature of the issue, and partisanship. Presidents tend to be more influential on foreign affairs issues, for example, than in domestic policy areas because of their traditional leadership role in this issue area. Members of the president's party are more likely to be influenced by his position than are those of the opposition.[130] Finally, there is an institutional tension between the two branches that diminishes the administration's influence, all other things being equal.[131]

These general propositions held true in the case of post-Watergate reform legislation. During the last days of the Nixon administration, Congress actively considered special prosecutor legislation for obvious reasons. During the Ford administration, the executive was able to influence the Senate on the issue because it was able to marshal support among moderate Republican senators, and a few Democratic ones, for its position that a prosecutor independent of the executive would be unconstitutional. This influence should not be overstated. The administration was not able to forestall some action by the Senate, and the failure of the House to act was based more on its opposition to and distrust of the executive than on any agreement. It is indisputable that President Carter's support for this legislation was important to its eventual passage in 1978. As long as presidents opposed the legislation on constitutional grounds, opponents had an explanation for their opposition.[132] Once that was removed, it became almost impossible to be against an independent special prosecutor.

The influence of partisanship and agreement with the executive is also evident in this case, although less so perhaps than on other issues. The electoral fallout of Watergate had yet to hurt Mr. Ford, but Congress had already felt its force, placing moderate congressional Republicans in a difficult spot. On the one hand they wanted to support their president, but on the other their electoral concerns pushed them toward support for some kind of congressional action, however limited. What resulted was a position that supported the idea of a special prosecutor in principle but sought to place that special prosecutor under executive control. This position, of course, is the classic symbolic one: were the proposal to be adopted, it would serve the electoral needs of the members while having virtually no impact on the problem that gave rise to the legislation in the first place.

Ultimately, the natural tension between the Congress and the executive that always exists, but was aggravated by Watergate, worked against executive influence on this issue. Congress's continued efforts to legislate in this area had more impact on the Department of Justice than the department had on the legislation finally adopted. Throughout debate on this issue, the executive branch continued to express its concern about the potential for encroachment on executive power. Had it not been for the already existing concerns of some members of Congress and the broad-based agreement among experts outside of government that this was a legitimate concern, it is likely that such protestations by the executive would have fallen on deaf ears. Until Carter, the executive took the position it was expected to take and had been taking on all issues involving congressional–executive relations. Consequently, its views were suspect, and those views were taken seriously only by those who already had reservations about constitutionality.

The Senate Government Operations Committee hearings on the Watergate Reorganization and Reform Act demonstrate the senators' impatience with the Department of Justice's opposition to its efforts. During the testimony by a department representative, Senators Weicker and Percy used the occasion to express their dissatisfaction. Weicker said: "I am trying to impress upon you gentlemen, that there is a necessity of heroic efforts in this area to reestablish faith in our justice agencies. . . . Please do not view this legislation as something coming along, as another piece of legislation in normal times. It is not. The public . . . wants to reestablish that faith, but they have to have something to hold onto, and unfortunately, just the good words of you gentlemen will not do the trick, any more than my own."[133]

Percy was angered by the failure of the department to submit testimony prior to the hearing. He also wanted to know when the committee could expect the proposals for reform that a department spokesman had hinted at earlier in his testimony. Percy chided the department: "This is a matter that has shattered the country. It is a matter that I should think would be of very, very high priority at the Justice Department . . . we have introduced legislation; it has had months to sit there; and we hoped it would be appraised and analyzed by the Department. . . . we would be hesitant to go into a mark-up session on the legislation . . . when you come here today and say there are highly creative imaginative things being considered."[134]

The committee did delay action on the bill until the department announced its internal reforms. On January 23, 1976, the department wrote to Ribicoff explaining its reorganization plan. The centerpiece of the plan was a new Public Integrity Section within the Criminal Division. The decision to create the new section was based upon a study done within the department which concluded that the Criminal Division's ineffectiveness in dealing with charges against public officials "derived from an outmoded and inefficient organizational structure in which enforcement of anti-corruption statutes and related matters was scattered among disparate sections."[135] Congress found this reorganization an inadequate solution to the problems raised by Watergate. It proceeded with its own efforts to respond to the scandal.

The executive branch's influence on this issue was minimal. Its views, as a rule, were suspect because its opposition was predictable. To the extent that it did influence the outcome it was because of the links between its position and those of influential elites. Until the Carter administration, the Department of Justice had worked in opposition to the creation of any special prosecutor arrangement that might infringe upon its constitutional responsibility for faithful execution of the law. That opposition no doubt slowed the legislative process but never fully stopped it. A new president and a new attorney general ensured that the effort would continue and, finally, succeed. Moreover, the issues raised in this five-year debate and the way in which the Congress resolved these issues through compromise would have important implications for the way in which the final arrangement was structured.

THE SPECIAL PROSECUTOR
PROVISIONS OF 1978

The final product of the five-year effort to create an independent special prosecutor reflects the tensions inherent in our constitutional system. These tensions, brought out in the legislative debate, revolve around an ambiguous separation of powers based upon a vague delineation of the executive, legislative, and judicial functions, which is complicated by an intricate system of checks, balances, and shared responsibilities. Attempting to resolve these tensions in a specific statutory scheme was bound to be fraught with complications and compromises, and the final product reflects these difficulties.

The special prosecutor provisions incorporated in the Ethics in Government Act of 1978 attempted to strike a balance between the executive responsibility for enforcement of the laws and the congressional desire to ensure the appearance of independence for a special prosecutor charged with investigating the executive branch. This balance was accomplished by dividing the responsibility for implementing the act between the attorney general and a special panel of judges created under the act.

The act required that the attorney general, upon receiving specific allegations of federal criminal law violations by certain high-ranking executive branch officials, conduct a preliminary investigation into the charges.[136] He had ninety days within which to conduct the investigation and was not permitted to utilize the compulsory process to obtain information during that time.[137]

At the end of this limited investigation, the attorney general had to determine whether or not the charges warranted further investigation or prosecution. If so, he was required to file a report on his findings with a special division of the Court of Appeals for the District of Columbia, requesting the appointment of a special prosecutor.[138] If he determined that the charges did not warrant further action, he was also required to file a report with the panel, explaining his decision to go no further with the case.[139]

The special division of the court was to consist of three senior or retired circuit judges, appointed by the chief justice of the Supreme Court.[140] The panel was responsible for selecting a special prosecutor, defining his jurisdiction, receiving the reports of the attorney general and the special prosecutor, and determining whether or not the reports would be made public.[141]

Although the panel appointed the prosecutor, the attorney general had the power of removal for "extraordinary impropriety." Should the attorney general remove the special prosecutor, the court could review that decision if the special prosecutor requested such review.[142] The attorney general's decision to request the appointment of a special prosecutor was not reviewable.[143]

Clearly, the provisions of the act reflected congressional acknowledgment of the uncertainty surrounding the extent to which the president was to control law enforcement activities. Thus the attorney general was given the authority to trigger the act and to remove the special prosecutor. The court panel, however, was given responsibility for appointment of the special prosecutor, this provision deriving from the belief that the prosecutor must be, and must be perceived to be, independent of the executive.

Given the constitutional debate outlined previously, we can view the resulting special prosecutor provisions as an effort to compromise over issues concerning the separation of powers that were raised by each side in the debate. However, the issues were not conclusively resolved and appeared again during the debate over reauthorization.

EXPLAINING CONGRESSIONAL ACTION

The legislative history of the independent counsel provisions reveals that the choice of a judicially appointed, temporary independent counsel mechanism was the result of the interaction of various environmental and internal institutional forces working on members of Congress. There were a number of alternatives open to Congress as possible responses to the Watergate experience. It chose this particular arrangement because none of the other possibilities seemed to satisfy the various goals held by members concerned about this issue. These goals differed among the members, but each was met by the final arrangement adopted. Most generally, a large number of members was convinced by public opinion polls and the elections of 1974 and 1976 that some action should be taken to help to restore public confidence in government after Watergate. This was essentially a symbolic goal that could have been met in a number of different ways. What form the action would take was determined by individual members whose policy goals had been shaped in the crucible of Watergate. That experience taught them that there was great potential for obstruction of justice by the executive when it is called upon to investigate itself. For these people, any legislative response would require the elimination, or at least the reduction of the potential for, this problem of conflict of interest. For some of these people there was an additional desire to find a way sufficiently to insulate from political pressure the person called in to remove the conflict of interest problem. The Saturday Night Massacre had precipitated a constitutional crisis with lasting impact. It was something to be avoided in the future. Finally, for many of these actors there was the additional concern about constitutionality. Members of Congress occasionally make misjudgments about the extent of their constitutional powers, but few, if any, set out to adopt knowingly an unconstitutional act. We can assume that all of the members had as one of their goals the creation of an arrangement that would be constitutionally sound. All of these goals are reflected to some extent or another in the special prosecutor provisions of the Ethics in Government Act of 1978. A decision about how effectively these goals have been met can only be made by studying the implementation of the provisions in the political process.

FOUR

IMPLEMENTATION AND CONGRESSIONAL OVERSIGHT

The constitutional issues raised during consideration of the special prosecutor provisions continued to have an impact on the implementation of the provisions during the first decade of their existence. Legal challenges to the provisions plagued investigations by the special prosecutor until 1988, when the Supreme Court finally addressed the issue in *Morrison v. Olson*. Further, the role of the attorney general in triggering the arrangement, adopted in order to meet the constitutional concerns, had important implications for how the provisions were interpreted and applied.

This chapter discusses the implementation of the provisions, focusing on congressional oversight of that implementation. Such a focus permits an explanation of the role Congress has played in this process and of why it altered the provisions as it did in 1982 and in 1987 through the reauthorization process. The study of the intersection between implementation and congressional oversight makes more clear the interactions that have occurred between Congress, the courts, the independent counsel, and the Department of Justice.

CONGRESSIONAL OVERSIGHT

As a rule, members of Congress lack incentives for engaging in systematic oversight of the implementation of legislation that they pass. Oversight is not viewed as serving their interest in re-election.[1] Members are more or less likely to engage in oversight depending upon the presence of certain "opportunity factors," including legal authority, staff resources, the subject matter (especially its visibility and complexity), committee structure, the status and priorities of a particular member of a committee, and relations with the executive branch.[2] Meaningful oversight is still not assured even with the existence of all of these factors unless certain "conversion factors" exist, or arise, as well. This conversion may be caused by strong disagreement with the executive branch on a policy or external events such as crises or scandal.[3]

Congressional oversight of the implementation of the special prosecutor provisions has followed predictable patterns. It has been neither intensive nor ongoing. It has been sporadic, occurring at times when the statute is being considered for reauthorization. The level of scrutiny and the nature of the changes adopted during the reauthorization in 1982 differ from those in 1987 because of differences in committee leadership, in relationships between oversight committees and the executive branch, and in the impact of external events.

Throughout the first decade of the act's existence, there continued to be two groups of members with different levels of interest in the issue of special prosecutors. The movers and shakers on this issue were a handful of individuals on policy-oriented committees with policy interests in the questions of ethics in government generally, and the special prosecutor particularly. Outside this small group, there was a much larger group of members who valued the provisions for their symbolic import. The specific changes wrought in the law can be attributed to the former group, the continued existence of the provisions to the latter.

1982: A NOD TO EXECUTIVE POWER

Between 1978, when the Ethics Act was passed, and 1983, when it came due for reauthorization, several events occurred that forced a re-examination of the constitutionality of the special prosecutor arrangement: the appointment of the first three prosecutors under the act, a civil suit challenging the provisions' constitutionality, and a new administration hostile to the act. These occurrences provided impetus for a review of the constitutionality and desirability of the 1978 arrangement.[4] They had the effect of converting the opportunity factors that existed within Congress on this issue into a period of relatively meaningful oversight and scrutiny of the provisions. The provisions themselves provided Congress with the legal authority to engage in oversight. In fact, the sunset provision that required reauthorization in five years made it certain that some kind of review would occur.[5] These provisions did not guarantee, however, that that review would be a thoughtful and careful one. Other factors and events determined that outcome.

The interest of the chair and ranking minority member of the Subcommittee on Oversight of Government Management of the Committee on Governmental Affairs, Sen. William Cohen (R-Maine) and Sen. Carl Levin (D-Michigan), and individuals on their staffs[6] was particularly important in ensuring careful review. This subcommittee is one created specifically for oversight. In addition, the subject matter involved a "good government" issue, one often viewed as having some electoral benefits as well as being interesting from a policy standpoint. Finally, in the early years of the Reagan administration the relationship between Congress and the president was fairly good. It was friendlier between the president and the Senate because the Republicans had gained control of that body in 1980, but even the House was more cooperative than might be expected given its Democratic control. As a result, the president's views on an issue would be given greater weight, especially in the Senate, than they would be in different circumstances.

The events emerging from the early implementation of the provisions had the effect of magnifying the executive's concerns about their constitutionality. In 1979 a special prosecutor was appointed to investigate allegations that Hamilton Jordan, Jimmy Carter's chief of staff, had used cocaine at Studio 54, a New York City discotheque. In 1980, similar allegations of cocaine use by another Carter staffer, Timothy Kraft, prompted appointment of a second special prosecutor. In each case the accused was cleared of criminal charges at the conclusion of a six-month grand jury investigation.[7] These lengthy and expensive[8] investigations into charges generally ignored by United States attorneys when made against ordinary citizens, prompted the Department of Justice to push for more discretion in triggering the act. Former Attorney General Benjamin Civiletti argued that the standard for appointment was so broad that it amounted to a "hair trigger," severely limiting the attorney general's discretion and forcing the request for a prosecutor in cases where one should not be appointed.[9]

The Kraft case was important as well because the question of the constitutionality of the provisions was raised again. After a special prosecutor was appointed by the court panel, Kraft's lawyers filed a civil suit seeking a preliminary injunction against the special prosecutor and a judgment of the constitutionality of the act.[10] The suit contended that Gerald Gallinghouse, the prosecutor, was "exercising Executive power and authority in violation of the Constitution of the United States."[11] The constitutional argument was based on the issues concerning separation of powers that were raised in the first legislative debate. The suit specifically questioned the interference of the judiciary in the appointment of one responsible for law enforcement; the presumption that one granted all the powers of the attorney general was an "inferior officer"; the designation of a panel of judges assembled for appointment purposes as a "Court of Law"; and the restriction on the executive removal power that permitted removal only for "extraordinary impropriety."[12]

The response by Common Cause, as amicus curiae, reiterated the arguments in the first debate supporting Congress's power to create the mechanism. It concluded by stating that the act "is fundamentally, a pragmatic law . . . evolved directly out of a prolonged national scandal that exposed the full potential for corruption and conflict in these very executive branch officials with the primary duty to enforce the law. . . . In this context . . . the Supreme Court's admonition that the constitutional separation of powers is a . . . 'common sense' doctrine must control."[13]

Had *Kraft v. Gallinghouse* been decided, the constitutional debate over the provisions might have been settled. As it was, Gallinghouse cleared Kraft of the charges prior to a decision being rendered, and the case was dismissed as moot.[14] Nevertheless, the suit and each side's memorandum in the case became important grist for the reauthorization mill.[15]

Finally, the question of constitutionality was raised by the new attorney general, William French Smith, in 1981. In a letter to the Senate legal counsel, Smith wrote, "In some or all of its applications, the Act appears fundamentally to contradict the principle of separation of powers erected by the Constitution. . . . If the Department's position is sought in future litigation, we would espouse views consistent with the above and addressed to the specific facts of the case."[16]

With this controversy in mind, the Senate Subcommittee on Oversight of Government Management began reauthorization hearings in 1981. All sides of the debate were represented, and most agreed that some change was necessary. In particular, there was a good deal of concern over the attorney general's statement,[17] and efforts centered on responding to the constitutional questions while keeping some sort of independent mechanism on the books.

The Amendments of 1983 (the bill was signed by President Reagan on January 3, 1983) reflect consideration of the executive's concerns regarding separation of powers. They increased the attorney general's discretion in triggering the act while maintaining appointment by the panel of judges. The standard for triggering the act was lowered so the attorney general could consider the specificity of the allegations and the credibility of the accuser.[18] In response to charges that the restrictions on removal interfered with executive power, the standard for removal was lowered to "good cause."[19] In addition, the special prosecutor was urged to follow Department of Justice prosecutorial guidelines, "except where not possible."[20]

The reauthorization amendments were based upon the experience with the Jordan and Kraft cases, which demonstrated the need for increasing executive authority in the process. While opponents of the provisions were able to use these cases to their advantage in making their argument for executive power, they would not have been able to accomplish much had there not also been agreement among the act's supporters. The fact that these cases had occurred in a Democratic administration helped to ensure bipartisan agreement that some change was necessary. Further, the American Bar Association also took the position that these cases demonstrated a need for change.[21] Common Cause was less troubled by the Jordan and Kraft cases than other interest groups, but its approach to the issue of special prosecutors has always been that as long as the principle of independence is maintained by judicial appointment, the details of the administration of the provisions can be altered without undermining their value to public confidence. Consequently, while it saw no need to expand executive authority, it saw no great danger in it either.[22]

The amendments of 1983 demonstrate the continued effort in Congress to balance the various goals of the provisions. The symbolic and independence goals continued to be met by maintaining the judicial appointment of the independent counsel. The constitutional goal was met by expanding the attorney general's authority to trigger the act and in lowering the standard for removal. It also appears that Congress became more concerned about what had seemed a relatively minor concern during the original conception of the provisions: that is, the desire to minimize the harm done to targets of special prosecutor investigations who may well be cleared of the charges against them. Members saw firsthand the damage that could be done to individuals subject to the provisions. The amendments changed the name of the special prosecutor to independent counsel in order to remove the Watergate stigma attached to the former. Another provision was added that permitted the court panel to reimburse attorneys' fees for targets who were not indicted.[23]

On the other hand, the goal of removing the potential for or actual conflict of interest by the attorney general was not served by the amendments. Rather, that longstanding problem may have been aggravated. By giving the weight that it did to constitutional and individual targets, Congress was forced to interfere with this other substantive goal. That decision would come back to haunt it during the tenure of Attorney General Edwin Meese.

INTERLUDE: 1983–1987

During the five-year period following the first reauthorization of the provisions, a number of important events occurred in their implementation that acted as conversion factors encouraging careful oversight of the provisions during the next round of reauthorization. There were more cases arising that required the appointment of independent counsel, and most of these cases were more public than the first three. In addition, several key appeals court decisions affected the implementation of the act, and there was a proliferation of constitutional challenges on the part of targets of independent counsel investigations. Finally, there were critical changes in leadership positions both in Congress and the Department of Justice that affected their relationship.

Events Related to Independent Counsel Provisions

Between 1982 and 1987 there were five independent counsels publicly appointed to investigate members of the Reagan administration. The appointments for cases involving Edwin Meese (twice), Lynn Nofziger, Michael Deaver, and the Iran-Contra scandal were higher profile than earlier cases had been because of the individuals and the nature of the charges involved. The Meese cases especially seemed to point to the need for independent counsel because they involved the attorney general himself.

The Olson case was far less prominent in its early stages, first, because of the lag between the time the Environmental Protection Agency controversy occurred (1981–1982) and the time an independent counsel was appointed (1986), and second, because Theodore Olson, from the Department of Justice Office of Legal Counsel, was much less a "public figure" than the targets of the other investigations. Olson's case gained its notoriety when his constitutional challenge was made public and when it became apparent that his case would be reviewed by the Supreme Court.

The legal challenges to the independent counsel statute by Michael Deaver, Oliver North, Lynn Nofziger, and Theodore Olson[24] served to renew interest in and concern about the constitutionality of the provisions.[25] It now seemed inevitable that one of these cases would find its way to the Supreme Court. Because of its relative obscurity, few suspected that the Olson investigation would "carry the ball" on this question.[26]

During the 1987 reauthorization hearings, the Olson challenge was pending. It was still a sealed case before the U.S. Court of Appeals for the D.C. Circuit, but members of Congress were aware of its existence. Naturally, they were also aware of the more public, but unsuccessful, attempts by Deaver and North to have their cases dismissed on constitutional grounds.[27]

It was clear that the constitutional questions would have to be examined carefully during the upcoming reauthorization.

In addition to the constitutional challenges, the federal courts were asked to interpret specific parts of the provisions relating to the role of the attorney general in triggering the process. These cases raised questions about the extent of the attorney general's discretion in triggering the provisions, the extent to which the attorney general's decisions were subject to judicial review, and the role to be played by private individuals in the enforcement of the act. Following on the heels of the first reauthorization, the disposition of these cases further solidified the attorney general's discretion in implementing the provisions.

During William French Smith's tenure as attorney general, there were three attempts by individuals to force Smith to trigger the act by conducting preliminary investigations into their allegations against executive officials. In each case their arguments were supported by the district court to which they brought the case but were reversed on appeal.

In 1983 two suits were filed seeking to compel Smith to initiate preliminary investigations. *Nathan v. Attorney General* involved allegations that top level Justice Department officials had engaged in a conspiracy to cover up FBI involvement in the shooting of Communist Workers' party members in Greensboro, North Carolina. Plaintiffs, who were private citizens affected by the shooting, sought appointment of a special prosecutor to investigate these charges. They contended that Smith had failed to conduct a preliminary investigation within the ninety days required by the act. The department moved to dismiss the case on the grounds that plaintiffs lacked standing to sue.[28]

The court denied the attorney general's motion. It held that the act conferred a procedural right upon the person making the allegations against covered officials. The judge argued that if this procedural right were not redressed, then "the entire statutory scheme, designed to focus attention on the claims of criminal misconduct in high places, is meaningless. To hold otherwise would be to declare that the Ethics in Government Act is merely a pious statement of pure political import designed to assuage the public's concern for abuses of trust that followed Watergate."[29]

Having recognized the procedural right, the court addressed the question of whether it could compel Smith to appoint a special prosecutor. It concluded that since a grand jury had returned indictments against some of those involved in the shooting, it would be inappropriate to order the appointment of a special prosecutor who might complicate the situation. Instead, the court ordered Smith to conduct a preliminary investigation under the act into the allegations presented by the plaintiffs.[30]

The 1984 Court of Appeals decision, sought by both sides in the case, has important implications for concerns about the enforceability raised by the district court. In reversing the lower court's decision, the three judges offered separate opinions, each addressing a different aspect of the case.[31] The opinion of Judge Bork was the most interesting. Bork reversed on the grounds that the court had no jurisdiction in the case because "the Ethics in Government Act creates no private right of action to compel the Attorney General to conduct a preliminary investigation."[32] After examining the legislative history of the act, Bork concluded that there was no evidence of congressional intent to create a private right of action.[33] The judge also raised the recurring question of executive power in law enforcement:

> If the execution of the laws is lodged by the Constitution in the President, that execution may not be divided up into segments, some of which courts may control and some of which the President's delegate may control. It is all the law enforcement power and it all belongs to the Executive. Given the area of constitutional doctrine and tradition in which this case falls, . . . we may not lightly impute to Congress an intent to remove prosecutorial discretion from the Executive and place it in the courts and private parties.[34]

In arguing against the private right of action, Bork pointed to Congress's decision to place the triggering mechanism in the hands of the attorney general and its subsequent amendments in 1982 increasing the attorney general's discretion.[35]

The other 1983 case, *Dellums v. Smith*, involved a similar effort by private citizens and a member of Congress to compel the attorney general to conduct a preliminary investigation, this time into allegations that the president and his foreign policy advisors were violating the Neutrality Act through their support for Nicaraguan rebels.[36] Again, Smith sought dismissal for lack of standing and jurisdiction, and again, the district court denied the motion, ruling that the act, by its very purpose, conferred a procedural right to plaintiffs. The court ordered Smith to conduct the investigation.[37] The department responded by requesting an altered judgment based on the facts that the actions in Nicaragua had been authorized by the president and that the department had a nonprosecution policy for federal executives who violate the Neutrality Act. In 1984 the court rejected these arguments, stating that the act favored investigation as long as the allegation could "reasonably be construed as involving a federal crime."[38] It went on to argue that the purpose of the law would be defeated if the standard for enforcement were the opinion of the attorney general on a disputed question of law.[39] In 1986 an appeals court overturned this decision, arguing that Congress intended no private right of action in enforcement of the law.[40]

In the 1984 case of *Banzhaf v. Smith*[41], Banzhaf, a public interest lawyer, sought an order to compel Smith to conduct an investigation into allegations that top Reagan campaign officials illegally obtained Carter debate documents in 1980. The department had conducted a lengthy investigation into the allegations and concluded that there was no evidence of criminal behavior by any of the officials named. This investigation was not conducted under the Ethics Act provisions, as the investigators concluded that no evidence was revealed that made the allegations "specific" enough to trigger the act.[42] The difference between the two investigations lies primarily in the act's requirement that after ninety days the attorney general must make a judgment and report that judgment to the division of the court. The department investigation lasted about eight months, and no final report was filed with the court.

The district court determined that Banzhaf had standing and that it had jurisdiction based on the *Dellums* and *Nathan* decisions. (The reversal of *Nathan* had not occurred at this time.) Beyond these issues, the court argued that the allegations were clearly "specific" under the requirements of the act, as evidenced by the department's own extended investigation and by the facts presented by Banzhaf.[43] The court also raised the issue of the department's accountability under the arrangement. The judge argued that if the department's position was correct, "That entire process can be short-circuited by the simple device of a refusal by the Attorney General . . . to initiate the required investigation. For if there is no standing to sue, there will be no accountability: no one could require the Attorney General to conduct a preliminary investigation in accordance with the Act, to report to the special judicial panel, or to apply in appropriate cases for the appointment of Independent Counsel."[44] Judge Greene denied the department's motion to dismiss.[45] Later that year he ruled that the attorney general must seek the appointment of a special prosecutor under the act, having failed to meet the ninety-day time limit for the preliminary investigation. In doing so, he rejected the department's new contentions that such an order would violate the separation of powers by infringing on the executive power over

law enforcement. The court argued that Article II, section 2, and supporting case law provided ample justification for the judicially appointed special prosecutor; that for the same reasons, the independent counsel had
constitutional authority over the cases covered by the act; and finally, that
it had the authority to order the attorney general to perform a ministerial
duty required by statute.[46]

The Court of Appeals for the D.C. Circuit found that the district court
lacked jurisdiction to adjudicate Banzhaf's claim. It held that Congress had
intended to preclude judicial review at public request of the attorney general's discretion to trigger the act. Furthermore, the act contained provisions designed to avoid the "premature airing" of charges against covered
officials. The court argued that permitting judicial review would undermine
these provisions by "airing charges preliminarily in the District Courts."
After examining these structural considerations, the court turned to the legislative history of the act and noted that earlier versions of the provisions
contained private right of action clauses but that they had been dropped
from the final bill. On this basis, the district court's decison was vacated.[47]

While there is little doubt that the appeals courts are correct in judging
that Congress intended to preclude private suits to enforce the act,[48] these
conclusions raise questions about the usefulness and importance of the provisions. If the attorney general has unreviewable discretion in determining
when to trigger the act, how effective is it in eliminating the actual or apparent conflict of interest that the attorney general presumably has in these
cases? How accountable is the attorney general in this statutory scheme, especially after these court decisions cementing his discretion in triggering the
act? These questions were at the heart of concerns raised during the second
reauthorization, in 1987.

Larger Political Events

During the same time that the independent counsel statute was directly under attack, there were several larger events that shaped the political environment within which the second reauthorization would take place. The most
important of these were the appointment and confirmation of Edwin
Meese as Attorney General, the election of 1986, and the decline of President Reagan's power with the onset of the Iran-Contra scandal.

Looking back, a convincing argument can be made that Mr. Meese did
more to ensure that the independent counsel would become a permanent
part of the political landscape than any other single individual, with the no-

table exception of Richard Nixon. The irony, of course, lies in the fact that Meese believed the mechanism to be an unconstitutional usurpation of executive power and worked during his tenure to have it overturned, or at the very least, to limit its impact. It was these efforts, combined with the fact that he had twice been the target of independent counsel investigations himself, that convinced many of the continued need for the arrangement. Meese's efforts to limit the impact of the statute are discussed later in this chapter and again in Chapter 6. It is sufficient to say at this point that his actions as Attorney General appeared to represent precisely the kind of behaviors that the provisions were designed to counteract. It should also be noted that after his bitter nomination battle, Meese's relationship with many members of Congress was at its best strained, and at its worst, outright hostile.

In the midterm elections of 1986 the Republicans lost their six-year hold on the Senate, and the Democrats returned to majority status. This change was viewed as a political defeat for Ronald Reagan since he had campaigned actively on behalf of his party's candidates and because the Republican-controlled Senate had been very important to his early legislative successes. Its importance to the independent counsel issue was in its effect on the chairmanship of the Subcommittee on Oversight of Government Management, the body with oversight responsibilities for the independent counsel provisions. Sen. Carl Levin became the new chairman, and he adopted a much more confrontational style in his dealings with Meese than William Cohen had.[49] This is not to suggest that Cohen had not taken oversight seriously during his chairmanship, for he had. But his approach to dealing with the Justice Department was more deferential and less combative than Levin's and consequently his relationship with Justice Department officials was more congenial.[50] While Cohen continued to have influence in the subcommittee's deliberations, he was no longer in control of its operations, and the nature of oversight changed. With Meese as Attorney General, Levin as subcommittee chairman, and the Democrats once again controlling both houses of Congress, it was almost inevitable that any changes adopted in 1987 would not favor the executive branch's position on this issue.

President Reagan's influence in Congress and beyond had been seriously diminished by 1987, especially when compared to his standing in the early years of his first term when the first reauthorization occurred. This decline in influence has been attributed to the loss of a Republican majority in the Senate in 1986, which meant he also "lost the intellectual force and the political maneuvering room afforded him by Republican Senate leaders," and to the "political body blow" of the Iran-Contra scandal that erupted at the end of 1986.[51]

The combination of these events created a political environment in which there was certain to be close and critical scrutiny of the the Department of Justice's role in the implementation of the independent counsel provisions and widespread consensus that despite any changes that might be made in the law, the essential parts of the mechanism would remain unchanged. Given this environment, it would have been extremely surprising if Congress had moved to abolish or to restrict significantly the independent counsel provisions.

1987: REPRIMANDING MEESE

Reauthorization efforts began in 1987 with a Senate subcommittee investigation into how the provisions had been implemented since 1983. Staff members were refused access to files in the Department of Justice but were granted access to the records of the special court panel. What they discovered was "a pattern that was very disturbing."[52] The investigators found that the department had engaged in "reinterpreting" the statute in a way that permitted it to conduct "pre-preliminary" investigations, some of which took significant amounts of time. These "threshold inquiries" permitted the department to dispose of cases without triggering an investigation covered by the reporting requirements of the act. Further, they found that the department, in disposing of cases, was applying standards that it was not permitted to apply under the statute. The most important of these were "no criminal mind" and "no reasonable prospect of conviction." The Senate report of this investigation concluded that "contrary to the statutory standard, in 50% of the cases handled by the Justice Department since 1982 in which it declined to conduct a preliminary investigation of a covered official, it relied on factors other than credibility and specificity to evaluate the case."[53]

The investigation also uncovered problems with the attorney general's interpretation of the recusal requirements, the "good cause" removal standard, and the status of independent counsel and their staff vis-à-vis the department in the statute.[54] In each case, the report criticized the degree to which Meese had interpreted the provisions to his, or the department's, benefit despite indications to the contrary in the statute.[55] In opening the Senate hearings on reauthorization, Senator Levin accused the department of making an "indirect assault" on the provisions, of "trying to undermine the process through the back door after being so unsuccessful using the front door."[56]

The main thrust of the changes proposed and adopted in 1987 was to eliminate these interpretative practices by the department. There was also some concern about the special division of the court's interpretation of its role and about the mounting criticisms of the lack of accountability of independent counsel, the costs of these investigations, and the length of time spent in investigating.[57]

The process by which changes in the provisions were adopted in 1987 provides another example of the way in which a complex interaction of factors shapes final legislative outcomes. The 1987 reauthorization amendments were shaped by policy differences among members within and between the two houses of Congress, the soured relationship between Congress and the executive branch, the influence of the American Bar Association and Common Cause, and the cloud of constitutional challenges looming in the background. The result was a set of amendments that attempted to meet three of the essential goals of the original legislation: to control the attorney general's conflict of interest, to remain constitutionally sound, and to maintain an arrangement that would meet the symbolic need to reassure the public.

The Symbolic Goal

Rhetorical position taking on the symbolic value of the judicially appointed independent counsel continued to be in the forefront of considerations of changes to the provisions. Although the Department of Justice proposed presidential appointment of the independent counsel, the effort was futile. Senator Levin called up the traumatic memories of Watergate, accusing the Department of wanting to return to "where we were in 1973 when we saw headlines about 'Nixon forces firing of Cox; Richardson, Ruckleshaus quit.'. . . what you want to do is say let's just forget what has happened in the 1970's with that Saturday Night Massacre. . . . I think you are going to find the Congress resisting that advice."[58]

The value of the arrangement in assuring public confidence was repeatedly mentioned in public statements on the issue. For example, Levin, in his exchange with a Department of Justice representative during the Senate hearings, said, "This is not some dry academic legal exercise . . . about some dry statute. What we are talking about is the confidence that people have in their government to do justice to high officials who are suspected or accused or where there is evidence of criminal wrongdoing."[59]

In testimony from representatives of the ABA and Common Cause, the symbolic value of the provisions was also emphasized, "The ABA is convinced that it is imperative for the administration of justice and the continued public confidence in the fairness of our system of justice that the Congress reauthorize the independent counsel provisions."[60] "Common Cause strongly supports the reenactment of Title VI. . . . The Independent Counsel provisions are essential to preserving public confidence in the fair and ethical behavior of public officials."[61]

Even people with reservations about the constitutionality and/or fairness of the provisions based their decision to support the provisions on their symbolic value. Sen. Warren Rudman (R-New Hampshire) wrote, in additional comments added to the Senate committee report, that despite his "serious concerns" about the provisions, he had voted to report the amendments to the full Senate because "Senators Levin and Cohen have argued quite effectively that a mechanism is needed to provide for the investigation and, if necessary, the prosecution of certain designated Federal officials . . . whose close working or personal relationship with the President could threaten the public's confidence in the Attorney General's objectivity."[62]

Further evidence of the perceived symbolic importance of the provisions can be inferred from the floor votes in the House and Senate on the reauthorization bills. For example, in the House the final vote for passage was 322 to 87. But in preliminary votes on floor amendments designed to limit the usefulness of the act and offered by members hostile to the provisions, the votes were considerably closer. Almost all of the House Republicans and a few Southern Democrats joined in support of these emasculating amendments.[63] Similar discrepancies occurred in the Senate votes between the final vote (85 to 10) and votes on hostile amendments.[64]

Most of the attempts to limit the impact of the independent counsel occurred out of the limelight. Few attacks on the provisions were full-scale frontal assaults. Given the political environment in 1987, it was very difficult to oppose publicly the independent counsel provisions, regardless of one's private convictions. Consequently, opponents tended to attack the provisions in more subtle ways, usually through offering amendments that would limit the effectiveness of the arrangement or decrease its popularity.[65] Two examples of these efforts that appeared neutral on their face included proposals to limit the reauthorization period and to apply the provisions to

Congress. The first was to extend the reauthorization for only a short period of time (one to two years) without any changes. Advocates of limited reauthorization argued that the Congress should wait until the Supreme Court had ruled on the constitutionality before reauthorizing for extended periods of time. The motive behind limited reauthorization appears to have been a hope that the Court would find the arrangement unconstitutional, or, if it did not, that the "anti-Meese" sentiment would have died down sufficiently, making further encroachments on the attorney general's discretion less likely.[66]

The second major effort to undermine support for the arrangement came in the form of an amendment making the independent counsel provisions applicable to members of Congress. This amendment had delayed passage of the original bill in 1978, and its proponents apparently hoped it would have a similar impact in 1987. Debate on the floor of the House had been scheduled for September 30, 1987, but the bill was "abruptly jerked" from the calendar on September 28, when it became apparent that Republicans intended to press the issue of applicability to Congress. Congressman Newt Gingrich "linked Democrats' uneasiness over the amendment with the growing number of ethics probes and criminal investigations of Democratic members."[67] The impasse was eventually resolved, and the House debated and approved the bill in late October of 1987. Similar efforts were made in the Senate but the amendment was defeated there as well. Opponents to the provision to include Congress argued that the conflict of interest problem did not exist when the Department investigated members of Congress, so no independent prosecutorial arrangement was necessary.[68] The relative closeness of the votes on these amendments compared to the final votes on bills that contained neither amendment suggests that once these attempts had failed, appearances required support for the bill in the final vote.

Perhaps the best example of the power of the symbolic argument can be found in the fact that President Reagan signed the reauthorization bill despite his professed belief that the provisions unconstitutionally usurp executive power. During the congressional debate, there was much speculation that Reagan would veto the bill.[69] But after it passed both houses of Congress, Reagan signed the bill into law "over the advice of top aides and despite strong personal reservations."[70] He said he signed "because it was necessary to ensure public confidence," even though he believed that the new restrictions on the attorney general only served to "aggravate the infirmities" of the arrangement.[71]

Removing Conflict of Interest

In contrast to the reauthorization in 1982, the goal of controlling conflict of interest on the part of the attorney general was a major consideration in 1987. The oversight investigation had demonstrated the consequences of the 1982 amendments and the Court of Appeals' decisions when combined with an attorney general who was hostile to the provisions. Consequently, Congress adopted a number of "clarifying" amendments designed "to deal with Ed Meese."[72] Key among these amendments were provisions limiting the criteria to be considered in deciding whether to begin a preliminary investigation to "only" specificity of allegations and credibility of the source;[73] limiting threshold inquiries to fifteen days and requiring the attorney general to inform the special court panel when a preliminary investigation is begun;[74] requiring the attorney general to provide a prior, written recusal decision when he becomes personally involved in a case covered by the provisions, whether he recuses himself or not;[75] and limiting the attorney general's ability to use "state of mind" criteria to dispose of cases to only those cases where a preliminary investigation has provided "clear and convincing" evidence to that effect, in which case a written report to the special panel is required.[76] Clearly, these changes were designed to rein in the attorney general's ability to interpret the act contrary to congressional intent. The new reporting requirements add a measure of accountability for the attorney general that was missing prior to 1987.

Constitutional Concerns

The specter of the constitutional challenges loomed large over the entire reauthorization proceedings and also had an impact on the final changes adopted. While supporters of the act were convinced of the constitutionality of the arrangement, there was less certainty about whether the Court of Appeals for the D.C. Circuit and the Supreme Court would agree. The former had already handed down the decisions supporting the attorney general's discretion under the act, and the latter had issued two opinions in recent years that had been based on a reading of the doctrine of separation of powers that seemed to favor the executive.[77] The key to the provisions' constitutionality was generally considered to be the temporary nature of the arrangement, the limits on the independent counsels' jurisdiction, and the role granted the attorney general in the process. For this reason, efforts to augment the special court panel's ability to expand the jurisdiction of the independent counsel over the opposition of the attorney general were rejected. Instead, the attorney general was encouraged to give "great weight" to a request for expanded jurisdiction by independent counsel, but he was not required to grant the request. A decision to refuse such a request was held to be nonreviewable by the court panel.[78] Supporters of the act feared that the efforts at expanded jurisdiction might undermine the limited nature of the provisions and, therefore, their constitutionality.[79]

Maintaining Independence

Finally, Congress struggled with the issue of the accountability of the independent counsel but in the end rejected any specific proposals that might limit its independence. It did accept a provision requiring the filing of status reports by the independent counsel, at six-month intervals, detailing the costs and predicted expenditures of the investigation.[80] It also adopted language encouraging the special court panel to appoint independent counsel who "will be prompt, responsible, and cost-effective" in carrying out their investigations.[81] But these provisions were essentially symbolic, giving a nod to concerns about cost and delay but imposing no restrictions that would clearly limit expenses or length of investigations. Congress's desire to keep the independent counsel truly independent worked against efforts to make them formally accountable.

CONCLUSIONS

The factors working for the continuance of the 1978 independent counsel provisions throughout their history have included the memory of Watergate (and particularly the Saturday Night Massacre), the perception by a significant portion of Congress that the provisions are symbolically important to ensure public confidence in unbiased law enforcement, the efforts of several members of Congress and their staffs who are influenced by the aforementioned factors but also by strong policy interests in government ethics, and support from interest groups with high levels of credibility on this issue. Forces working to limit the effect of the provisions and the amount of change adopted in reauthorization have included the constitutional questions about the arrangement, the executive branch opposition to it, and the influence of key members of Congress in behind-the-scenes bargaining over the scope of specific provisions. These forces clearly have not been able to have any substantial impact on the existence of the provisions but have been able to influence their structure at the margins and their implementation in very significant ways. The ten-year implementation history outlined in this chapter further demonstrates the way in which internal and external factors shape legislative outcomes.

Prospects for Change

This issue has a way of going away for five years at a time. What happens at each authorization will depend on the experience of the five years in between. What happens in the last year before reauthorization is the key to it all.[82]

The first ten years of the existence of the independent counsel provisions demonstrates the truth of this statement. Consequently predictions about likely changes during the 1992 reauthorization must be speculative. The question of the costs of independent counsel investigations is likely to be raised again.[83] During these times of tight money and large deficits, opponents of the provisions can gain more sympathy on this issue than on direct attacks on the arrangement. Further, the constitutional arguments have been blunted by the court's decision in *Morrison v. Olson*. The problems encountered by the independent counsel's office in the Iran-Contra case are also likely to be subject to discussion. Independent Counsel Walsh has struggled with significant problems in obtaining and using evidence because of the national security implications of the case.[84] The length and expense of the investigation, especially given the meager "results," are also likely to be scrutinized.[85] The 1990 Court of Appeals decision setting aside Oliver North's convictions calls into question the very usefulness of the investigation.

It is always possible that the president may veto the reauthorization bill, although this seems unlikely in an election year. In the end, the factors most likely to shape reauthorization will be political ones: the relationship between Congress and the executive (and more specifically, between the oversight committees and the Department of Justice) and the distribution of power between the Democrats and Republicans in Congress. Since 1992 is a presidential election year, a shift of partisan power in Congress or the White House could result in conditions very differrent from those in 1982 and 1987. What seems inevitable is that the independent counsel arrangement will continue to exist in some form. The memory of Watergate, which drove the initial adoption of the provisions and which might have faded by this time in different circumstances, was kept alive by the Iran-Contra scandal and by Edwin Meese's tenure as Attorney General. A majority in Congress is likely to remain convinced that the symbolic value of the act is such that the provisions, in some form, must be maintained. Finally, the Supreme Court's acceptance of the provisions in *Morrison v. Olson* has heightened their legitimacy. It is to this decision that we now turn.

FIVE

IS THE SPECIAL PROSECUTOR
CONSTITUTIONAL?

Special prosecutor investigations during the first decade after the Ethics Act was enacted were plagued by the recurring question of their constitutional legitimacy. The Reagan administration's hostility toward the provisions added further to the uncertainty. It was inevitable that the courts would have to address this question, and by the latter part of the decade the issue was ripe for judicial review. There were four ongoing special prosecutor investigations, three that resulted in criminal indictments and prosecutions (Deaver, Nofziger, Iran-Contra) and a fourth that raised difficult questions about the extent to which a special prosecutor could expand her jurisdiction to pursue allegations of wrongdoing (Olson). It was this last case that ultimately addressed the central constitutional questions of the arrangement.

This chapter examines more closely the constitutional debate about the independent counsel provisions of the Ethics Act. It does so through a discussion of the cases challenging the arrangement, with a particular focus on the Supreme Court's 1988 decision in *Morrison v. Olson*. As we trace the development and resolution of this particular case, we can see clearly the two sides of the argument over the special prosecutor's constitutional legitimacy.

CASES BEFORE *MORRISON V. OLSON*

The first constitutional challenge to the special prosecutor arrangement came early in its history. Timothy Kraft, the subject of the second Ethics Act investigation, filed a civil suit against the special prosecutor shortly after his appointment. The special prosecutor sought dismissal of the charges against Kraft before the district court had the opportunity to decide *Kraft v. Gallinghouse*. The case was dismissed as moot.[1]

The other early litigation requiring courts to interpret the provisions did not focus on the constitutional questions. The focus of the *Dellums*, *Banzhaf*, and *Nathan* cases was the attorney general's discretion under the act, not the authority of the special prosecutor. Nonetheless, the courts involved in these cases did contribute to the constitutional debate. In

Banzhaf v. Smith, District Court Judge Greene rejected the Department of Justice's argument that forcing the attorney general to conduct a preliminary investigation would violate the doctrine of separation of powers. The judge found that the appointments clause provided adequate constitutional support for a judicially appointed prosecutor and supported the prosecutor's authority over cases covered by the act. Consequently, Greene argued, the attorney general's authority under the act was merely ministerial, his discretion was intentionally and constitutionally limited, and a court could order him to carry out his ministerial duty.[2] In arriving at this conclusion, Judge Greene had to make a preliminary judgment as to the constitutionality of the provisions themselves.

The Court of Appeals for the D.C. Circuit never directly addressed the central constitutional questions of the special prosecutor arrangment in its rulings in favor of the Department of Justice in *Banzhaf* and *Nathan*. However, there were hints in the opinions that suggest that some on the court would be sympathetic to the executive branch's concerns about the provisions. In each case the court placed great value on the ability of the attorney general to exercise discretion in law enforcement. Judge Bork in particular demonstrated his belief that the executive's power over law enforcement was not easily divisible, stating that all law enforcement power "belongs to the Executive."[3]

These cases would be used later to support both sides of the debate. On the one hand, they validated the important role given the attorney general in the appointment of the special prosecutor, permitting supporters of the act to argue that executive power was not seriously threatened by the provisions. Alternatively, the cases endorsed the concept that the attorney general's authority over law enforcement was extensive and that it flowed from the broad grant of power to the executive to take care that the laws are faithfully executed, supporting opponents' arguments that the provisions were an unacceptable intrusion into executive power and discretion in law enforcement.

The most prominent challenges to the constitutionality of the special prosecutor arrangement came from Michael Deaver and Oliver North. Early in 1987 the District Court for the District of Columbia was petitioned by Deaver and North to enjoin the investigations of the special prosecutors working on their cases. In *Deaver v. Seymour*,[4] Michael Deaver sought to enjoin Whitney North Seymour from filing a perjury indictment against him, arguing that Seymour lacked the constitutional authority to pursue the indictment. Judge Jackson denied the request because Deaver had a remedy available to him after indictment and because he had failed to demonstrate that he was likely to win on the merits of the case. While admitting that the special prosecutor arrangement was "a constitutional hybrid which neither the framers of the Constitution nor any court since expressly contemplated," the judge argued that the available precedent suggested "that the arrangement, on its face, will probably not be found to offend the Constitution."[5]

In *North v. Walsh*[6] defendant North sought to enjoin Lawrence Walsh from investigating his involvement in the Iran-Contra scandal. North argued that the special prosecutor provisions violated the principle of separation of powers. In response to concerns that the Iran-Contra investigation might be derailed by the constitutional challenges, Attorney General Meese offered Walsh a collateral appointment with the Department of Justice.[7] Walsh accepted the terms of the appointment and continued his investigation. In a second challenge North argued that the attorney general lacked the authority to make this appointment and that the arrangement was further flawed because officers exercising executive power must be removable by the president at will. Under the attorney general's regulations, Walsh continued to be protected by the "good cause" removal standard.

The district court dismissed the cases, holding that the question of constitutionality was not ripe for review. The case had not yet resulted in either an indictment or prosecution, and North had failed to demonstrate sufficient hardship that would warrant the court's early involvement in the constitutional questions. Despite this procedural dismissal of the complaint, the court did give several indications that it was not sympathetic to North's constitutional contentions. In explaining why it was acting with restraint, the court pointed to the importance, and extended implications, of the constitutional questions at issue: "North's arguments do not merely challenge the legality of the Office of Independent Counsel. His rather doctrinaire approach to the separation of powers issues would require the Executive to reserve all prosecutorial powers for itself. Such a requirement would call into question the constitutionality of vesting prosecutorial power in independent agencies and other institutions."[8]

Judge Parker also indicated his belief in the constitutionality of the provisions in his discussion of the presumption against early judicial intervention in ongoing criminal investigations. He wrote that Walsh "was appointed and is acting pursuant to a law enacted by Congress and signed by the President, a law which carries the presumption of constitutionality."[9] More importantly, in a footnote to that statement, the judge argued that

North's "rigid vision of the separation of powers doctrine is not supported by our constitutional structure of government" and went on to cite case law that adopted a flexible approach to questions concerning separation of powers. In the next footnote, he discussed the important role of the attorney general in the process and the statutory limits placed on the independent counsel.[10]

On appeal the D.C. Circuit Court remanded the case to the district court, ordering that it determine whether the case could be decided on other grounds, including the authority of the attorney general to delegate law enforcement powers to the independent counsel, and the relationship between the independent counsel and the special division of the court that had originally appointed him.[11] Relying on the precedent established in the Watergate case, the district court concluded that the attorney general's action was appropriate and within his authority. It also determined that the relationship between the independent counsel and the special division of the Court was so limited as to warrant no immediate consideration of the constitutionality of the act.[12]

While these more public cases were garnering headlines, the Olson investigation was slowly moving toward a constitutional confrontation that would make it the case that finally reached the Supreme Court. In the meantime, the Deaver and North suits served to renew public debate about the constitutionality of the provisions[13] and provided the first early indications that the provisions would ultimately be upheld.

MORRISON V. OLSON

The Dispute

The dispute that the Supreme Court addressed in its 1988 decision arose out of a bitter confrontation between the Congress and the president that had occurred five years earlier. In 1982 many in Congress had become concerned about what they perceived as political manipulation by the Environmental Protection Agency of the Superfund program designed to deal with the cleanup of toxic waste. Two House subcommittees with oversight responsibility for the EPA became embroiled in a legal dispute with the EPA, the Justice Department, and the president over the release of certain documents that they deemed relevant to their investigations.[14] The two sides were eventually able to reach a political accommodation on the issue, but many

House members involved in the investigation were angered by the role played by the Department of Justice in the executive privilege dispute. They asked the House Judiciary Committee to investigate the department's role more carefully.

Between February 1983 and December 1985 a subcommittee of the House Judiciary Committee carried out an extensive investigation of the participation of the department in the EPA controversy. On December 5, 1985, it issued a three-thousand-page report including the suggestion that Theodore Olson, assistant attorney general for the Office of Legal Counsel in the department, had lied to the subcommittee during its investigation. It also accused Deputy Attorney General Edward Schmults and Assistant Attorney General for the Land and Natural Resources Division Carol Dinkins of obstructing the congressional investigation by witholding relevant documents.[15]

On December 12, 1985, House Judiciary Committee chairman Peter Rodino requested the appointment of an independent counsel to look into the allegations made against the Justice Department officials. After a lengthy preliminary investigation, the Public Integrity Section of the department recommended that the allegations against Schmults, Dinkins, and Olson be turned over to an independent counsel. It suggested that all three should be subject to the investigation because the case appeared to involve "a seamless web of events" that could not be adequately investigated in isolation. It concluded that any effort to separate the allegations and individuals out would be "artificial" and "may impede the independent counsel's ability to fully explore the allegations."[16] After reviewing this report, the deputy assistant attorney general for the Criminal Division, John C. Keeney, ruled that only Olson should be subjected to investigation by independent counsel. Due to the large number of recusals because of personal interests in this case, the attorney general had appointed William F. Weld, the U.S. attorney for Massachusetts, as a special assistant for advice. Weld recommended that the allegations against Schmults and Olson, but not Dinkins, be turned over to an independent counsel. On April 10, 1986, Meese referred only the allegations against Olson, for lying to Congress, to the special division of the court for independent investigation.[17]

The special court panel originally appointed James C. McKay to investigate the allegations. McKay resigned a month later after determining that he had a conflict of interest. His chief deputy, Alexia Morrison, was appointed in his place on May 29, 1986. After beginning her investigation, the independent counsel began to be concerned about the way in which her jurisdiction in this matter had been carved out. There appeared to be no criminal behavior in Olson's statements if they were taken alone, but the office had serious concerns about the role Olson might have played in a broader conspiracy to obstruct the congressional investigation. Deputy Independent Counsel Earl Dudley, Jr., explained:

The House Judiciary report did not think it was just a problem of whether Ted Olson told the truth. The report suggested a conspiracy at the highest levels of the Department of Justice to obstruct the inquiry into the EPA dispute. Six months into our investigation we were fairly strongly of the view that if we took only Olson's testimony, that it was literally true if misleading. But we were concerned that the Committee may have had a point about what was going on at Justice. Our jurisdiction had been carved up in a very peculiar way and on the basis of what we could see, without being able to include Dinkins and Schmults in our review, there was a lot more reason to ask questions about them than about Olson.[18]

On November 14, 1986, Morrison requested an expansion of her jurisdiction in a letter to the attorney general. A month later she received a reply from Deputy Attorney General Arnold I. Burns explaining that Meese had refused an expansion of her jurisdiction to include Dinkins and Schmults. Early in January 1987 she took her request to the special division responsible for her appointment. In its filings in response to her request, the Department of Justice gave its first indication that it might join in a constitutional challenge to her authority.[19] After hearing arguments from both sides, the court panel ruled on April 2 that it lacked the authority to overrule the attorney general's decision to exclude Dinkins and Schmults from her jurisdiction. However, it did give her permission to investigate whether or not Olson had been engaged in a conspiracy to obstruct the investigation. The panel also ruled that the arrangement was constitutional.[20]

The independent counsel quickly impaneled a grand jury and in May and June it subpoenaed Olson, Dinkins, and Schmults to testify before it. All three moved to quash the subpoenas, challenging the constitutionality of Morrison's authority. The independent counsel provisions of the Ethics Act were upheld in the district court, struck down by the court of appeals, and upheld by the Supreme Court. A closer look at each court's opinion will make the various arguments for and against the arrangement more apparent.

The District Court's Opinion

Chief Judge Aubrey E. Robinson, Jr., of the U.S. District Court for the District of Columbia held in *In Re Sealed Case* that the independent counsel provisions represented a "measured response" by Congress to the problem of the executive investigating itself. "Congress chose to use its authority . . . to create a mechanism to guarantee the integrity and independence of criminal investigations in matters where the Department of Justice has real or apparent conflicts of interest. By carefully assigning the functions necessary for the accomplishment of its purpose, it has constitutionally addressed an important national need."[21]

Robinson found support for the provisions in the language of the Constitution and in previous decisons of the Supreme Court. He held that the powers of the special division of the court responsible for appointment were supported both by Article III and by the appointments clause of Article II, granting Congress the power to vest appointment of inferior officers in "courts of law." He concluded that the independent counsel was clearly an "inferior officer" within the meaning of the appointments clause because of the limitations placed on her authority, the fact that special prosecutors are not listed among the primary officers specifically mentioned in the Constitution, and the belief by Congress that the independent counsel was inferior demonstrated by the decision to vest appointment in the court panel. The judge found no "incongruity" in placing this appointment in the courts given Congress's clear intent to remove the executive's conflict of interest and the limitations placed on the court panel in overseeing the independent counsel.[22]

Addressing the more general contention that the arrangement violated the principle of separation of powers, the judge argued that Supreme Court precedent requires a flexible and common sense reading of the doctrine. Citing the Court's opinions in *United States v. Nixon, Humphrey's Executor v. United States*, and *Weiner v. United States*,[23] Robinson ruled that the restrictions on removal and the lack of presidential supervision in the arrangement were justified given Congress's desire to make the investigation independent. The very purpose of the statute required that that independence be protected.[24]

On the procedural matters before it, the court denied the motion to quash the subpoenas. On August 19, 1987, it held Dinkins, Olson, and Schmults in contempt for refusal to comply with the subpoenas. It then stayed the contempt charges pending an expedited appeal to the D.C. Circuit. The case was argued before a three-judge panel of the Court of Appeals on September 16, 1987. Amicus briefs asking for reversal of the district court were filed by the Department of Justice and Michael Deaver's attorneys. Amicus briefs supporting the district court were filed by Iran-Contra Independent Counsel Lawrence Walsh, the Senate legal counsel, a group of members of the House of Representatives, the American Bar Association, Common Cause, and Public Citizen. Despite this support, Morrison and Dudley were certain they had lost when they saw that the panel included two Reagan appointees and they heard the questions from the bench during oral argument.[25] They were right.

The Opinion of the Court of Appeals

On January 22, 1988, the Court of Appeals for the D.C. Circuit held that the independent counsel provisions were unconstitutional. The 2-to-1 decision, written by Judge Laurence H. Silberman, found that the provisions constituted an unacceptable intrusion into the executive power over law enforcement and gave the special panel of the court inappropriate powers.[26] Judge Ruth Bader Ginsburg dissented. In order to arrive at its conclusions, the court traveled a rather tortuous route around a well-established body of precedent to the contrary.

The court was asked to address essentially three related questions. First, did the process by which the independent counsel was appointed violate (1) the appointments clause of Article II, (2) the limitations placed on the judiciary in Article III, and (3) the doctrine of separation of powers? Second, did the restrictions on removal ("good cause") violate Article II by interfering with the president's power to execute the laws faithfully? Third, did the provisions, taken as a whole, violate the principles underlying separation of powers because they weakened the "constitutional structures that serve to protect individual liberty?"[27] The court answered "yes" to each of these questions.

The court focused first on the appointment arrangement in the provisions. It began by rejecting the argument that the independent counsel was an "inferior officer" within the meaning of the appointments clause. Deciding whether an officer is indeed inferior, said the court, required it to ask: "Is she in the exercise of her duties . . . a mere aid and subordinate of the head of a department or does she instead employ such independence of authority as to place her on the principal officer side of the appointments dichotomy?"[28]

Having asked this question, the court concluded that despite the limited supervisory role given the attorney general, the independent counsel could not be considered to be his inferior. It argued that her authority was "so broad as to compel the conclusion that she is a principal officer"; that, in fact, her authority was "unchecked by the President himself"; and, that the appointment was not temporary in a technical sense since it removed the attorney general's power altogether in these cases and it was "coterminous with the investigation," however long it might take.[29] The court believed that the case could have been disposed of on these grounds alone, but it chose to address the other questions as well since an appeal to the Supreme Court appeared likely.

The court turned next to an examination of the more general Article II issues raised. It argued that because the power to prosecute was so potentially dangerous to individual liberty, the framers structured the governmental prosecution process to check the arbitrary abuse of the power. Thus, Congress was given the power to make the criminal laws, the executive the power to initiate prosecutions, and the judiciary the power to judge impartially the cases brought forward by the executive. Especially important to this analysis was the court's focus on the executive power to initiate, or refuse to initiate, prosecutions. It argued that a unitary executive was created in order to ensure the accountability of the prosecutor. "For no federal government function is it more vital to the protection of individual liberty that ultimately the buck stops with an accountable official—the President—than in the prosecution of criminal laws."[30]

Judge Silberman contended that the Ethics Act provisions interfered with the concept of executive control over law enforcement in three ways. The removal of appointment from the executive interfered with the principle of accountability in a unitary executive, for the power to appoint was essential to maintaining a "responsive and accountable" executive.[31] Next, Silberman argued that the "good cause" removal standard placed unacceptable limitations on the President's power to remove "purely executive" officers at will. The 1926 Supreme Court decision *Myers v. U.S.*[32] held that removal at will of officers doing "purely executive functions" was necessary in order for the president to execute the laws faithfully. Silberman held that the independent counsel was "charged with an indisputably executive function" (law enforcement) and that consequently, the removal restrictions violated the *Myers* principle.[33] Finally, the judge objected to the power given to the special court panel to review an attorney general's decision to remove the independent counsel. He saw no difference between this provision and one that would require the attorney general to ask the court panel for removal power. "Not content with eliminating the President's implicit power to direct or influence the independent counsel," Silberman wrote, "Congress went further to render the President impotent to affect the independent counsel's behavior." Consequently, the arrangement "strikes at the very heart of the unitary executive doctrine."[34]

The judge next examined the argument that the act, taken as a whole, violated the principle of separation of powers. He concluded that the act constituted "a serious encroachment" on executive authority and rejected the argument that the arrangement was necessary, and therefore, justified. He found no actual conflict of interest to exist in the cases covered by the act and suggested that the act was a partisan overreaction to Watergate. The provisions gave Congress a powerful weapon to use against the executive, for "repeated calls for independent counsel may, like a flicking left jab, confound the Executive Branch in dealing with Congress." While some conflict would always exist between the branches, Silberman argued that the "legal obligation" imposed by the statute had the effect of altering "the political equation" to the advantage of Congress.[35] In doing so, it intruded in an unconstitutional manner on the power of the executive, and thus violated the doctrine of separation of powers.

Finally, the Court of Appeals addressed the Article III issues raised by the independent counsel provisions and found violations of the Constitution here as well. The role played by the special court panel in appointment and supervision of the independent counsel was found to be beyond the Article III provision that limits the jurisdiction of federal courts to cases and controversies. Silberman contended that the ability to define the jurisdiction of the prosecutor was not a simple ministerial task but rather one requiring the exercise of policy discretion more appropriate for the executive than for a court of law. Further, he questioned the role of the court panel both in issuing interpretive orders that were also not within the case and controversy limitations and in the ability of the panel to review the decision of the attorney general to remove an independent counsel. He concluded, "Intimate involvement of an Article III court in the supervision and control of a prosecutorial office undermines the status of the judiciary as a neutral forum for the resolution of disputes between citizens and their governments."[36]

In her dissent, Judge Ginsburg relied extensively on the large body of precedent that appeared to support the independent counsel arrangement. She argued that the Supreme Court's separation of powers jurisprudence relied on two basic questions. Does the arrangement in question impermissibly transfer the executive function to another branch? Is there any undue intrusion into executive prerogatives? The judge found no reason to answer either question in the affirmative. In order to answer the questions, she said, the court should consider the "actual effects of each apparent limitation." Using this "fluid, functional approach," Ginsburg found the Ethics Act provisions to be only very limited intrusions into the executive sphere with corresponding strong justifications for such intrusion. The arrangement, she wrote, "is a carefully considered congressional journey into the sometimes arcane realm of the separation of powers doctrine, more particularly, into areas the framers left undefined. . . . It is a measure faithful to the eighteenth century blueprint, yet fitting for our time."[37]

In a majority opinion that "ranges far and wide,"[38] Silberman worked his way around the body of precedent on the appointments clause and separation of powers to conclude that the provisions had serious constitutional flaws. His position was supported by the "unitary executive" arguments from the executive branch[39] and by two recent Supreme Court decisions that seemed to support the position. "Make no mistake about it," one commentator on the case warned, "the Morrison case is but the latest effort, an aggressive effort, by the executive to mold the separation of powers doctrine into a means of inflating the powers of the executive under the rubric of the vested but imprecise duty to execute the laws faithfully. The effort succeeded in Chadha and Bowsher."[40]

In its 1983 decision in *INS v. Chadha*[41] (striking down the use of the legislative veto) and its 1986 decision in *Bowsher v. Synar*[42] (finding unconstitutional the automatic cut provisions of the Gramm–Rudman–Hollings Deficit Reduction Act) the Supreme Court appeared to be retreating on its traditional view of the separation of powers as a fluid and flexible doctrine. In *Chadha*, seven members of the Court viewed the use of legislative veto provisions in congressional acts as an unconstitutional violation of the doctrine of separation of powers. In an opinion that had the effect of invalidating approximately two hundred such provisions placed in legislation over a period of five decades,[43] the Court argued that the constitutional roles of the legislature and the executive branch in the passage of legislation are clearly spelled out in the Constitution. The requirements that both houses of Congress approve the bill and that it be presented to the president for approval or veto (Article I, sections 1 and 7) were viewed by the Court as the only constitutional means of making legislation. Finding that the legislative veto was a legislative act and that it did not go through this process, the Court concluded that the practice was unconstitutional.

The language used by the majority in its decision reflected a rigid interpretation of the separation of powers. Consider, for example, the following passages from the majority opinion:

> the fact that a given law or procedure is efficient, convenient, and useful in facilitating functions of government, standing alone, will not save it if it is contrary to the Constitution. Convenience and efficiency are not the primary objectives—or the hallmarks—of democratic government.[44]

> The Constitution sought to divide the delegated powers of the new federal government into three defined categories, legislative, executive, and judicial, to assure, as nearly as possible, that each Branch . . . would confine itself to its assigned responsibility. The hydraulic pressure inherent within each of the separate branches to exceed the outer limits of its power, even to accomplish desirable objectives, must be resisted.[45]

When contrasted with the view of separation of powers held by Justice White in his dissent, the comparative rigidity of the majority's conception becomes more apparent.

> The legislative veto is more than "efficient, convenient, and useful.". . . It is an important if not indispensable political invention that allows the President and the Congress to resolve major constitutional and policy differences, assures the accountability of independent regulatory agencies, and preserves Congress' control over lawmaking.[46]

> the wisdom of the Framers was to anticipate that the nation would grow and new problems of governance would require different solutions. Accordingly, our Federal Government was intentionally chartered with the flexibility to respond to contemporary needs without losing sight of fundamental democratic principles.[47]

Interestingly, even White suggested that he would be less tolerant of certain "inventions" than others. In a statement that Judge Silberman read as having direct implications in the special prosecutor case, White wrote, "I do not suggest that all legislative vetoes are necessarily consistent with separation of powers principles. A legislative check on an *inherently executive function, for example that of initiating prosecutions, poses an entirely different question*"[48] (emphasis added).

Similar comparisons can be made between the majority opinion and White's dissent in *Bowsher*, where the Court found that the Gramm–Rudman deficit reduction plan violated the separation of powers because of the authority given to the comptroller general to make automatic cuts if targets are not reached by Congress. The majority believed that this arrangement violated the separation of powers because it gave executive powers to a congressional officer.

Given these opinions, and the highly formalistic view of the separation of powers that drove them, it seemed entirely possible that the Supreme Court would uphold the decision of the Court of Appeals for similar reasons.[49] The provisions' defenders were forced to explain how this case differed from the legislative veto and the Budget Act, while their opponents emphasized the similarities among the cases.[50] There was no dispute that the powers being exercised by the independent counsel were ones usually lodged with the executive. The question was whether or not Congress could vest the appointment of someone exercising those powers in a court of law and whether it could place limits on the ability of the executive to control that person. When the independent counsel's office tried to predict the outcome of the case, it had difficulty coming up with a majority for either position.[51] After oral arguments before the Supreme Court, each side claimed that its position appeared likely to prevail.[52] Thus, there was a good deal of uncertainty about the likely outcome of the case before the high court.

The Opinion of the Supreme Court

In *Morrison v. Olson* a 7 to 1 majority reversed the Court of Appeals and found the independent counsel provisions to be constitutionally valid. Supporters of the provisions hailed the Court's apparent return to a more flexible approach to the separation of powers while opponents criticized the Court's lack of consistency in applying the doctrine. For example, members of Congress praised the decision because it gave them "more breathing space to legislate on sensitive interbranch issues" and because it would mean that they "didn't have to have absolute, perfect, pristine separation of powers among the branches."[53] Opponents of the law read the case more narrowly[54] but also criticized the Court for its failure to see the threat to the executive embodied in the provisions and its use of the necessity justification in upholding the statute.[55] After a more careful look at the arguments of Chief Justice Rehnquist in the majority opinion and at Justice Scalia's dissent, we shall return to this debate over the appropriateness of the Court's decision.

The Court focused its attention on three central questions regarding the arrangement. It asked first whether the appointments clause of Article II was violated by the judicial appointment of independent counsel. It concluded that it was not. Next, it asked whether or not the role played by the judicial panel was a violation of Article III. Again, it found no violation, although it expressed some reservations about some of the panel's activities. Finally, it asked whether the provisions violated the principle of separation of powers by unduly interfering with the ability of the president to execute the laws faithfully. It answered this question in the negative as well. In general, it found the statute to be a carefully crafted one that could withstand constitutional challenge.

Rehnquist began by addressing the issues raised by the judicial appointment of the independent counsel. He found that the independent counsel did indeed constitute an "inferior" officer for the purposes of appointment because the duties, jurisdiction, and tenure of the counsel were limited by the statute and because the attorney general's power of removal implied that the counsel was of inferior rank. Further, the chief justice rejected the argument that the appointments clause did not permit interbranch appointments (i.e., appointment of an executive officer by the judiciary). Relying on the "plain meaning of the words" and on substantial precedent to the contrary, he found no evidence in the language of the clause, nor in its history, to prohibit such appointments. Given Congress's desire to insure independent investigation in these cases, Rehnquist found judicial appointment to be a logical way to accomplish this end.[56]

Rehnquist found first that Article II, through the appointments clause, provides an additional, and independent, source of judicial power and that therefore, the failure of Article III to include appointment of inferior officers is clearly not a bar to such action. He went on to argue that the ability of the court panel to define the jurisdiction of the independent counsel was a power incident to the enumerated power to appoint and therefore was not in violation of Article III. He also noted the constraints placed on the panel in the defining of jurisdiction, most notably that it had to be "demonstrably related to the factual circumstances that gave rise to the Attorney General's investigation and request for the appointment of the independent counsel in the particular case." In a footnote Rehnquist further pursued this question of jurisdiction, arguing that the provisions do not give the court panel the power to expand the independent counsel's jurisdiction without such a request from the attorney general.[57]

Rehnquist turned next to the challenges to the particular responsibilities of the special panels that could not be so easily identified as incidental to appointment. These included receiving reports from the attorney general and the independent counsel, referring new charges to the independent counsel, granting the attorney general extensions for preliminary investigations, deciding when to make certain reports available to the public, granting reimbursement of attorneys' fees for targets of investigations who were not indicted, and terminating the office of independent counsel when its work was complete. He found nothing in Article III that "absolutely prevents Congress from vesting these other miscellaneous powers in the Special Division." In order to draw this conclusion, he argued that the purpose of the traditional view that courts should not exercise executive or legislative powers is to ensure that the judiciary does not unduly encroach upon the powers of the other branches. In this case Rehnquist found these miscellaneous powers to be essentially ministerial, not inherently executive in nature, and "directly analogous to functions that federal judges perform in other contexts." No threatening intrusion into executive functions existed.[58]

The Court was more troubled by the power given to the special panel to terminate the office of independent counsel, for it at least implied a more supervisory role for the judges. In order for the provisions to be constitutionally sound, the Court said that they had to be interpreted narrowly, as only giving the panel the power to shut down the office when all of its work had been accomplished. The power was clearly not to be seen as equal to the attorney general's power of removal for "good cause."[59]

In completing his analysis of the Article III concerns, Rehnquist discussed the alleged threat of the provisions to the "impartial and independent federal adjudication of claims" by the judicial branch. He rejected the argument that such a threat exists, pointing out that the act gave the court panel no power to review the actions of the independent counsel or of the attorney general with regard to the counsel. "Accordingly, there is no risk of partisan or biased adjudication of claims regarding the independent counsel by that court." Rehnquist went on to note that the provisions forbid the judges on the panel to participate in any case arising under the provisions that comes before the Court of Appeals. This makes the panel "sufficiently isolated" so as to raise no problems for impartial adjudication of cases where independent counsel have been named.[60]

The majority ended this discussion with a warning that demonstrates the extent to which it relied upon the specific statutory limitations of the act in finding it constitutional. "We emphasize, nevertheless, that the Special Division has *no* authority to take any action or undertake any duties that are not specifically authorized by the Act. The gradual expansion of the authority of the Special Division might in another context be a bureaucratic success story, but it would be one that would have serious constitutional ramifications."[61] The Court then noted two instances where the special panel had engaged in activities not expressly granted by the provisions (issuing advisory opinions and ordering postponement of an investigation). While the propriety of these actions was not before the Court, it did note that such actions were not authorized by the act and that "the division's exercise of unauthorized powers risks the transgression of the constitutional limitations of Article III."[62]

In the early parts of the opinion Rehnquist had managed to avoid the question of whether *Chadha* and *Bowsher* were controlling in this case. The opinion avoided expressing any particular theory of the doctrine of separation of powers but in method did not stray far from the two previous opinions, relying on such interpretive devices as the plain meaning of the words and the framers' intent. In answering the broadest question in the case, however, Rehnquist was forced to address this question head on. Did the act as a whole violate the separation of powers by impermissibly intruding on executive power? There seemed no way to answer this question without expounding a theory of what that doctrine entails. It was still possible, of course, that the Court might conclude that while the appointments clause and Article III were not offended by the provisions, that the rest of Article II was. Nevertheless, the implications of the first two sections of the opinion made it all but inevitable that the court would answer this question in the negative as well. But in doing so it had to modify to some extent the rigidity of the theory that had driven *Chadha* and *Bowsher*.

Rehnquist focused first on whether the restrictions on removal of the independent counsel interfered with the president's ability to execute the laws faithfully. In holding that the restriction was valid, he distinguished the case from *Bowsher* and from the earlier *Myers* precedent. In each of these cases the Court had struck down the congressional action because Congress claimed for itself a role in the removal of officers carrying out executive functions. In the *Morrison* case, however, no such congressional usurpation existed, for the removal power remained with the executive. The chief justice went on to argue that the precedent on removal should not be interpreted as requiring a strict functional analysis that looks only at whether the officer is performing a purely executive function or some other kind of function. Rather, the test of legitimacy for removal requirements should be understood as depending on the extent to which the provisions "interfere with the President's exercise of the 'executive power' and his constitutionally appointed duty to 'take care that the laws be faithfully executed' under Article II." He said, "The real question is whether the removal restrictions are of such a nature that they impede the President's ability to perform his constitutional duty."[63] The "good cause" removal standard was able to withstand such a test, for it involved an inferior officer with limited tenure, duties, and jurisdiction. "Although the counsel exercises no small amount of discretion and judgment in deciding how to carry out her duties under the Act, we simply do not see how the President's need to control the exercise of that discretion is so central to the functioning of the Executive Branch as to require as a matter of constitutional law that the counsel be terminable at will by the President."[64]

In the final part of the opinion Rehnquist addressed the question of the entire impact of the act on the doctrine of separation of powers. He acknowledged that the Court had been fairly strict of late in requiring that legislative arrangements comport with the doctrine, relying on the framers' intent that the structure of government act "as 'a self-executing safe-guard' against the encroachment or aggrandizement of one branch at the expense of the other." But, cautioned the Chief Justice, "we have never held that the Constitution requires that the three Branches of Government 'operate with absolute independence.'" He further distinguished this case from those in which the Court had struck down legislative actions by noting that here there was no effort by Congress to take executive power for itself. It had no power to supervise or control the independent counsel. Further, there was no judicial usurpation of executive power since the judicial appointment was permitted by the appointments clause. Finally, while it was "undeniable that the Act reduces the amount of control or supervision that the Attorney General and . . . the President" have in these cases, Rehnquist noted the continued influence of the attorney general throughout the process and found this to be "sufficient control over the independent counsel to ensure that the President is able to perform his constitutionally assigned duties."[65] The independent counsel provisions violated neither specific provisions of the Constitution nor the theory of the separation of powers that underlies the document.

Scalia's Dissent

Justice Scalia was clearly angered by the majority's opinion. In an emotionally charged and frequently bitter dissenting opinion, he attacked the Court's decision both for its specific interpretation of the Constitution and precedent and for its failure to adopt a formalist approach to the separation of powers. His dissent is important because it presents the constitutional arguments against the independent counsel arrangement more effectively than the Court of Appeals by focusing on the theory of the unitary executive and the threat the provisions pose to executive power. Additionally, it raises important questions about the operation of the provisions in practice where the majority opinion focuses almost exclusively on the carefully crafted limitations in the language of the statute itself. While as a matter of constitutional law Scalia is wrong, the value of his dissent remains, for it poses questions about the practical implications of the statute that should not be ignored.

Scalia began by discussing the framers' view that the separation of powers was essential to the attainment of "just government." Not willing to rely on simple "parchment barriers," they gave each branch certain powers that would enable it to resist encroachment from the others. Scalia argued that the fortifications given the executive were the power to veto legislation[66] and the creation of a unitary executive (in contrast to a bicameral legislature) better able to carry out the grant of "executive power" given him in Article II. Power was allocated in a way that would preserve the equilibrium of the system, and it was believed that the grant of all executive power to the president would enable him to resist outside encroachments on that power.[67]

The relevance of this issue is clear in the case before the Court, for, Scalia wrote, "That is what this suit is about. Power." While some constitutional disputes about this power distribution may come to the Court as wolves "in sheep's clothing," Scalia argued that in this case, "this wolf comes as a wolf." He traced the history of the dispute, pointing to the bitter confrontation between the Congress, the president, the EPA, and the Justice Department that started it all. Given this heated political context, Scalia contended that the attorney general had little choice but to appoint an independent counsel when the House Judiciary Committee requested it, for "merely the political consequences (to him and the President) of seeming to break the law by refusing to do so would have been substantial." And while no judicial review of a failure to request appointment exists, Scalia argued that there is a more political review exercised by Congress. "The context of this statute," said Scalia, "is acrid with the smell of threatened impeachment."[68]

Once the realities of the politics of the arrangement are revealed, Scalia believed one could not help but decide that the arrangement violated the principle of the separation of powers. He criticized the majority for focusing on the technical details at the expense of any meaningful analysis of separation of powers. The focus of his opinion was on such an analysis, taking as its starting point a test of whether the provisions unconstitutionally intrude on executive power. He concluded that they clearly did because two central questions must be answered in the affirmative. Is criminal investigation and prosecution a purely executive power? Yes, he said. "Does the statute deprive the President of exclusive control over the exercise of that power?" Again, yes. Scalia rejected the argument that while limited by the statute, the executive control was sufficient to pass constitutional muster. For example, the majority's contention that the attorney general's power to remove for good cause is a source of continued power for the executive was "somewhat like referring to shackles as an effective means of locomotion." In essence, the statute created a prosecutor exercising core executive functions without any meaningful way of holding her accountable to the executive.[69]

Scalia went on to argue that the problem that the statute was designed to address was one that could be solved by the separation of powers system. He noted that past executive misconduct had been exposed and punished without such a statutory arrangement. It followed that while there was no actual need for the provisions, they served instead to "deeply wound the President, by substantially reducing the President's ability to protect himself and his staff. That is the whole object of the law."[70]

Justice Scalia also rejected the majority's Article II appointments clause analysis, claiming that the independent counsel was clearly not an inferior officer. The limitations placed on the ability of the executive to control her clearly implied that she was not subordinate to anyone. He accused the Court of misinterpreting the limitations placed on her power. In reality, he argued, she remains in office until she thinks her work is done, and despite her comparatively small area of jurisdiction, within that jurisdiction her power was unlimited. In this part of his opinion, Scalia adopted the same line of reasoning as did the Court of Appeals, focusing on the perceived lack of accountability on the part of the independent counsel.[71]

Concluding his dissent, Scalia contended that the creation of an unaccountable prosecutor raised serious questions of fairness and due process. He noted that the safeguard against the abuse of vast prosecutorial power has always been the political accountability of the executive responsible for appointing the prosecutor. The key value of adhering to the unitary executive theory in the area of prosecution, in particular, was the benefit gained by this accountability. In the special prosecutor process, no one is held accountable for a bad appointment and no politically feasible way exists to get rid of, or rein in, such an appointment. While no such abuses of power may have occurred thus far, Scalia argued that "the fairness of a process must be adjudged on the basis of what it permits to happen, not what it produced in a particular case." He concluded that in upholding the arrangement, "I fear the Court has permanently encumbered the Republic with an institution that will do it great harm."[72]

CONCLUSIONS

The Court's decision in *Morrison* was an important one for two reasons, one having to do with its specific implications for the independent counsel process, the other having to do with its general meaning in analyzing the separation of powers. Its specific importance derives from its contribution to resolution of the constitutional uncertainty that had surrounded the independent counsel arrangement from its inception. In upholding the constitutionality of the provisions, it secured the ongoing investigations in the Olson and Iran-Contra cases and the convictions in the Deaver and Nofziger cases. Moreover, the decision alters the balance in the debate over the continued existence of the provisions because it makes it more difficult for opponents to argue that the arrangement infringes to an unconstitutional extent upon the power of the executive. The fact that the opinion was authored by no less a conservative than William Rehnquist and had the support of seven justices gives great weight to the proponents' position. There will continue to be some who argue that the Court was wrong, but that argument will have little impact on the majority in Congress, which has always believed the arrangement to be constitutionally sound. It is also unlikely, however, that the provisions' supporters will do much in the way of altering them to grant increased independence for the special prosecutor.

The Court's decision clearly rests on what it sees as the carefully constructed limits on the independent counsel and the court panel. Any attempts to alter those limits might open up the provisions to renewed attack. At this point, there is little incentive to do anything to the provisions, for as they stand they have the endorsement of a large majority on the Supreme Court.

More generally, *Morrison v. Olson* is important because it appears to signal a readjustment in the Court's separation of powers jurisprudence. After two decisions (*Chadha* and *Bowsher*) that seemed to herald a new formalism in the analysis of separation of powers, *Morrison* and several cases that follow it suggest that the Court is unwilling to follow the formalist approach to its logical conclusion (or at least to the conclusion that many conservatives hoped it would come to): that the theory of the unitary executive requires major restructuring of the modern administrative state.[73] The Court's recent separation of powers decisions seem, on their face, to be inconsistent, for they rest on apparently contradictory "theories" of separation of powers, depending upon whether they are striking down legislative acts (rigid) or upholding them (flexible). Gary Goodpaster concludes:

> The Supreme Court likes and uses both formalism and functionalism, but does not give much guidance about what triggers one mode of analysis and justification over another in particular cases. This is a familiar, if unsatisfactory, position in constitutional law: two lines of cases using two kinds of analysis leading in different directions to different results, with the Court in the position to pick and choose, but with no evident principled basis with which to pick and choose.[74]

There is more sense to the Court's analysis of separation of powers questions than its critics imply. The Court's decisions rest on consideration of the textual and implied powers of each branch, its recognition of the particular political context surrounding each separation of powers case, and, perhaps, in its evaluation of its own powers and its historical role as referee in separation of powers disputes. When we consider these concerns as a whole, we see that Morrison was decided correctly and was not the "revolutionary" decision that Scalia contends in his dissent. In fact, it has been suggested that "adoption of Scalia's position at this point in our history was much more likely to revolutionize the conduct of government."[75]

When reading the carefully controlled language of the majority's opinion in *Morrison*, it is difficult to take seriously Scalia's prediction that the

Court has given Congress an open invitation to usurp executive powers. Rehnquist looks to the language of the text. He relies on the plain meaning of the appointments clause. He examines its history and usage. Having done all of this, he concludes that the appointment arrangment in the statute is not a violation of the clause. It is firmly rooted in the text of the Constitution and in the precedent interpreting that text. Harold Krent argues convincingly that the formalist and functionalist debate over the Supreme Court's analysis of separation of powers misconceives that analysis and ignores the subtleties in it that give it an underlying logic. Krent suggests that the Court's decisions have at their base a "deceptively simple principle . . . : that the Constitution circumscribes the power of the branches by limiting the ways each can act."[76] While the Constitution leaves the boundaries between the branches ambiguous, it clearly places limits on "how and when each branch can act." If we understand this to be the core of the separation of powers arrangement, then neither a rigid, mechanistic view nor a practical, flexible view is adequate to the task of analyzing the separation of powers in a meaningful way. Krent finds that the Supreme Court follows a two-step process in its analysis of disputes concerning the separation of powers. It asks whether the branches have acted within the constitutional limits placed on their actions. If they have, but a conflict between the branches is nonetheless unavoidable because of the overlapping of powers, then the Court asks what "is the best way to accommodate the overlapping powers of the branches?"[77] In seeking such an accommodation, the Court balances the "potential for disruption" of one branch's powers with the justification or need of the other branch to act.

This approach takes into account both the formal limitations on the power of each branch and the ambiguity and overlap of powers that keep the system flexible and able to adapt to its world. The Court is taking an inherently sensible approach to separation of powers that is no more "inconsistent" than the Constitution itself. What remains to be considered, however, is what factors influence the way in which the Court strikes the balance when conflict between the branches is inescapable. It is at this point that the Court's recognition of the political realities of the case and its view of its own role in the separation of powers are likely to influence its analysis.

The background facts of separation of powers disputes are frequently charged with high-powered political ramifications. Deputy Independent Counsel Earl Dudley, Jr., argues that in the *Morrison* case there were two major political problems standing in the way of a Court decision against the independent counsel. The first problem was the implications of such a move for the validity of the "myriad arrangements of the administrative state."[78] While a constitutional challenge to independent regulatory agencies had clearly been on the conservative agenda during the Reagan administration, a majority on the Court clearly was not willing to participate in the dismantling of an administrative arrangement that it had helped to legitimate. Striking down the independent counsel arrangement on the basis of the theory of the unitary executive would clearly have been a major step in that direction.

The other major political problem facing the court was more directly related to the independent counsel. The immediate consequence of a decision to strike down the provisions would have been to make invalid two recently obtained convictions under the act, to dissolve the ongoing investigation of Olson that instigated the suit, and, perhaps most importantly, to call into question much of the work of the Iran-Contra independent counsel. Further, the provisions had had the support of the Department of Justice when they were originally passed in 1978, President Reagan had signed both reauthorizations into law in 1982 and 1987, and he had actively participated in the request for the appointment of independent counsel in the Iran-Contra case in late 1986. Dudley writes:

> It is difficult to envision a more unappetizing political setting in which to invite the Court to adopt the broadest view of untrammeled executive power in its history. If the Reagan administration had come before the Court with an unblemished reputation for public probity and if the Justice Department had opposed the legislation from the start on principled separation of powers grounds, their opposition at least would have had the credibility of their ideology behind it. . . . it is impossible to fault the Supreme Court for declining to rescue this particular Executive from a dilemma at least in part of its own making by adopting a breathtaking view of executive prerogative for which even the administration had been unwilling to contend in the legislative process.[79]

In cases concerning separation of powers it seems inevitable that the political facts should shape the outcome. The Court could not divorce itself from the pending constitutional crisis provoked by Watergate when it decided *United States v. Nixon*. The battle between Truman and Congress over the invocation of Taft–Hartley could not be ignored in the steel seizure case. These political facts are woven into the fabric of separation of powers cases. They cannot be removed or ignored without altering the meaning of the case itself. The *Morrison* Court correctly took them into account in the case of the independent counsel.

Finally, some members of the Court may be influenced in their analysis of separation of powers by whether or not the judiciary is given a role in the disputed arrangement. In several of the Court's separation of powers decisions, including *Morrison*, the judiciary has been implicated in the dispute. When it is, the Court appears to be reminded of the value of a flexible approach to the separation of powers. Perhaps this lies in the value of knowing thyself and thus, believing that ambiguous grants of power are not dangerous in the hands of the "least dangerous branch." This view may underlie the *Morrison* Court's willingness to accept duties that were not clearly "judicial" under the independent counsel arrangement, minimizing the threat that such an exercise of power might pose to individuals or the executive.

This view seems to be more clearly expressed in the Court's 1989 decision in *Mistretta v. United States*[80] which upheld the constitutional validity of the U.S. Sentencing Commission. The commission was challenged on the grounds that it violated the separation of powers by giving federal judges the power to set binding criminal sentencing guidelines. It was argued that such an arrangement was an unconstitutional delegation of legislative power and that the exercise of lawmaking power by judges violated Article III. The Court rejected this argument and adopted, far more clearly than it had in *Morrison*, a pragmatic, flexible approach to separation of powers. While admitting that the commission was "an unusual hybrid in structure and authority," the Court could find nothing in the Constitution or the doctrine of separation of powers that would "prohibit Congress from calling upon the accumulated wisdom and experience of the Judicial Branch in creating policy on a matter uniquely within the ken of judges."[81] The opinion suggests that the "intractable dilemma" of sentence disparity justifies the delegation of legislative power to the judiciary because it is so well suited to resolving this difficult problem. This faith in the judiciary may have also affected the Court's decision in *Morrison*.

The Court made the right decision in *Morrison* because it recognized the broader consequences of striking down the independent counsel arrangement. It was able to use the opinion to step back from the slippery slope of formalism down which it had appeared to be headed after *Chadha* and *Bowsher*. Had it pursued this formalist approach in *Morrison* and adopted Scalia's view of the extent of executive power, it would have taken a major step toward finding independent regulatory agencies unconstitutional, a decision with enormous consequences for the modern administrative state and for the expansion of executive power. While its decisions in *Bowsher* and *Chadha* reflected a concern about a perceived expansion of congressional power, its decisions in *Morrison* and more recent cases demonstrate that the Court is likely to be suspicious of too broad a reading of executive power as well. As the referee of the separation of powers system, the Court appears to favor neither of the two major combatants.[82] Its analysis of the separation of powers suggests that it will examine each dispute with a mind to the text of the Constitution, the balance of power of the two branches, and the political background facts of each case.

Resolution of the constitutional dispute does not resolve the questions about the practical and political consequences of creating an independent prosecutor for cases involving executive officials. Scalia's dissent must be taken seriously even by those who disagree with his constitutional analysis, for he raises two significant challenges to the way in which the provisions are implemented. He does so in the context of his argument that the provisions are a significant intrusion into executive power. Despite the statutory limits placed on the independent counsel, Scalia argues that in reality the counsel is accountable to no one. Political circumstances make it virtually impossible for the attorney general or the president to exercise any real control over the counsel. His contentions raise two questions that can only be answered by an in-depth look at how the provisions have operated in practice. How much influence does the attorney general exercise in the independent counsel process? How accountable is the independent counsel? It is on these questions that the next two chapters focus.

SIX

THE ATTORNEY GENERAL
AND CONFLICT OF INTEREST

Due to the constitutional uncertainties about judicial appointment and executive responsibilities for law enforcement, the Ethics Act arrangement gave the attorney general a critical role in the appointment of a special prosecutor. It is the attorney general who has responsibility for triggering the mechanism. After receiving allegations of criminal conduct by certain high-level executive branch officers, the Justice Department has ninety days in which to conduct a preliminary investigation into the charges. If within that time the attorney general determines that the allegations do not warrant further investigation or prosecution, he files a report with a special three judge panel of the D.C. Court of Appeals explaining that decision. If he is unable to make that determination, he must request that the panel appoint a special prosecutor (or independent counsel) to carry out further investigation and/or prosecution.[1]

The legislative history of the act has indicated that the role of the attorney general has been a key point of focus during reauthorizations. His statutory role was also of importance to both the majority and dissent in *Morrison v. Olson*. The majority emphasized the importance of the powers given to the attorney general in its argument that the provisions limited, but did not completely remove, executive influence in the process. Justice Scalia, on the other hand, argued that the statutory role was, in practical terms, meaningless, for the attorney general's discretion was eliminated by the political pressures surrounding the triggering of the act.

This chapter examines the attorney general's role in implementation of the provision of the Ethics Act. It discusses the contending issues of conflict of interest and prosecutorial discretion that are at the root of the powers granted to and limitations placed upon the attorney general by the statute.

THE PROBLEM OF CONFLICT OF INTEREST

Conflict of interest occurs in the legal process when "a lawyer may be seen as having a personal or professional interest in a matter that may differ from the interests of his public or private client, or in which a lawyer may be seen as switching sides or betraying the confidences of a former public or private client."[2]

The problem of conflict of interest as addressed by the process of assigning a special prosecutor derives from political interest. The problem of political interest when the executive investigates itself was an important issue throughout congressional consideration of special prosecutor legislation. One observer noted: "While partisan considerations are understandably a component of most executive decisionmaking, criminal laws should be enforced without partisan bias. The partisan instincts of the executive collide most noticeably with the supposedly nonpartisan nature of law enforcement when the executive branch investigates itself and prosecutes the crimes of government officials."[3]

Political conflict of interest is a special problem for the U.S. attorney general and the Department of Justice. The concentration of law enforcement and all other legal functions in one Department of Justice may exist nowhere else in the free world.[4] This concentration of functions places conflicting pressures on the person who holds the office of attorney general. Navasky noted this "tension between law and politics which is built into the attorney general's office" in his study of the department under Robert Kennedy. He argued that the attorney general is faced on the one hand with his obligation to the law and on the other with his personal loyalties to the president and his executive colleagues. These loyalties may conflict with his official role.[5]

Luther Huston's study of the Department of Justice examines this question of divided loyalties and concludes that the department really has three masters: the Congress that created it, the courts that oversee it, and the president who appoints its top officials. Huston asserts that the lawyers in the department are "impaled upon a three-horned dilemma. They must approach enforcement of a law mindful of the purpose and intent of Congress. . . . They must interpret and adhere to rules promulgated in decisions of the Supreme Court. And they must not deviate further than the law requires from the policies of the presidential administration of which they are a part."[6]

As one of the earliest presidential advisors, the attorney general has traditionally become part of the president's "inner cabinet." In this capacity, he may be called upon for advice in areas far from his expertise and for help in developing and executing the president's policies.[7] As a member of the cabinet and chief legal officer of the United States, the attorney general "necessarily has close and continuing relationships with the President."[8] In fact, Arthur S. Miller argues that "it seems to be a fair generalization to say that the Attorney General is enmeshed in the administration. In his advisory capacity to the president who must 'take care that the laws be faithfully executed,' the government's chief legal officer is drawn increasingly into the political arena."[9]

Until the Civil War, the attorneys general acted under the authority of the Judiciary Act. In the post-war period responsibilities for the administration of justice were greatly increased, both in size and in complexity. As legal problems grew, various departments began seeking legal advice from individual lawyers outside the attorney general's office. Primarily as an economy measure, Congress decided to create a Department of Justice with the duty of coordinating and controlling litigation and providing uniform legal advice throughout the federal government.[10] This history weakens the argument that the duties of the department can only be carried out by the department. Their combination into the Department of Justice in the 1870s was more a matter of convenience and efficiency than of constitutional theory.

Charges of conflict of interest in the executive investigating itself became a problem early in the department's history and continued to be a problem in the twentieth century. The first department, under President Grant, was implicated in the Whiskey Ring scandal of the 1870s. The president's personal secretary and a close friend were accused of diverting hundreds of thousands of dollars in federal tax revenues to a group of whiskey distillers. Lack of attention to the charges in the Justice Department and lack of confidence in the department by key congressmen led to an investigation outside the department, with Treasury Department officials playing a leading role.[11] During this century the Teapot Dome, the tax scandals, and Watergate all led to decisions to appoint independent prosecutors to investigate and prosecute the charges of official corruption that arose from the scandals. In each case, the attorney general was either implicated in the scandal or accused of dragging his feet in pursuing the criminal allegations. Finally, since World War II, presidents have tended to appoint as attorney general men who have played key roles in their election campaigns. Consequently, these attorneys general have continued to act as political as well as legal advisors, a situation making charges of conflict of interest more likely.[12]

This historical context was not lost on supporters of a mechanism for identifying an independent prosecutor. They suggested that Teapot Dome and Watergate were "only the tips of the icebergs that continuously float in the political waters."[13] The special prosecutor provisions outlined in the

Ethics in Government Act have as one of their goals the elimination of the conflict of interest, which exists when the the Department of Justice, and especially the attorney general, investigates executive colleagues. It should be noted that in the modern debate, the conflict of interest problem is two dimensional. Proponents of the independent prosecutor sought to eliminate not only true conflicts of interest but also the appearance of such conflicts. They argued that because the attorney general and his subordinates are presidential appointees and prosecuting attorneys, they have "an obvious political conflict of interest" when investigating colleagues in the executive branch. Consequently: "Conflicts of this sort are doubly incapacitating. They prevent unfettered and vigorous prosecution of those who should be prosecuted. Equally important, they breed public distrust of decisions not to prosecute which may be entirely justified on their merits . . . The appearance of conflict is as dangerous to public confidence in the administration of justice as true conflict itself. Justice must not only be done; justice must also be seen to be done."[14]

The task of removing both the actual and apparent conflict of interest from the Department of Justice is a formidable one. Questions remain as to the effectiveness of the special prosecutor arrangement in resolving this problem. It has been argued that allowing the attorney general to trigger the appointment of a special prosecutor does nothing to remove either the conflict of interest or the appearance thereof and that the conflict of interest problem can only be resolved by removing the attorney general from the process.[15]

This study of the implementation of the provisions by the attorney general supports the contention that the conflict of interest problem is not removed under the present arrangement. But given the constitutional uncertainties surrounding the debate about independent prosecutors, Congress had little choice but to include the attorney general in the early stages of the process. After *Morrison* it seems all the more apparent that some role for the attorney general must be maintained. Further, acknowledging that the attorney general's continued influence in the process is problematic does not mean that the Ethics Act has accomplished nothing in this regard. The reporting requirements in the provisions place new obligations on the attorney general to explain his decisions in covered cases. This new measure of accountability permits, at least, political review of some of his actions, even though judicial review has been severely restricted.

PROSECUTION AND THE NECESSARY
EXERCISE OF DISCRETION

As in most policy debates, there are competing concerns in the issue of use of an independent special prosecutor. Congressional actors had to balance their concerns over conflict of interest with their recognition that law enforcement is usually viewed as an executive function with a necessary discretionary component. In *Principles of Federal Prosecution* the guidelines for federal prosecutorial decisionmaking begin with the identification of the existence and importance of prosecutorial discretion. The guidelines state that in the federal justice system "the prosecutor has wide latitude in determining when, whom, how, and even whether to prosecute for apparent violations of federal criminal law."[16]

The *Principles*, while recognizing the desire for uniformity in the application of federal criminal law, point to the need to maintain the responsible exercise of prosecutorial discretion toward the end of fair administration of justice. Since "different offices face different conditions and have different requirements," the *Principles* emphasize the need to allow flexibility in law enforcement.[17] The good to be gained from the flexible exercise of prosecutorial discretion has long been recognized. In what is essentially a treatise on constraining discretion, Kenneth Culp Davis admits: "Discretion is a tool, indispensable for individualization of justice. All governments in history have been governments of laws and men. Rules alone, untempered by discretion, cannot cope with the complexities of modern government and of modern justice."[18]

The constitutional basis for prosecutorial discretion has been found by the courts to be the executive responsibility for faithful execution of the laws. The attorney general and other federal prosecutors are executive officers. The courts have recognized the executive nature of the power they exercise when endorsing the doctrine of prosecutorial discretion. The doctrine "also musters support from the concept of separation of powers."[19]

Early case law began by establishing that the attorney general, as the "hand of the President in taking care that the laws of the United States . . . be faithfully executed," was responsible for the direction and control of suits involving United States' interests.[20] The courts have also regularly found that the doctrine of separation of powers forbids them from forcing prosecutors to carry out certain functions of law enforcement. For example, in 1925 a federal court held that "the federal courts are without power to compel the prosecuting officers to enforce the penal laws, whatever the grounds of their failure may be. The remedy for inactivity of that kind is with the executive and ultimately with the people."[21] A series of decisions since then has endorsed the idea that federal prosecutors must have wide discretion in initiating prosecution and that federal courts may not intervene in the exercise of executive discretion in law enforcement.[22]

Broad-based prosecutorial discretion has not been endorsed universally. In 1972 a federal district court did hold that the attorney general's discretion is constrained by constitutional and statutory standards and that "the doctrine of prosecutorial discretion has never insulated conduct from review on charges of bad faith, fraud, or illegality."[23] Furthermore, there have been scholarly arguments against blanket acceptance of prosecutorial discretion. Davis argues that uncontrolled discretion is "like a malignant cancer" that forms the basis for much of the injustice in our legal system.[24] Palmer has rejected the idea "that the Attorney General has an unlimited inherent right to determine to prosecute in all matters." He contends that in exercising power that "originates solely from Congress, the Attorney General is acting principally as an agent of Congress, and is, therefore required to follow congressional instructions. Accordingly, any discretion exercised by the Attorney General would exist only through the grace of Congress."[25]

Despite these caveats, the vast body of case law supports very broad discretion on the part of prosecutors, including the attorney general. A study of congressional efforts to remove politics from federal law enforcement drew this conclusion regarding executive power and prosecutorial discretion: "Appendaged to the Constitution, begotten and nourished by the Supreme Court and grown weighty with the preponderance of authority, the . . . doctrine will prove difficult to displace. Prosecutorial discretion and law enforcement may not be exclusive or illimitable functions of the executive branch, but they are, according to the prevalent view, prerogatives of the executive and are not easily severed from that branch."[26]

In its search for a way to eliminate the conflict of interest that arises when the executive investigates itself, Congress had to balance that concern with considerations of prosecutorial discretion and law enforcement. This balance was not easy to strike given the interrelatedness of the two concerns. The source of conflict of interest lies in the ability of the attorney general to make discretionary judgments about whether to pursue charges against a colleague. The nature of that decision is at the core of prosecutorial discretion and conflict of interest. In the end, Congress failed to solve completely the problem of conflict of interest because it could not escape from the horns of this dilemma. The court cases involving enforcement of the Ethics in Government Act provisions highlighted this problem.

The general conclusion that can be drawn from the decisions by the courts of appeals during William French Smith's tenure as attorney general is that there is no legal means for forcing the attorney general to implement the provisions of the act in particular cases. Private individuals, Congress, and the courts may not legally second-guess the attorney general's decision to close an investigation before the act is triggered or before an independent counsel is appointed. If he concludes that no appointment is necessary, he must explain his actions to the special division of the court. However, should the court disagree with him, there is no legal recourse to alter that decision. Only political pressure can force the attorney general to trigger the act or to seek the appointment of an independent counsel.[27]

The special panel's decision in *In Re Olson* adds more weight to the argument that in the early stages of the process the attorney general's discretion is unreviewable. There, the panel refused to overrule Attorney General Meese's decision to limit the jurisdiction of the independent counsel to allegations against Theodore Olson.[28] The Supreme Court further strengthened that position in *Morrison v. Olson*, interpreting the judicial power in oversight of the procedures as being very narrow and limited.[29] The courts clearly have played a significant role in endorsing the amount of discretion given the attorney general in the early stages of the independent counsel process.

THE ATTORNEY GENERAL AND THE EXERCISE OF DISCRETION

What are the practical implications of the role given the attorney general in implementation of special prosecutor provisions in the Ethics Act? It is difficult to identify the precise number of times the attorneys general have exercised their discretionary judgment under the act, since so much of the earliest stage of the process is obscured from public view. A former Public Integrity Section lawyer estimated that during the first seven years that the provisions were in effect, close to one hundred allegations against covered officials were received by the department, but most were frivolous or insufficiently specific to trigger a preliminary investigation. He estimated that as many as fifteen of these charges led to preliminary investigations.[30] A more formal estimate was derived for the purposes of the 1987 reauthorization hearings. Based on Department of Justice reporting, the Senate investigation found that thirty-six cases implicating covered officials had been handled by the department between 1982 and 1987. Eleven triggered preliminary investigations and eight led to the appointment of independent counsel. Two of these appointments never received public attention and were not officially announced by the court panel.[32] Since that study, one more prosecutor has been publicly appointed to investigate former HUD Secretary Samuel Pierce. On their face these figures clearly demonstrate that the attorney general is exercising discretionary judgment in the early stages of the independent counsel process. This filtering system is clearly desirable, at least to some extent, for eliminating frivolous and unfounded charges against vulnerable public officials. But it also indicates that the attorney general continues to exercise a good deal of discretion outside the public spotlight, a situation that may create opportunities for conflict of interest. It is clearly not the case, as Scalia suggests, that the attorney general is forced to seek appointment of an independent counsel any time allegations against covered officials arise. A closer look at specific cases where the attorney general and the department have exercised this unreviewable discretion demonstrates the significant amount of control that the attorney general continues to have in deciding whether a preliminary investigation is triggered, in declining to seek appointment of an independent counsel, in defining the jurisdiction of independent counsel if one is appointed, and in influencing the outcome of cases taken to trial.

The Carter Peanut Warehouse Case

In early 1979 the White House revealed that the Justice Department was conducting an investigation into whether money from the Carter Peanut Warehouse business had been illegally diverted into Jimmy Carter's 1976 presidential campaign coffers. The investigation grew out of an ongoing probe into Office of Management and Budget Director Bert Lance's alleged mishandling of funds while working at the National Bank of Georgia.[32]

The Justice Department and Attorney General Griffin Bell faced a sensitive decision about how to conduct the investigation into the warehouse allegations. In March 1979 it became evident that the department was considering some sort of "special counsel" office with responsibility for the investigation. Congressional Republicans were placing pressure on the department to appoint an independent special prosecutor. While recognizing the need "to appear unbiased in the conduct of probes involving the president and his family," officials within the department expressed their opposition to turning the case over to someone outside of its control. Deputy Attorney General Benjamin Civiletti told reporters, "If we set a trend for handling such cases outside the department, then it [the department] really does begin to deteriorate from an administration of justice standpoint. . . . We will have little Justice Departments here, there, and everywhere. We could have justice depending on how loud people scream."[33]

On March 20, 1979, Attorney General Bell announced the appointment of Paul Curran, a New York City Republican lawyer, as special counsel to conduct the investigation. Curran was given the responsibility of carrying out the probe, but Bell stopped short of giving him the powers of a "Watergate-style" special prosecutor. Since the alleged misconduct and initial investigation had taken place prior to passage of the Ethics Act, the department argued that the special prosecutor provisions did not apply. Special Counsel Curran was to be required to have any indictments or witness immunity grants approved by Philip Heymann, assistant attorney general for the Criminal Division.[34]

The attorney general's decision to avoid an Ethics Act appointment was criticized loudly by congressional Republicans. Senate Minority Leader Howard Baker suggested, "The parallel with Watergate is inescapable." Seven Republican members of the Senate Judiciary Committee urged Bell to appoint an Ethics Act prosecutor, arguing that Curran was not sufficiently independent.[35] After several days of criticism, some Democrats in Congress joined their Republican colleagues in urging greater independence for Curran. Senate Majority Leader Robert Byrd, expressing his disappointment over the department's strict interpretation of the special prosecutor legislation, urged that Curran's charter include guarantees against arbitrary removal.[36]

Throughout the public debate over the extent of his authority, Curran continued to state his belief that he had been granted sufficient independence. The need to have an indictment decision reviewed by the department did not bother him. "I knew," he said, "that I would do a good and thorough investigation and thus a revision of my decision would not stand up. So to me the charter issue was academic, cosmetic. I wasn't pushing for a change because I was satisfied that I would not be bothered. I never felt there were strings attached."[37]

Nevertheless, Attorney General Bell ultimately bowed to the furor raised by the press and the Republicans and altered Curran's charter. He granted Curran "full Watergate-style prosecuting powers," agreeing not to interfere with or countermand any of the special counsel's decisions. Calling the criticism that had occurred largely partisan, Bell argued that the limits on Curran's independence were "just a red herring. It was something to talk about and write about and argue on the Senate floor about. It didn't amount to nothing [sic] so I just decided to take it out."[38]

In October 1979 Curran announced his conclusion that there was no basis for criminal prosecution of anyone implicated in the investigation. Curran sent a 180-page report outlining his investigation and findings to Congress and the Department of Justice.[39] Curran's investigation was praised as thorough and "entirely persuasive,"[40] and the issue quickly faded from view, lost in the shadows of the latest scandal developing on the political scene—Hamilton Jordan's alleged use of cocaine.

Attorney General Bell's discretion in overseeing the Carter warehouse case was constrained by the political pressure he encountered from the press and congressional Republicans. However, an important point demonstrating his continued influence in the case should be made. He was able to sidestep the Ethics Act provisions, ensuring that the appointment decision would be his, and not the court panel's. By maintaining the authority to make the appointment, he was able to define Curran's role as that of "special counsel" rather than "special prosecutor." A *Washington Post* editorial recognized the importance of this semantic distinction, noting:

> The quarrel over nomenclature is not so frivolous as it might at first seem. It concerns the language of scandal, and the power of word association. . . . A good many people once close to [Richard Nixon] feel a deep interest in suggesting that all presidents must be, to one degree or another similarly touched by corruption. The very phrase "special prosecutor" evokes the Nixon-Watergate period. That is why the Republicans are attempting to attach it to the Carter administration—and why the Carter administration is struggling . . . to avoid it.[41]

The Carter-Mondale Luncheon Case

In November 1978 the FBI received allegations that President Carter and Vice President Mondale had attended a White House luncheon for prominent businessmen at which funds to repay the Democratic party's 1976 campaign debt were solicited and possibly received. The alleged behavior was a violation of 18 U.S.C., section 603, which prohibits the solicitation or receipt of political contributions in any public area occupied by a public official in the conduct of official duties.

The allegations were followed by an article in *New York* magazine which stated that several large contributions were made to the Democratic party by persons attending the unpublicized luncheon on the same day it occurred.[42] The Department of Justice determined that the charges triggered the Ethics Act special prosecutor provisions and conducted a preliminary investigation. After the investigation revealed that the purpose of the luncheon had been to thank contributors for help already received, that President Carter had been present only for the first hour of the luncheon and for the purpose of thanking those present for their past support, and that the vice president had been in Canada at the time, the attorney general found the matter to be "so unsubstantiated that no further investigation or prosecution is warranted, and that no special prosecutor should be appointed."[43] In addition, the court panel granted Bell's request that his report be made public because "the circumstances of the White House luncheon. . . have already been the subject of a news article, and continued public comment is foreseeable."[44]

Attorney General Bell's report reveals that the decision that a special prosecutor was not needed involved, in part, the interpretation of the statute forbidding the alleged behavior. Bell noted that there were only four known criminal prosecutions under section 603 and that the intent of the statute was to protect federal employees from being solicited for campaign funds. He asserted that "the activity in question here, a social gathering of past and potential contributors who are not federal employees, in a White House dining room, falls outside the concern of the statute."[45]

There is evidence that the attorney general's discretionary decisionmaking in this case went beyond just interpreting 18 U.S.C., section 603. At this time the department, particularly the Criminal Division, was engaged in interpreting its responsibilities under the Ethics Act as well. Assistant Attorney General Philip Heymann has revealed that the attorney general "was miffed" in this case because the allegations came to him late in the ninety-day period and that he did not have much time to decide whether or not he wanted to appoint a special prosecutor. Consequently, this case was important in motivating the department to regularize its procedures in implementing the act. Heymann identified the luncheon case as "an important step in the process when the attorney general decided to make public his report when he did not request a special prosecutor. We felt that we could call the close ones the way we wanted if a public report was made."[46]

After the luncheon case, the attorney general made it clear that he wanted earlier notice of these cases, and lawyers in the Public Integrity Section were given responsibility for setting up procedures for "picking up these allegations early so that we could make a quick determination about whether or not they were frivolous."[47] Aside from the patently frivolous cases, there were considered to be three levels of allegations which indicated varying degrees of discretion applied by the attorney general in their resolution. The first category involved cases, such as the luncheon one, in which the question to be answered was whether the alleged act was a crime as a matter of law. The department believed it "had a lot of power to decide this." The second category covered cases in which the central questions were ones of fact. In these cases, the department felt it could only dispose of very straightforward cases. Complicated fact-finding was to be left to a special prosecutor. The most troubling cases fell into a third category: "How do we dispose of a case when it is a matter of prosecutorial discretion? The Jordan case fell into this category. No one would ever be prosecuted for this alleged crime, especially in the district in which it occurred. But we felt that we had no power to refuse to turn the case over to a special prosecutor for this reason given the way the law read at the time."[48]

The Carter-Mondale luncheon case exemplifies the important role the attorney general plays in implementation of the special prosecutor provisions. The department's ability to determine whether a particular law is applicable to the alleged criminal behavior demonstrates that the attorney general still has considerable discretion.

Richard Allen, Japanese Watches, and Financial Disclosure

Changes in procedures did occur between the Carter and Reagan administrations, based on the expanded discretion granted the attorney general in triggering the act in the 1982 amendments.[49] Attorney General William French Smith was faced, in late 1981, with several allegations against National Security Advisor Richard Allen. Smith's handling of these allegations further illustrates the importance of the Attorney general's discretion in applying special prosecutor provisions of the Ethics Act. The *Washington Post* ran an article on November 21, 1981, which alleged that Allen had received two watches from Japanese journalists in exchange for arranging an interview with Mrs. Reagan.[50] The allegation involved possible violations of 18 U.S.C., sections 201(g) and (c), which prohibit public officials from accepting anything of value in exchange for performance of an official act. It was determined that under the Ethics Act, a preliminary investigation was warranted. At the close of that investigation, Smith decided that the allegations did not warrant further investigation or prosecution because there was "wholly insufficient evidence concerning a material element—intent— necessary for prosecution under 18 U.S.C. sec. 201(g) or 18 U.S.C. sec. 201(c)."[51]

After outlining the sometimes inconsistent statements of the people involved in the case, Smith explained the basis for his conclusion that criminal intent was absent from the case. In order for Allen to have violated the law, Mr. Smith wrote, "He would have to have known that the watches were given to thank him for an official act or to influence him in an official act. Such knowledge could not be established because . . . the watches were given to Allen under circumstances where Mr. Allen could reasonably have believed they were personal gifts not linked to any official act."[52]

Three days after the watch allegation became public, another *Post* story revealed that some information on Allen's financial disclosure report was inaccurate.[53] Specifically, it stated that Allen had not given the correct date on which he sold his consulting firm after accepting a position in the Reagan administration. The FBI investigated the charges, but Smith determined that these allegations did not trigger the Ethics Act and thus did not require a limited preliminary investigation, a determination of whether or not a special prosecutor was needed, or a formal report to the court panel.

Smith did release a public report explaining his decision to drop these allegations against Allen. First, he argued that the relevant criminal statute (18 U.S.C., section 1001), which prohibited "knowingly and willingly" falsifying disclosure forms, while "technically applicable" was only applied by the department in "aggravated circumstances." Concluding that the errors in Allen's form were inadvertant, he decided that the statute should not apply in this case.[54] Second, Smith explained his conclusion that the special prosecutor provisions had not been triggered. He contended that the Ethics Act was triggered only when the department received "specific information" of a federal criminal offense. Since the relevant criminal statute described the offense as knowing and willful falsification, Smith argued that in order for the provisions to be triggered, the allegation received would have had to have been a charge that Allen had knowingly and willfully falsified his disclosure forms. A news story stating that there were inaccuracies on Allen's form did not amount to "specific information of a federal offense." In interpreting the Ethics in Government Act disclosure requirements, the attorney general concluded: "From a practical standpoint, it cannot have been Congress' intent to have all errors on disclosure forms regardless of intent, constitute 'specific information.'. . . If the Special Prosecutor provisions were triggered whenever an error in these forms is discovered, the Department of Justice would be conducting countless preliminary investigations where there is no reasonable possibility of a criminal prosecution."[55]

In looking at Attorney General Smith's role in the handling of the Allen allegations, we can see the critical importance of the attorney general's discretion in interpreting the law. Smith's decisions in the incidents that led to the court cases cited previously further serve to highlight the centrality of the attorney general to the process. While Smith was criticized for his interpretation of when the act applied and when it did not,[56] he was successful in protecting his department's prerogative in triggering the provisions.

The Faith Whittesley Allegations

Attorney General Edwin Meese experienced more scrutiny and oversight in his handling of Ethics Act cases than any of his predecessors because of the ethics questions surrounding him when he entered office and because of his adversarial relationship with those with oversight responsibilities in Congress. Consequently, it seems likely that Mr. Meese would have experienced greater pressure than other attorneys general to use the independent counsel arrangement. Even in this instance, however, the oversight and subsequent efforts to restrict or control the attorney general's discretion tended to be concentrated around reauthorization efforts. During the 1987 reauthorization process, Meese's critics pointed to several incidents in which the attorney general had exercised his discretion in interpreting the provisions in a way that maximized his control of the process and distorted the intent of the provisions.

Faith Whittesley, a personal friend of the attorney general and ambassador to Switzerland, was the subject of several allegations of official misconduct in 1986. The Justice Department received allegations that the ambassador had improperly used money that had been donated to the embassy. Whittlesley was accused of using the funds to entertain friends, and included in this allegation was a party held for Meese and his staff. It was further alleged that Whittesley had given a job to the son of one of the donors of this money shortly after the gift was received. Finally, Whittesley was accused of obstructing justice by threatening to dismiss the deputy chief of mission for cooperating with an investigation of these allegations.[57]

After a Department of Justice investigation into the allegations, the attorney general concluded that further investigation was not warranted and, consequently, that no independent counsel was needed. He reached these conclusions by making assessments about the evidence that were not permitted by the statutory standards guiding the attorney general's discretion. His report argued that while the funds had been improperly used, there was no evidence to suggest that the ambassador had any knowledge that the use of such funds was restricted. Regarding the job given to the donor's son, Meese found no evidence of quid pro quo despite the fact that the job was given around the same time as the donation was received. Finally, the attorney general concluded that the conflicting versions of accounts of the events leading to the allegation of obstruction of justice indicated that, under similar circumstances, a private citizen would not be prosecuted. In addition, there was no reason to believe that a prosecution would be successful were it to be pursued.[58]

In pursuing an investigation into the allegations and in closing the case as he did, Meese violated several standards within the Ethics Act provisions. His "thorough inquiry" into the initial allegations of misuse of funds was never reported to the special division of the court, despite the fact that it revealed "specific and credible" evidence that is supposed to trigger a preliminary investigation, the results of which are to be reported to the court panel. Meese closed the investigation on the basis of his belief that there was no intent on Whittesley's part to violate the regulations involving the use of funds. A report of a preliminary investigation on other allegations against Whittesley revealed this earlier inquiry. After the case received public attention the attorney general released his earlier report.[59]

The Whittesley example demonstrates the amount of discretion and influence given the attorney general at the earliest stages when allegations against covered officials are received. Without press attention, which then triggers inquiries from congressional overseers,[60] there is no way to know what allegations come in and what decisions involving interpretations of facts and law have been made in disposing of the cases. If no report is made to the court panel, there is no legal means to hold the attorney general accountable at this stage of the process. The 1987 congressional oversight investigation found that since 1982 the department had closed more than two-thirds of the cases involving covered officials (twenty-five of thirty-six) prior to conducting a preliminary investigation that would require a report to the court panel. In most of these cases the department conducted "threshold inquiries," that were an average of two and one half months in duration and that resulted in determinations that there was insufficient evidence to trigger a preliminary investigation. In some of these cases, including the original investigation into the Whittesley allegations, that determination was based not on specificity or credibility of evidence but rather on a determination that the subject lacked criminal intent.[61] The substantive difference between many of these "threshold inquiries" and preliminary investigations under the Ethics Act is difficult to discern. As the Senate committee report pointed out, "In some cases, these inquiries have lasted months, and involved elaborate factual and legal analyses."[62] For example, the department took six weeks to investigate the Whittesley allegation. During that time, it sent two investigators to Switzerland, France, and around the United States. Almost fifty interviews were conducted. This in-depth investigation led to the attorney general's conclusion that no statutory preliminary investigation was warranted. The Senate investigators clearly saw this practice as troublesome: "It is not clear why the Department of Justice has adopted this practice. Some have suggested that the Department is conducting preliminary investigations in all but name to avoid statutory reporting requirements that attach after a 'preliminary investigation' has taken place. Since these reporting requirements are the primary means of ensuring the Attorney General's accountability for decisions not to proceed under the statute, Congress intended them to attach in all but frivolous cases."[63]

In a later preliminary investigation into the allegations against Whittesley, Meese concluded that no independent counsel should be appointed. He based his conclusion on his belief that given the results of his investigation "a reasonable prosecutor would not seek an indictment." He argued that appointment of an independent counsel would be "unjust" because no harm had resulted from Whittesley's behavior and that she was under a good deal of stress at the time of the incident.[64] Again, in reaching these conclusions, Meese interpreted his decisionmaking power under the statute in a troublesome, if not outright incorrect, way. Archibald Cox told the Senate oversight subcommittee:

> The Attorney General's decision appears to be based partly on sympathy that he believed the Ambassador should be accorded. Reliance on grounds of compassion is precisely the sort of consideration inappropriate for one involved in a conflict of interest. The Attorney General had worked together with the Ambassador in the White House and had been entertained by her in Switzerland. Could anyone in his position, sensitive to conflict of interest, be sure that his judgment that compassion was due was wholly uninfluenced by personal, official or political association?[65]

While the reporting requirement for preliminary investigations ensured that the errors in Mr. Meese's interpretation of the statute would become known in this case, the court decisions cementing the attorney general's discretion in these matters ensured that such errors can only be corrected in the advisory sense. The Senate subcommittee could criticize Meese's actions but no one could do anything about correcting particular errors in past cases. The Whittesley case prompted much concern among congressional overseers and spurred some of the changes in the language of the statute during the 1987 reauthorization. One congressional staff member noted that the Whittesley case demonstrated "the one big flaw in the process. We still have to trust the Attorney General to trigger the statute and we don't know if he doesn't."[66]

The EPA/Justice Controversy

The attorney general's influence in the process is further illustrated along another dimension in the Olson case, which arose out of the EPA controversy of 1981–1982. The details of that case have been discussed in the previous chapter. The important issue in that case with relevance here was the attorney general's critical role in setting the jurisdiction of the prosecutor. In making this decision Meese played an important role in significantly shaping the investigation of the independent counsel.

In setting the jurisdiction of the prosecutor, Meese determined that only the allegations against Theodore Olson, for lying to a congressional committee, warranted independent investigation. In evaluating the allegation against Deputy Attorney General Edward Schmults (obstruction of a congressional investigation), Meese concluded that there was not enough evidence of criminal intent. He handled similar allegations against Assistant Attorney General Carol Dinkins in like fashion, finding insufficient evidence that she took these actions with criminal intent. He made these decisions even though the department's Public Integrity Section had recommended that the allegations against all three Department of Justice officials be sent to an independent counsel because they seemed to involve "a seamless web of events" that necessitated an investigation of all three individuals.[67] The result of Meese's referral of only the Olson allegations was to place significant limitations on the independent counsel's ability to investigate the case. That decision was not necessarily wrong nor was it made with some sort of devious intent, but the situation exemplifies the attorney general's ability to exercise a great deal of control in this case. It was not illusory or meaningless and it was further strengthened by the court panel's refusal in *In Re Olson*[68] to expand the jurisdiction of the independent counsel against the wishes of the attorney general. The jurisdictional decision clearly constrained the independent counsel's ability to act. One of her deputies described it as "requiring us to go into the investigation with clipped wings."[69] In comparing her experience with this case to past prosecutorial experience, Morrison believed that she had had greater power as an assistant U.S. attorney than she had had here, primarily because of the limitations on her jurisdiction: "The jurisdiction problem demonstrated the difference between the normal prosecution where you get a file on a case or a person and you follow it wherever it may lead you. In these cases, the focus on a particular person and the ability to place limits on the jurisdiction clearly have the potential for limiting the ability to investigate a case along whatever lines it leads you. We had to make alot of jurisdictional decisions, asking ourselves, 'can we look at this?'"[70]

Meese's use of the criminal intent standard in refusing to pass on allegations against Dinkins and Schmults was also criticized during reauthorization. Such determinations are problematic under a statute that seeks to restrain the attorney general's discretion because they are frequently dependent on conflicting testimony and ambiguous evidence. The Senate subcommittee report stated: "Criminal intent is extremely difficult to assess, especially in the early stages of an investigation. Further, it often requires subjective judgments which should ideally be left to an independent decisionmaker. It is not the type of factual question that the Attorney General should be resolving in light of his limited role in the independent counsel process and lack of access to important investigative tools such as grand juries and subpoenas."[71]

Iran-Contra and Classified Documents

The Iran-Contra case provides further evidence of the significant role that the attorney general can play in affecting the conduct and the outcome of independent counsel investigations. In retrospect, it is remarkable that North and Poindexter were tried at all, given the very complicated questions of classified information that entered these cases.[72] Decisions by the executive branch, and particularly the attorney general, regarding the use of classified documents by the defense seriously hampered the prosecution by delaying the proceedings and by forcing the independent counsel to drop the most significant charges against the defendants.

Throughout 1988 and 1989 the trial of Oliver North was delayed by the complicated legal wrangling between the attorney general, the independent counsel, the defense, and the district court over the best way to handle the myriad classified documents the defense claimed were relevant to the case.[73] The procedures for deciding on the admissability and availability of classified information in criminal trials is provided for in the Classified Information Procedures Act of 1980 (CIPA).[74] The statute was designed to try to avoid "graymail" by criminal defendants whose job or alleged crime might make classified information relevant to their defense. "Graymail" results when the government is forced to drop a prosecution because of the danger to national security of the threatened exposure of the classified information by the defense. The CIPA attempted to balance the right of the defendants to a fair trial with the need of the government to protect classified information. The balance is sought through the establishment of pretrial discovery and trial procedures governing the use of the information. The act requires defendants to give advance notice of their intent to use classified information in their defense and to describe the information and its relevance to their case.[75]

The court is required to conduct an in camera hearing as to the use, relevance, and admissability of the information. If the court decides that the classified information is necessary to the defense, the government may offer substitute information that either admits the relevant facts contained in the information or is a summary of the information contained in the classified document. The court may deny the motion for substitution if it believes that the substituted information would not adequately protect the defendant's right to a fair trial. The government ultimately decides whether the classified information is used at the trial. The attorney general may submit an affadavit certifying that the disclosure of the information would lead to "identifiable damage" to the national security. Once the affadavit is filed, the court must decide whether the case can go forward without the information. If not, the court may dismiss the indictment.[76]

The CIPA procedures were designed to ease the "friction" that occurs between the Justice Department and intelligence agencies when prosecutions involving classified information arise.[77] When the statute was written, no one anticipated that a CIPA case might pit an independent counsel against the attorney general and the intelligence agencies combined,[78] which is precisely what happened in the Iran-Contra case. The attorney general and the intelligence agencies worked in tandem, sometimes as Walsh's adversaries, in the proceedings before the court regarding CIPA decisions. In the seven months before the trial the CIPA process worked fairly smoothly. Walsh challenged none of the twenty CIPA orders issued by Judge Gesell. But final authority over what information could be disclosed remained with the attorney general and the intelligence agencies. "That authority," argues one observer, "enabled them to impose broad de facto limits on Walsh's freedom to prosecute, even though the independent counsel law barred them from controlling his prosecution directly."[79]

Only significant compromises by the independent counsel allowed the North case to go forward at all. In November 1988 Judge Gesell announced that he would begin North's trial in January of the next year and that he intended to give North "wide latitude" to use documents to challenge the credibility of government witnesses. Gesell indicated that he did not intend to dismiss the case unilaterally and that if the trial were to be stopped, it would have to occur through the exercise of the presidential pardon or the filing of CIPA affidavits by the attorney general.[80] On December 1, President Reagan announced that he did not intend to pardon North prior to the trial but that he would have to move to prevent the disclosure of some of the secrets North claimed were essential to his defense.[81] After intense negotiation between Walsh and Attorney General Thornburgh, during which Thornburgh made it clear that the government would not permit the disclosure of some of the information Gesell had found to be essential to North's defense, Walsh announced on January 5, 1989, that he would seek dismissal of the central conspiracy charges against North. Gesell agreed to dismiss the two charges only after the attorney general certified that the interests of national security required that the documents be kept secret. Thornburgh submitted a sworn affidavit to that effect on January 13, and the charges were dropped. "There is no way known to the court," Gesell said, "or found in any of the cases, to force the attorney general to prosecute a case the attorney general doesn't want to prosecute."[82] During the next year Walsh was forced to drop the same conspiracy counts in the other cases.

The impact on the independent counsel's case was profound in the sense that it permitted Walsh to focus only on the narrower charges involving North's personal behavior (lying to Congress, destroying documents, accepting an illegal gratuity) and not on the central issue of the scandal, the conduct of a foreign policy in contradiction with the laws of the United States: "The guts of the original indictment lay in its first two counts, which examined the full sweep of the defendant's covert plan to sell arms to Iran and to direct the profits to the Nicaraguan contras. . . . In contrast to these two core charges, the rest of the original twenty-three count indictment focused upon epiphenomena, not the heart of the affair."[83]

The impact of the attorney general's decisions on the ability to prosecute the Iran-Contra cases is clear. And it raises some troubling questions about the potential for conflict of interest that continues to exist within the executive branch despite the existence of the independent counsel. Michael Tigar, a professor of law at the University of Texas argues that the attorney general's influence in the North trial potentially undermines the value of having an independent counsel. "The idea," he said, "was to ensure that the foxes didn't have custody of the hen house. Now it turns out . . . that the foxes are in charge of the hen house when it really matters."[84]

CONCLUSIONS

It is important to consider the implications of this evidence for the goal of removing conflict of interest from the handling of these cases and for the Scalia argument that the role given the attorney general is meaningless in practice. Control over most allegations against high-level executive branch officials remains within the discretion of the attorney general, as it did prior to the act. Since this discretion has been judged to be unreviewable, the potential for conflict of interest that existed prior to Watergate remains in the current arrangement and the role of the attorney general is not simply a legal nicety with no substance.

In placing great importance on the symbolic goal of restoring public confidence in impartial justice, creators of the Ethics Act viewed independence for the special prosecutor as an essential ingredient in any statutory arrangement. Ensuring this independence would be the solution to the problem of conflict of interest. It is perhaps in keeping with this symbolic theme that Congress did more to address the appearance of conflict than it did to eliminate the potential for or actual conflict of interest. Faced with a powerful counterargument based on the constitutional authority of the attorney general over law enforcement, Congress proceeded to place what has since been ruled to be unreviewable authority to trigger the whole process in the hands of the very official whose discretion the act is supposed to restrain.

There are those who make the argument that, even though the attorney general's discretion to trigger the provisions has been ruled as unreviewable, the act is still enforceable through the political process.[85] Of course, political enforcement is what we had prior to the act. Past decisions to appoint special prosecutors to investigate serious allegations of misconduct by the president or his subordinates have come about as the result of political pressure.

The implementation of the Ethics Act special prosecutor provisions has been controlled to a significant extent by the Department of Justice and the attorney general. The department has continually expressed its distaste for the legislation. Having control over the triggering process has allowed the attorney general to exercise his prosecutorial discretion to minimize the perceived intrusion of the act upon the department's prerogative in law enforcement. The department successfully lobbied Congress in 1981 and 1982 to amend the provisions in a way that enhanced the attorney general's discretion. Its participation in the suit challenging the constitutionality of the provisions helped to restrain Congress in its 1987 amendments. It has also been victorious in having its discretion in triggering the act and in shaping the independent counsel's jurisdiction upheld in the federal courts. The effect of these court decisions is to make the provisions all but unenforceable except by political pressure.

Finally, the Iran-Contra case highlights another potential conflict of interest problem. The role of the attorney general and the intelligence agencies in making CIPA decisions in independent counsel cases raises two important questions: "Were decisions by the attorney general to withhold documents made on the basis of legitimate national security concerns, free of any motive to thwart the independent counsel's prosecution? Can any high-level government official whose work routinely offered exposure to classified data ever be successfully prosecuted for crimes related to that material?"[86]

It was the perception of the creators of the special prosecutor provisions that the attorney general's involvement in cases against colleagues was undesirable. But in structuring the provisions as they did, they failed to deal adequately with the perceived problem. Given the conflicting aims of ensuring symbolic independence, eliminating conflict of interest, and protecting executive authority over law enforcement, it is little wonder that the conflict of interest problem was not eliminated.

SEVEN

ACCOUNTABILITY, INDEPENDENCE, AND THE SPECIAL PROSECUTOR

How accountable is the special prosecutor? This question has been at the core of the debate over the use of the independent arrangement. In popular government accountability is valued highly. This central political value makes any independent office vulnerable to criticism and the special prosecutor arrangement has been no exception. Critics claim that the limited power of removal given the attorney general is politically meaningless because the shadow of the Saturday Night Massacre still hangs over any efforts by the department to control an independent counsel. Justice Scalia claimed that special prosecutors, as set out in the Ethics Act, are answerable to no one, not even the president of the United States.[1] Even supporters of the arrangement agree that the independent counsel cannot be removed for refusing to follow a direct order from the president.[2] Many defense attorneys for targets of independent counsel investigations claim that the investigators are completely unrestrained as they go over every inch of their potential defendants' lives looking for evidence of wrongdoing. One claims that the independent counsel provisions "are the worst engine for the deprivation of constitutional rights that I can imagine."[3]

Theodore Olson, one of the targets of an independent counsel investigation, recalls the experience as a traumatic one. "I felt like a piece on a chess board," he said. "It was one of the most devastating and frightening things that had ever happened to me. My life's work was appearing before courts in D.C. and now I faced the prospect of appearing as someone charged with a crime." Olson did not see his experience as unique, but rather as a natural result of the flaws in the independent counsel statute. "It unavoidably makes the case more important than it should be because there are no time or resource constraints on the independent counsel. With the Department of Justice the availability of resources inevitably affects decisionmaking."[4] Olson and others argue that the lack of similar restraints on the independent counsels encourages them to pursue cases when it is not warranted.[5]

Criticisms of this type must be taken seriously. The benefit of an independent counsel is presumably that it ensures impartiality and public confidence. The question remains, at what cost? At least part of the answer can be found by examining the way in which independent counsel offices have operated in the political and legal systems. By understanding the relationships that develop between the independent counsels' offices and various other actors in the system, we can test these challenges to the independent arrangement. The findings suggest that while theoretically there is cause for concern over the lack of formal constraints on the independent counsel, in practice there have been a number of meaningful constraints on the exercise of that power. These constraints arise out of the practical political realities of the separation of powers system. While statutory constraints may be limited, the independent counsel do not operate in a vacuum. In the process of pursuing a criminal investigation, the prosecutors are forced to depend upon, and interact with, many other actors in the system who can either aid or interfere with the investigation. While the memory of Watergate helps to ensure that these actors are more likely to aid than to hinder the investigation, they nonetheless have at their disposal various constitutional and practical political means to protect their prerogatives. Consequently, the concerns about "runaway" special prosecutors are supported more by abstract constitutional theory than by reality.

There are many studies of the way in which prosecutorial behavior is shaped by the political system within which a prosecutor must operate.[6] While the independent counsel replaces the regular prosecutor in the Ethics Act cases, he or she must still work within the same legal and political system and must interact with the same legal and political actors. How does the "independence" of the prosecutor affect relations with other actors in the system? How do these relationships resemble or differ from the traditional relationships of regular prosecutors? Where do the independent prosecutors obtain the resources they need to pursue their investigations and how do these resources differ, if at all, from those of a regular prosecutor? What criteria influence the decision to prosecute if not those traditionally provided by other actors in the system? What are the constraints, if any, on the discretion of the special prosecutor? How does the high visibility of the prosecutors and the cases they handle affect the decisionmaking process of the office? We can answer these questions by studying the interaction of the federal special prosecutor's office with the other relevant actors in the federal system.

THE INTERDEPENDENT SPECIAL PROSECUTOR

The legislative history of the special prosecutor provisions demonstrates congressional efforts to reach a compromise between the symbolic goals of "restoring public confidence" and a more practical recognition of the inevitability and desirability of allowing for some controlled institutional inter-action to exist in the process. The amendments to the law that resulted from reauthorization hearings of the 1980s demonstrate a shift in emphasis to these more practical considerations while attempting to maintain the symbolic independence of the prosecutor. As a result, the same statute contains both elements that tend to promote independence and others that recognize the desirability of interdependence. An examination of the way in which these various elements manifest themselves in the implementation of the act will point out the consequences of such an arrangement for both independence and accountability in the special prosecutor arrangement.

Relations with the Department of Justice

Through the provisions of the Ethics Act, Congress sought to eliminate the supervisory authority of the attorney general over the attorneys who would traditionally handle cases of public corruption. The provisions of the act that formally inhibit relations between the Justice Department and the special prosecutor include the appointment of the special prosecutor by a panel of three judges, rather than by the attorney general;[7] the grant to the special prosecutor of "full power and independent authority to exercise all investigative and prosecutorial functions and powers of the Department of Justice, the Attorney General, and any other officer or employee of the Department of Justice";[8] the power of the special prosecutor to select a staff and determine its duties and salaries;[9] the prohibition against appointing anyone who works for the United States government, thus excluding any current department employees;[10] and the requirement that any ongoing Department of Justice investigations relating to the matters within the special prosecutor's jurisdiction be suspended unless the special prosecutor permits their continuance.[11]

On the other hand, the statutory incentives for interaction include the attorney general's authority to trigger the appointment of a special prosecutor;[12] the permission for the special prosecutor to consult with the U.S. attorney for the district within which the alleged crime occurred;[13] the special prosecutor's ability to request resources such as staff and information from the department, and the requirement that the department provide that assistance;[14] the requirement that the special prosecutor comply, "except where not possible," with established criminal enforcement policies of the department;[15] the full authority to drop the case prior to investigation if consistent with these departmental policies;[16] and finally, the power of the attorney general to remove the special prosecutor for good cause.[17]

The actual behavior of the special prosecutors, their staffs, and the Department of Justice officials follows fairly closely the relationship outlined and anticipated by the statute. The 1982 changes in the act, which encourage more consultation by the special prosecutor with the department, demonstrate the recognition that such consultation is desirable for the uniform application of the law.

All of the actors in the relationship between the special prosecutors and the Department of Justice emphasized their conscious efforts to remain aloof from each other. In interviews, before Congress, and in their final reports, the special prosecutors emphasized their feelings of independence from the department. A Department of Justice official in the Carter administration confirmed that "each special prosecutor was rigorous in avoiding contact with the Department of Justice."[18] This "rigorous" avoidance of relationships with the department varied over time and with different prosecutors, depending upon their perception of the extent to which their independence would be threatened by such contacts. Some prosecutors were more likely than others to make frequent contacts with the Public Integrity Section for advice in interpreting laws or applying prosecutorial standards.[19] Two special prosecutors accepted parallel appointments from the department when constitutional challenges were raised while two others refused similar offers because they believed such appointments would interfere with their independence.[20]

Despite the general lack of sustained contact described by all participants, it was affirmed again and again that there was the need for some contact, primarily of an administrative nature. In each of the investigations under the act, it was necessary for the special prosecutors to meet with Department of Justice officials to obtain the results of its preliminary investigation. In addition, this initial meeting was used several times by special prosecutors to affirm their authority and to gain the attorney general's assurance of cooperation in the investigation.[21]

In a strictly administrative sense, then, there exists for the special prosecutor an initial dependence on the attorney general for the raw material with which to pursue the investigation. The special prosecutor must get the initial allegation and results from the preliminary investigation of the Department of Justice. Having done so, there is no evidence to suggest that this dependency continues. In fact, contact with the attorney general appears to cease at this point until the conclusion of the investigation. Exceptions to this trend appeared in the Olson and Iran-Contra investigations. In the Olson case the independent counsel engaged in negotiating with the attorney general for an expansion of her jurisdiction. In Iran-Contra, Lawrence Walsh had to have frequent contact with the attorney general's office to negotiate over the availability of classified documents.

While their contacts with the top Justice Department officials are minimal, special prosecutors have generally continued to seek information and advice from lower echelon department employees, including lawyers in the Criminal Division and field office personnel. A staff member in the investigation of Hamilton Jordan described the relationship with the U.S. Attorney's Office for the Southern District of New York as "friendly and informal," based primarily on working out the administrative details of setting up a grand jury.[22] Furthermore, the special prosecutor consulted with the chief assistant U.S. attorney for that district on how his office would handle similar allegations. He was advised that such cases were declined in that district. Nevertheless, Arthur Christy pursued the investigation.[23] The investigation into Secretary of Labor Donovan's alleged ties to organized crime required the special prosecutor, Leon Silverman, to obtain information from the Organized Crime and Racketeering Division of the department and to seek cooperation from the Eastern District of New York Organized Crime Strike Force in bringing witnesses before the grand jury. For example, Mario Montuoro, the primary witness against Donovan, was one of the strike force's major informants and the force tended to consider him its "private property." It sought the power to clear everything he said in Silverman's grand jury, but the special prosecutor refused, and the strike force cooperated.[24] Silverman described their relationship this way: "We had a close relationship with these people. If I was going to grant immunity to any of my witnesses I would call them first to see if they had anything cooking with that person. But the decision on whether to grant immunity was up to me. They never asked me why I wanted to grant it or questioned my judgment, so I never felt the need to be confrontational with them, although I was prepared to be. Good will was the order of the day."[25]

During both of the Meese investigations there were also contacts with the department, although participants tended to classify the relationship as part of the formal requirements provided for in the 1982 amendments on following departmental prosecutive policies. The first special prosecutor and his staff noted that it was necessary to seek guidance from the department with regard to its prosecutive policies on the financial disclosure laws.[26] James McKay cited similar experiences during his investigation into

Lynn Nofziger's and Edwin Meese's involvement in the Wedtech scandal: "We had frequent contact and a good working relationship. The statute required us to follow the procedures of the Department and we wanted to comply with this. We used them as a sounding board on various issues. Depending on the particular issue, we used experts in the PI Section or the Tax Division. We always consulted with the highest career level person—never with a political appointee."[27] Independent Counsel Alexia Morrison described her relationship with career attorneys at the department, especially those with the Public Integrity Section, as "fabulous." If it needed help, her office would call that section, pose a hypothetical question, and ask what procedures or policy the department would use in that situation. The career attorneys were "extremely helpful" in these conversations.[28]

While the Justice Department has demonstrated its willingness to cooperate with special prosecutors, department officials in both the Carter and Reagan administrations expressed their lack of enthusiasm for the act, based on their belief that the legislation institutionalized distrust of the department's ability to administer justice impartially.[29]

Given their lack of enthusiasm for the special prosecutor arrangement, why do these Department of Justice officials cooperate as they do? The answer may lie more in the legislative history of the act than in its formal provisions. The barrage of criticism leveled at the department for its role in the Watergate scandal remains in its institutional memory. While Department of Justice representatives resent the implication that they are not capable of handling these cases impartially, they recognize that the "special prosecutor is a political symbol which, since Watergate, has become a sacred cow."[30] A former official in the Justice Department during the Carter administration commented, "I feel sometimes like saying 'I am not a crook', but President Nixon has made all those words cheap and laughable."[31] Most members of the department appear resigned to the process and willing to comply with the statutory requirements for cooperation in order to escape further criticism. Some members of the Public Integrity Section even cite this problem of appearances as a justification for the act and seem less opposed to it than higher level political appointees.[32]

There have been several incidents where the department has been able successfully to defend its organizational prerogatives with regard to the statute. The first instance provided the department with the opportunity to demonstrate to Congress the down side of legislatively enforced independence for the special prosecutor. During the investigation into allegations that Timothy Kraft had used cocaine, Kraft's lawyers sought an injunction against the investigation and a declaratory judgment that the act was unconstitutional.[33] Special prosecutor Gerald Gallinghouse sought legal representation by the department and after initially receiving assurance of help, was advised by the attorney general that he should seek representation elsewhere. The prevailing hourly fee of Washington, D.C., law firms ($150.00 per hour) precluded Gallinghouse from hiring private counsel because he was "not authorized to commit the Department of Justice to such fees."[34] Attorney General Civiletti said that it was the department's judgment that "if we took to defend the special prosecutor it would be contrary to the exclusive prohibitions of the Act and we could be subject to criticism for that. We believed that it would be better within the spirit of independence of the special prosecutor that he have his own counsel."[35]

Common Cause came to the aid of the special prosecutor by filing an amicus curiae brief, arguing for the constitutionality of the act.[36] However, Gallinghouse completed his investigation, concluding that there was insufficient evidence against Kraft, and the case was dismissed before it could be judged on the merits.[37]

We have seen in the previous chapter the extent to which the Department of Justice, and especially the attorney general, has been able to protect its role in the process in the courts. The attorney general's discretion in conducting a preliminary investigation, requesting appointment of an independent counsel, and establishing the jurisdiction of that investigation have all been successfully defended by the department.[38] During his tenure as attorney general, Edwin Meese sought to establish further the influence of the department in the independent counsel process in two actions. He extended an offer of parallel appointments to all of the independent counsel operating at the time of the constitutional challenge mounted by Oliver North. James McKay (Nofziger and Meese) and Lawrence Walsh (Iran-Contra) accepted these appointments. This offer had the advantage of allowing Meese to support the ongoing investigations while still questioning the constitutionality of the arrangement. Obviously such parallel appointments would have been unnecessary if the arrangement were clearly constitutional.

Far more controversial was Meese's declaration that the independent counsel and their staff were employees of the Department of Justice for the purposes of conflict of interest laws and therefore subject to the same restrictions on outside employment. Had such a decision held, it would have had significant negative consequences for the independent counsel process. A few of the independent counsel and many of their assistants worked part time on the investigations and continued to carry a workload at their private firms. In many cases this private workload involved cases in which the United States was a party. Application of the conflict of interest rules would have forced them to give up these cases with significant financial impact on their practice. When the application of the rules was announced, one independent counsel working on a "minor case" that had not received public attention resigned from the position rather than be subjected to the rule.[39] A judge on the special court panel argued that the rule would render very difficult the task of finding private attorneys willing to take an independent counsel case.[40] The Senate oversight subcommittee identified this action by the department as one that "has had a significant and detrimental impact on the independent counsel process."[41] Whitney North Seymour argues that this "brainstorm" by the department "would have had the effect of stripping us of most of our qualified staff. I believe to this day that it was a deliberate attempt to emasculate the office."[42] In the end the attempt was defeated by the special court panel and by Congress in its 1987 reauthorization, which clarified the position of the independent counsel and their staff as "special employees" who are exempt from most of these rules.[43]

The evidence available on the interaction between the special prosecutors' offices and the Department of Justice suggests that Congress has been relatively successful at interrupting the relationship that would occur traditionally between the department and the attorney responsible for an official misconduct case of this sensitivity. Rather the relationship appears to be both more formalized and more unilateral in nature, with information, the main resource needed by the special prosecutor from the department, flowing to the prosecutor. While the 1982 amendments have the appearance of giving the department some policy control over the independent office in terms of the decision to prosecute, that control is made ambiguous by the inclusion of the phrase "except where not possible" in the consultation clause. The consultation remains at the discretion of the special prosecutor and the amount of help sought has varied among independent counsel. Nonetheless, as the evidence presented here and in the previous chapter demonstrates, the attorney general is not without influence in the process. That influence is less visible than it might have been before because it occurs early in the process or in more subtle and indirect ways.

Relations with Investigative Agents

The interaction between the offices of the special prosecutor and investigative agencies, particularly the FBI, differs somewhat from that in a regular prosecutorial relationship in the extent to which the prosecutor depends upon the agency to provide it with the evidence needed to make a prosecutorial decision. Because a regular federal prosecutor depends upon the investigative agency to provide the bulk of the material needed to make the case, guilt has generally been established when the prosecutor receives the case. The special prosecutor legislation collapses the investigation and prosecution stages of the criminal justice process. Consequently, the special prosecutor is less dependent upon the investigating agencies of the federal government for their input. Nevertheless, there continues to be a need for the resources that the investigative agencies control, particularly the agents' expertise and skills.

All of the special prosecutors have recognized the need to use agents of the FBI to conduct their investigations. A staff member in the Donovan investigation believed, "We couldn't have done this type of investigation without the aid of experienced agents. The Bureau really has the best and most experienced organized crime experts. Of course, a concern for divided loyalties is always something we should think about, but in this case it did not effect the investigation. We never felt any one of them was working for anyone but Leon."[44]

As a rule there was little concern about divided loyalties of the agents. In all cases the special prosecutors sought and received assurance from the director of the FBI that the agents would be on special detail and answerable only to the special prosecutor. In addition, they tended to select agents with whom they were familiar, either by reputation or through past career experiences.[45] Some offices also hired private investigators to assist them. Silverman explained, "In choosing investigators I wanted to use the FBI but to organize the staff in such a way that it never seemed to be captive of the FBI. I hired private investigators so that the investigation would not appear to be federally controlled."[46]

The investigations required the skills of special agents from other agencies as well. The Jordan and Kraft investigations used Drug Enforcement Administration agents, the Donovan investigation used Internal Revenue Service agents, and the Meese investigations required some consultation with IRS agents and Securities and Exchange Commission investigators. The SEC was conducting an investigation into possible stock trading violations by individuals also implicated in the Meese case at the same time as the Stein investigation was proceeding. There was an extensive investigation involving several agencies looking into the Wedtech scandal. All participants in the process characterize their relations with these investigative agencies, and particularly with the FBI, as extremely cooperative. An assistant in the Meese investigation felt that everyone "bent over backward to cooperate."[47]

When questioned about the nature of the relationship between the special prosecutor's office and the agencies, participants emphasized that it was not in any way a reciprocal arrangement. The special prosecutor received information from the agencies, but the agencies neither sought nor received information from the prosecutor during the investigation. For example, in the Meese investigation, a deputy special prosecutor worked very closely with the SEC investigators on the stock trading allegation and the agency gave him everything it had on a daily basis. But, he said, "our involvement was really a one-way street. I couldn't tell them anything about our investigation and they understood that."[48]

There are several conclusions to be drawn after examining the relations between the special prosecutors and investigative agencies. First, the statutory prohibitions against the attorney general using the compulsory process in his preliminary investigation have resulted in the special prosecutors choosing to begin by retracing the steps of the original investigation. They then carry out a far more extensive one by using agents on special assignment and by impaneling grand juries. Consequently, while the special prosecutors may have an initial dependence on the expertise of the staff of these agencies, their power to demand that the agents report only to them and to carry out an independent investigation virtually eliminates any ongoing dependency.

Second, because of the statutory grant of exclusive jurisdiction over allegations against the covered officials, related investigations by other agencies are either suspended or continued only with the special prosecutor's permission. Jurisdictional conflict between the agencies is eliminated because once the special prosecutor is appointed, "everyone seems to recognize that the office is the focal point of the investigation."[49] One staff member noted, "If you have a regular prosecutor dealing with this sort of case you have to deal with these other agencies on the same level, and you may share responsibilities, which makes the willingness to cooperate more difficult to obtain. With the special prosecutor, you have a narrow focus of investigation in which they are not permitted to be involved."[50]

James McKay's investigation into Nofziger's and Meese's involvement in the Wedtech scandal did encounter some problems because of the larger investigation taking place in New York. When conflicts arose they tended to be resolved in favor of the independent counsel. McKay recalls that there was a good deal of cooperation with the U.S. attorney's office for the Southern District of New York: "They were willing to abstain on some matters and transferred that part of the case to us, but they did stay involved. At first, there were problems with both of us subpoenaing the same witnesses. We didn't want to take over the whole Wedtech investigation. We were only interested in the covered officials. But our investigation did delay the work of the Southern District."[51]

Finally, the memories of Watergate also appear to encourage cooperation. "Very few people want to be seen as not cooperating with the special prosecutor. . . . Everyone cooperates because they know the public will examine the record and they fear that they will be seen as obstructionist."[52]

While the willing cooperation of other investigative agencies aids the independent counsel in many ways, there is an investigative disadvantage for the independent counsel that inheres in the process. In all of these cases preliminary investigations have been conducted by the Department of Justice with the aid of the FBI and other investigative agencies. The key witnesses have already been identified, and their names and roles in the case have been publicly revealed in media coverage. In many cases congressional investigations have occurred. For the "white collar" crimes alleged in these cases, this early investigation and publicity can have significant repercussions on the ability of the independent counsel to make a case. It can "tip off" both the targets of the investigation and the witnesses and informants whose testimony is needed. The kind of evidence frequently relied on in these cases is easily tampered with when subjects have advanced warning that they are going to be investigated. Participants in conspiracy can get their stories straight, knowing which meetings, dates, and conversations are of interest to investigators. One need look no further than the Iran-Contra scandal for evidence of this problem, although it is one mentioned by several participants in the process. Alexia Morrison noted that in the Olson case, "Everyone knew what everyone else had said. The PI section had investigated and written a 160 page report. Congress had issued a four volume report. Consequently, it was a very difficult case for us to get into. It had been well chewed over and we were handed a very cold trail. It had been chewed over in a way no other case I had ever been involved in had been."[53]

Relations with the Judiciary

Judges have a great deal of influence over prosecutors because they are key figures in reducing the uncertainty of outcomes in the system. Their ability to affect the output of the prosecutor's office provides a primary check on prosecutorial discretion. Their behavior provides cues to all of the actors in the system on future actions.[54]

It is difficult to assess the relationship between the special prosecutor and the judiciary for the first four cases under the act because none of the four progressed beyond the investigative stage. For these cases there is little evidence available to permit comparisons of the way independent counsel are affected by the judiciary, except in the area of influence on appointment. In the later cases there was clearly a significant role for the judiciary beyond appointment because each involved criminal indictments, criminal trials, and appeals to higher courts. These cases demonstrate that the judiciary provides an extremely important check on the use of power by independent counsel.

Appointment. Judicial selection is the method by which Congress sought to insure the independence of the prosecutor and is one of the primary statutory checks in the arrangement. Selection of the special prosecutor is "done in a very human way that is both personal and subjective."[55] A combination of factors affects the final choice of the panel of judges. The panel begins by identifying the case's "center of gravity": that is, where the alleged criminal behavior took place and where the majority of witnesses are. Once this is established, the panel identifies the attorneys practicing in that area who have had experience in these matters and have a good reputation at the bar and with the public. Party affiliation is also perceived to be important, other things being equal, for the appearance of impartiality.[56] The panel "examines minutely the possibility of conflict of interest" and engages in "an exceptionally broad inquiry into the past history" of candidates. The judges are interested in discovering "anything that might tarnish the candidate's reputation." They sometimes check into past cases that the attorney has been involved with and, in particular, are looking at whether or not the attorney has been a "publicity seeker." Reputation and appearances are very important considerations, and consequently many otherwise qualified attorneys are never considered because of associations that give the appearance of conflict of interest.[57]

Engaging a known quantity is a high priority, so, in practice, the "old-boy network" plays a major role in the selection. Both Silverman and Christy cite the fact that they were assistants to Judge Edward Lumbard when he served as U.S. attorney for the Southern District of New York as a factor influencing their selection.[58] Silverman also served with panel member Judge Roger Robb on the Advisory Committee on Criminal Rules for the U.S. Judicial Conference.[59] The selection of Gallinghouse was made at the suggestion of two federal judges acquainted with the New Orleans bar. He had also served as U.S. attorney for that district.[60] Jacob Stein was well known in the District of Columbia, having recently served as president of the District of Columbia Bar Association. In addition, he had defended Judge Robb's former law partner Kenneth Parkinson in the Watergate case. (Parkinson was the only defendant acquitted in that case.)[61] Seymour had worked with Judge Mansfield (a panel member from the Second Circuit) in several capacities. He had been a district judge when Seymour was a U.S. attorney and a circuit judge when Seymour served as president of the Federal Bar Association for the Second Circuit. Seymour had recruited Mansfield for help on several matters before the association.[62] James McKay knew Judge MacKinnon only slightly: they had met at a function where they shared their common interest in Scotland. He believes he was recruited after the panel consulted D.C. Circuit judges who were familiar with his work.[63] Alexia Morrison had been hired to be McKay's assistant in the Olson case, but after McKay resigned for conflict of interest reasons, he suggested to the panel that she be appointed. After an interview with the panel she received the appointment.[64] The implications underlying the Iran-Contra scandal made Lawrence Walsh the most desirable candidate for independent counsel because of his reputation and the depth of his background. Judge MacKinnon explained: "No one else really touched him on background and experience. He had been president of the ABA, involved in the Little Rock litigation, had foreign affairs experience, Department of Justice experience, had been a federal judge, had been a prosecutor with Dewey in his early career. . . . There was no one in America that came close. In addition, he met the fundamental requirement of being generally recognized as someone not influenced by political considerations."[65]

The major influence that the panel of judges has over the special prosecutor investigation is in choosing people whom it trusts to do a thorough and impartial job. This influence is enhanced when the judges select persons whom they have worked with in the past or with whom they are familiar. Statements by several of the special prosecutors demonstrate this perceived influence. Christy stated that he felt ultimately accountable to the panel and said, "Silverman and I both conducted ourselves in the way we knew Lumbard would want us to."[66] Silverman felt the appointment authority was the only check on the office. "If the judges are honest," he said, "then they appoint honest men to the position. Otherwise, there are no restraints. You just don't pick a bad person to do it."[67] Seymour argued,

"The independent counsel institution is perfectly workable if the panel picks experienced professionals. You don't need artificial restraints if you pick the right person. If you pick the wrong person those restraints won't mean much anyway."[68]

After the appointment, the panel has little influence over the special prosecutor's office. With the exception of the Olson case, no one involved cited any contact with the panel except for minor administrative requests. The only contact cited by the judges was signing orders or papers that were needed and in determining who the independent counsel had appointed as members of their staffs.[69] MacKinnon was adamant in his statement that the court panel "does not supervise the independent counsel and never has."[70] After the *Morrison* decision it is all the more clear that the court panel must play this very limited role after appointment. But its influence as a check on the power of independent counsel at the appointment stage should not be underestimated. Who holds the office clearly influences how that power is used.

Other Judges. Other judges in the federal court system act as constraints on independent counsel in the same way that they check regular prosecutors' power. Trial judges supervise grand juries, conduct trials, and rule on the various motions involving the conduct of the trial. Appellate judges reexamine the case with an eye to procedural fairness and the application of the law. There is no reason to believe that the impartial federal judiciary acts any differently with independent counsel than it does with other federal prosecutors. One might argue that in the independent counsel cases the trial judges scrutinize the cases even more carefully because of the greater likelihood of heightened scrutiny from both appellate courts and the public.

The trial judge in the Iran-Contra case clearly played a significant role in deciding the complex questions of what evidence may be used in the trials. His rulings on the national security protections required that the special prosecutor drop some of the charges he originally planned to pursue and alter his approach with others.[71] Further, the Court of Appeals for the D.C. Circuit, in setting aside the verdicts in the North case, has acted as an additional check on both the trial court and the prosecutor.[72] In the Deaver case the judge's refusal to permit Seymour to subpoena the Canadian ambassador had the direct effect of keeping the independent counsel from being able to offer evidence on one of the charges against Deaver. Deaver was acquitted by the jury on that charge.[73] We need not belabor the point. Trial judges provide a meaningful check on special prosecutors to the same extent, if not more so, than they do for regular prosecutors. To bring a case against a covered official, independent counsel are subject to the same impartial review of their actions, the same rules of evidence, and are required to provide for the targets of their investigations the same procedural protections as regular prosecutors.

The other judicial check that acts in the same way lies in the use of grand juries and trial juries. Prosecutors, both independent and regular, must have sufficient evidence to convince a jury that a crime has been committed. "One clear constraint on independent counsel," argued a deputy independent counsel, "is one that is on all prosecutors. They must ask themselves whether their case will pass 'the smell test' in front of a jury. Will they find criminal action beyond a reasonable doubt?"[74] There is virtually no incentive for any prosecutor, independent or otherwise, to pursue a criminal case that fails that test. To argue then that there are no checks on the independent counsel is, to say the least, disingenuous for it ignores the fact that independent counsel do not operate outside the established legal system in their pursuit of criminal cases. They cannot escape the requirement that their case against an individual be reviewed by an impartial judge and a jury of his peers.

Relations with Defense Attorneys

Defense attorneys at the federal bar tend to differ from most of their local counterparts in that they are part of the "establishment," are generally well connected politically, and belong to prestigious law firms. Their clients are better off financially and are likely to be banks, corporations, and prominent citizens. Neither side dominates in the relationship between these attorneys and independent counsel because both are interested in the successful and timely processing of their cases. Uncertainty about how the cases will be handled is reduced by the development of personal relationships between the attorneys. Cooperative interaction predominates because their relative equality places them in a "classic bargaining situation."[75] The relationship between defense attorneys and independent counsel is characterized by similarity in career paths and mutual respect, both of which facilitate cooperation. The ties between the defense attorneys and the special prosecutor's office may provide one of the greatest unintended checks on the special prosecutor's power.

The targets of investigations by special prosecutors hire prestigious defense lawyers. Those attorneys most often have graduated from top law schools, work for firms whose major clientele are part of the "establishment," and are well respected at the bar.[76] The special prosecutors and their staffs are linked with these lawyers because they are drawn from the same legal community. They too are private attorneys with "a suitable measure of recognition at the bar and with the public."[77]

An examination of the careers of the defense attorneys, special prosecutors, and their staffs, indicates a number of ties between these participants. Most interesting are the number of lawyers involved in the process who have had more than one experience with the special prosecutor process. Paul Curran, special counsel in the investigation of the Carter peanut warehouse allegations, served as defense counsel for Raymond Donovan. Hamilton Jordan's defense attorneys included Henry Ruth, formerly of the Watergate Special Prosecution Force, and John Aldock, future member of the special prosecutor office for the Meese investigation. The Meese investigation involved several former Watergate actors. Special Prosecutor Stein had represented a Watergate defendant, staff member George Frampton was a deputy on the Watergate Special Prosecution Force, and Meese's lawyer Leonard Garment helped to defend Richard Nixon. Bart Schwartz, a staff member in the Donovan case, was a defense lawyer for the Studio 54 owners who made the allegations against Hamilton Jordan. Jacob Stein, special prosecutor in the first Meese case, served as an attorney for Carol Dinkins in the Olson case and was also involved in the defense in the Iran-Contra case. Theodore Olson, the target of an independent counsel investigation, later represented former President Reagan in his dealings with the Iran-Contra independent counsel. One of Alexia Morrison's assistants left the investigation after his firm became involved in the representation of an Iran-Contra defendant. Morrison herself was criticized for representing the target of another independent counsel investigation during the time she was investigating Olson.

There are additional indications of linkages between the various attorneys. Special prosecutors tended to select either staff members with whom they had worked on private practice cases or persons recommended to them through the established network. Several of the attorneys involved had also served on professional committees together, and a large number of the attorneys had had experience in the local U.S. attorney's office, some of them with overlapping terms. In sum, there is every indication that the same linkages that exist in the community of regular prosecutors also exist among potential special prosecutors.

There is a good deal of interaction between the defense attorneys and the special prosecutor's office during the course of the investigation. This interaction is justified for the same reasons given by regular prosecutors: that is, to reduce the uncertainty of what might happen in the courtroom. In situations requiring a special prosecutor, this need to reduce uncertainty is enhanced by the sensational nature of the cases and the potential harm to a public official's reputation if frivolous charges are pursued. One staff member with extensive prosecutorial experience noted: "You need to know the theory of the defense in order to know if the case is worth prosecuting. You don't just base these decisions on probable cause. You want no stone unturned. To the extent that the defense is involved in this process, you are better able to determine whether a case is worth pursuing. So you naturally encourage them to come in and reveal their cases and have them tell you why you're wrong. You want to find out these things before you reach the courtroom."[78]

Once the case enters the more adversarial stage after indictment, there is a natural straining of this relationship. This seems to have occurred most prominently in the Deaver case. Seymour described the breakdown of communications as beginning after the decision to indict:

During the investigation, we had a lot of contact with them. We were very candid with them and gave them every chance to persuade us that we were wrong. They were able to do that several times. During the post indictment period the relations began to deteriorate. They filed their motion to stop the indictment without giving us any warning. Out of courtesy we had informed them that an indictment would be filed before we did it so that they would have some warning and could prepare their client for this. They abused their professional courtesy by bringing the proceedings without warning us. This alerted us to be careful and after that the relationship deteriorated badly. We wouldn't communicate with them except in writing.[79]

The generally cordial relations and mutual respect that exist in most cases between the defense and the special prosecutors act as a check on the prosecutors' exercise of discretion and steer them away from clearly unwarranted prosecutions. Several special prosecutors pointed to their reputations in the legal community as a constraint on their actions. For example, Silverman noted that "at this point in my career, I don't want to be thought of as a tool of anyone."[80] Jacob Stein believed that the only check on his power was "the quality of the people around me. I wouldn't have wanted to make an ass out of myself."[81] "Professionalism provides its own set of restraints," said Seymour. "There is an obligation to be fair, honest, and responsible in your dealings with defendants, witnesses, and their attorneys."[82] Finally, Alexia Morrison listed defense attorneys among the checks that she perceived to be on her use of power. "It was always our belief that defense attorneys would criticize us if we were not conducting ourselves properly and that they would go to the Attorney General with those complaints."[83]

The practice of drawing the special prosecutor from the private bar seems to serve as a major check on the abuse of discretion. Having been on both sides of the fence causes the special prosecutor to be more sensitive to the potential abuse of prosecutorial power. In discussing the restraints he felt as special prosecutor, Jacob Stein noted that in his thirty-seven years at the bar he had seen great abuses of power. He had always promised himself that in a similar situation, he would not act in that way.[84] One of Morrison's deputies, who had no prosecutorial experience, noted: "As a defense lawyer I was enormously impressed by the care and sensitivity that those with more prosecutorial experience displayed. I felt good in the sense that if other professional prosecutors give the defendant that much benefit of the doubt, then the world of prosecution is a better place than I thought it was. They looked at every angle including the one most favorable to the target."[85]

The ties that the special prosecutor offices have to the legal community provide important checks upon the possible abuse of the discretion to prosecute. This set of relationships, because it is private in nature, cannot be altered by the statutory requirements of independence. It may, in fact, be enhanced because the special prosecutors and their staffs are drawn from the private sector and will return to it at the completion of their investigation. Their reputations and careers depend upon the extent to which they are perceived by the private bar as having acted responsibly.

Relations with Political Actors

A major goal of the special prosecutor process was to remove "political" influence from the handling of cases against high-level executive officials. Given this goal, we would not expect to find much interaction between the special prosecutor and political actors. While there is little evidence to suggest that there is any concerted effort by political actors to interfere with the special prosecutor in his investigation, the arrangement does not remove all political considerations from affecting the process. The two sets of political actors that maintain some involvement in this process are the White

House and the Congress. However, the White House involvement has been in no way similar to the efforts by the Nixon administration to obstruct justice. Congress emerges as another potential check on the independent counsel, although not in any direct statutory way. Rather, Congress's actions may constrain the special prosecutor because each institution has interests that are potentially in conflict.

Most contact with the White House is for the purpose of interviewing witnesses (or the targets). This was true in the investigations of Jordan, Kraft, Meese, Nofziger, Deaver, and Iran-Contra. In the first Meese case in particular, large amounts of documentary evidence were required from the White House, including telephone logs and files on politically sensitive topics such as personnel selection. Unlike the Watergate investigation, however, the special prosecutor did not have to resort to the compulsory process to get this evidence. It was unnecessary to subpoena White House witnesses because they testified voluntarily. "Their pitch was 'we have nothing to hide so come and get whatever information you need.' "[86]

During his investigation of Michael Deaver, Independent Counsel Seymour also had to seek documents and testimony from persons in the White House. He characterized the relationship as "polite, correct, and grudging." He worked through the White House counsel's office when making requests for documents and witnesses and found that office to be "always courteous and cooperative within reason." The willingness of individual witnesses to cooperate varied. "Some were extremely resentful. They did not like us or our investigation. They had convenient lapses of memory. Some were aggressively hostile."[87]

The Iran-Contra investigation required extensive contact with the White House for the purposes of obtaining evidence. It has been estimated that during 1987 and 1988 the White House spent 12 million dollars for the collection and review of documents and the preparation of witnesses. Throughout 1987 the White House employed sixty lawyers and support staffers full time in this effort.[88] In addition, the White House clearly played an influential role in decisionmaking about classified documents for the trials. The impact of these decisions has been discussed elsewhere.

There is some indication that political concerns involving the presidency were considered by some members of the special prosecutor office. The Jordan investigators felt some time pressure because it was an election year and because Jordan held an important position and was needed by the president.[89] Gerald Gallinghouse purposely delayed his investigation of Timothy Kraft until the 1980 election was over.[90] A staffer on the Meese investigation stated that his office wanted to complete its work "substantially before November 6th because we didn't want to be accused of influencing the election."[91] Presidential elections are a political consideration not easily ignored, even with an independent, "nonpolitical," investigation.

The special prosecutor process does not remove congressional partisan concerns. Rather, Congress's statutory role in the process is structured along partisan lines. A provision of the act permits a majority of either party's members of the judiciary committee in either legislative body to "request in writing that the Attorney General apply for the appointment of an independent counsel."[92] The attorney general is not required to concede to the request of the committee members but must explain his decision not to proceed to the committee. The Democrats exercised this right in the Donovan, Meese, Olson, and HUD cases. The Republicans did the same in both the White House luncheon case and the peanut warehouse investigation during the Carter administration. Critics claim this congressional involvement makes the process "all very political. Calls for the special prosecutor are useful to the opposition party."[93] While this role for Congress does have the potential for politicizing the decision to seek appointment of an independent counsel it has little effect on the actual conduct of the investigation. Other congressional powers, of oversight and investigation, have greater significance as constraints on the operation of the office.

The special prosecutor statute outlines an oversight function for the "appropriate committees of Congress."[94] The Subcommittee on Oversight of Government Management of the Senate Committee on Governmental Affairs and the Subcommittee on Administrative Law and Governmental Relations of the House Judiciary Committee have assumed primary jurisdiction in this oversight process. In that capacity they held reauthorization hearings for the provisions in 1981, 1982, and 1987 seeking information from the special prosecutors and the Department of Justice on the implementation of the act. These are among the few instances in which the special prosecutors have provided information to the Congress. During reauthorization hearings only independent counsel who had completed their investigations were asked to provide information. The subcommittees have made a conscious effort to avoid inappropriate contacts with counsel when investigations are in progress.[95]

Congressional actors have also come into contact with the special prosecutors through committee action in the form of investigation and confirmation hearings. When this occurs, the conflicting institutional goals of Congress and the independent counsel can serve as a significant restraint on the independent counsel. Congressional investigations have frequently played an important role in exposing misconduct in the executive branch. This sort of oversight is an important way for Congress to resist abuse of power by the executive and to protect "the constitutional rights of the place."[96] No doubt, it may also be motivated by personal ambition or partisan desire to harm the opposition, but it is reasonable to conclude that congressional investigations can be important and appropriate means by which Congress checks the use of executive power. Further, investigations serve a valuable educative function for the public, both in the sense that they teach citizens about the workings of government and inform them of possible abuses of public trust.

A problem arises when exposure of misconduct leads to a criminal investigation and prosecution. It is at this point that the potential for conflict over institutional goals exists. The needs of a representative institution like Congress are frequently at odds with the needs of an office of the criminal justice system. Two major barriers to criminal prosecution are raised by congressional inquiries. The first is the publicity that inheres in an investigation of this type. The second is the ability of Congress to grant immunity in exchange for congressional testimony. In both cases one can identify clearly conflicting institutional interests between Congress and the prosecutor's office.

The congressional interests in investigation make it likely that such investigations will be widely publicized. In fact, for Congress to accomplish any of its goals, wide-ranging publicity is necessary. On the other hand, the prosecutors desire minimal publicity because of the impact that extensive exposure has on both the investigative and prosecutive stages of their cases. In the investigative stage, we have already discussed the way in which extensive publicity may have the effect of tipping off both the targets of the investigation and witnesses or informants whose testimony is necessary to make the case. In both Watergate and Iran-Contra, the prosecution stage of the case was complicated, and to some extent damaged, by the granting of immunity to witnesses appearing before the congressional committees.[97] Prosecutors are forced to prove that their cases have not been tainted by protected testimony. They may be forced to forgo the use of some evidence available to them because of the difficulty of proving that it is untainted and may have to litigate these issues before proceeding with their case in chief. They must also prove that none of their cross-examination is tainted. These problems are aggravated by the attendant publicity.[98] In both cases Congress perceived its interests in exposure of executive wrongdoing and

education of the public on the substantive issues raised in the cases as sufficiently compelling to justify the risk run to the effective prosecution of
criminal behavior in the scandal.[99]

The Senate Labor and Human Resources Committee carried out its own
investigation of Raymond Donovan during which the first allegations of
ties to organized crime surfaced. The allegations against Edwin Meese became public during the hearings of the Senate Committee on the Judiciary
on his nomination to be attorney general. When special prosecutors were
appointed in the Donovan and Meese cases, the committees turned over
their information to the investigation. The Senate Labor Committee attempted to stay involved in the process and on several occasions contacted
Silverman with offers of additional information.[100] The committee was involved as well in an ongoing investigation into the FBI's performance during its pre-confirmation check of Donovan. Silverman often felt caught in
the middle between the committee and the agency as FBI Director William
Webster would refer the committee's requests for information to him. He
"often got the sense that the Committee and Webster were trying to manipulate" him. Silverman's response was to tell Webster that if the agency
wanted to furnish the information, he had no objection. These exchanges
occurred regularly.[101]

The Senate Judiciary Committee did not seek information from Jacob
Stein during the first Meese investigation but did seek some clarification of
the final report once it was filed.[102] Committee investigators and opposition
party members were also the alleged sources of additional charges against
Meese that were leaked to the press during Stein's investigation.[103] Furthermore, it has been speculated that political considerations were the motive
for requesting an independent counsel appointment in the Meese case.
"There was terrific heat on that nomination," said a Stein assistant. "The
effect of the appointment was to remove the Senate Judiciary Committee's
jurisdiction by invoking the Special Prosecutor Act and therefore diffuse
the heat."[104]

Other investigations encountered potential problems with parallel congressional inquiries, but those independent counsels were able to negotiate
mutually satisfactory solutions that enabled each side to pursue its case.
The staff conducting the Olson investigation originally had difficulty obtaining documents from the House Judiciary Committee's earlier investigation into the Department of Justice's role in the EPA controversy. Eventually the documents were released.[105] Independent Counsel McKay was
concerned about the congressional desire to investigate the Wedtech scandal

at the same time that he was investigating the roles played by Nofziger and Meese in the affair: "Senator Levin's investigation into Wedtech caused us a tremendous amount of concern. We had a number of meetings and phone calls to discuss it and did come to an accommodation. They agreed not to call any of our witnesses. They sent us a list of names of people that they were considering calling and we marked off the ones we needed and then they didn't call them. They also withheld their final report until the Nofziger trial was over."[106]

The problems for the Iran-Contra investigation created by the grant of immunity were extensive. Elaborate procedures had to be developed within the prosecutor's office to avoid tainting the investigation through exposure to the immunized testimony. Significant delays in bringing the case to trial were caused by the pretrial motions based on the immunity claim filed by the defense.[107] It appears that the congressional grants of immunity to North and Poindexter for their televised testimony will negate much of the work of the special prosecutor in this case.

Relations with the Press

Almost every case handled by a special prosecutor had been subject to intense press scrutiny, prior to his or her appointment, because it involved a high-level executive official and the alleged abuse of the public trust. However, in this relationship there is usually no reciprocal exchange of information. All of the special prosecutors have established a general rule of refusing to comment to the press on the progress of their investigations. In most cases, the press has respected that rule.

Despite the general lack of interaction during the investigation, the press is nonetheless important to the process, and the special prosecutors recognize this fact. The mere existence of the press and the importance it seems to attach to these investigations has an important influence upon the special prosecutors. They are very conscious of the press attention focused on their investigations.

Prior to the appointment of a special prosecutor, the press plays an important role in bringing the allegations against the official to the attention of the public. Some of the information is gained through investigative reporting, but most seems to come from others involved in the early investigation of the charges. In the Donovan and Meese cases this information came from the committees involved with the confirmation of these officials. In the Jordan case the firm defending Studio 54 owners leaked the charge to the press after the Justice Department refused to reduce the tax evasion charges against the owners in exchange for the information on Jordan's alleged cocaine use.[108] The Deaver, Olson, and Iran-Contra allegations had been the subject of congressional investigations. The original allegations about the sale of arms to Iran appeared first in a Lebanese newspaper.[109]

The media tend to pay a good deal of attention to these kinds of allegations against public officials. According to a former Justice Department official, significant attention is focused on these cases because, "like Watergate, these are human stories . . . with overtones of the mighty doing wrong. What you have is a sort of national political morality play, with the appearance of powerful figures abusing the law and you get a vigorous public response."[110]

The potential impact that extensive press coverage may have on the investigation is recognized by the appointing judges. Besides expressing to the new prosecutors the absolute necessity of investigating the case on a confidential basis, the judges also try to choose a person who "understands public relations and the need not to talk to the press until something is completed. If you pick the right man and know enough about him, you know that he knows these things."[111]

The special prosecutors have been generally successful in preventing leaks during the course of their investigations, even though reporters continued to request information in the beginning of the investigation, often by posing leading or hypothetical questions. Information that did become public could be traced to witnesses before the grand jury or to their defense lawyers, who found the press attention useful for their own purposes. For example, one of Jordan's accusers held press conferences on the steps of the courthouse after appearing before the grand jury.[112] There were also witnesses before the Donovan grand jury who found it useful to talk to the press. According to Silverman there were times when "what I read in the *Washington Post* was a better summary of grand jury testimony than my own staff was putting together daily."[113] Stein, following the same rules of no comment, was able to keep his grand jury proceedings secret because his witnesses, primarily high-level government employees, had an interest in keeping quiet. However, it has been suggested that the leak several weeks before the conclusion of the investigation, regarding Stein's decision not to prosecute, came from Meese's lawyers.[114] During McKay's investigation of Meese, a leak involving the pipeline allegations had a damaging effect on the investigation: "It basically killed several things that we were doing on that, especially in terms of getting witnesses to talk with us. It started with a story in the *LA Times* and then a *Washington Post* reporter started a series of stories that sounded as though the information was coming from our office. It turned out to be coming from a paralegal in the law firm of [one of the people involved in the deal]."[115]

The special prosecutors' concerns about press influence seem to be demonstrated most clearly in their attention to writing their final reports. They regularly refer to their expectations of intense press scrutiny as the reason for choosing to write detailed and lengthy explanations of their actions in the report. Their general concern seems to be that the public recognize the thoroughness and impartiality with which their decision has been made. By contrast, U.S. attorneys do not release lengthy and detailed accounts of their decisions not to prosecute. In particularly sensitive cases they may issue press releases with brief explanations of their actions.

It is the link between the press and the public that leads the special prosecutors to feel the concern they do with press relations. Both special prosecutors and staff tended to emphasize the need to assure the public that a fair and impartial investigation had taken place as the goal of both the statute and their final report. Since any knowledge that the general public would have of the investigations would come from the press, the special prosecutors have been understandably concerned with how their efforts are interpreted in the popular media. They are dependent upon the press to provide public support and acceptance of their work.

The link between the press, the public, and the final report is perceived by independent counsel to provide an important measure of accountability in the arrangement. The fact that they must conduct their investigation in a "fishbowl"[116] and explain each of their actions encourages them to be cautious at every move. The report "responds to the dual concern of actual accountability and the appearance of accountability for the Independent Counsel. This is important given the great deal of statutory independence granted the office."[117]

There have been some occasions where relations between the press and the independent counsel were strained. Whitney North Seymour established a rule of refusing to take calls from reporters and found that most reporters left him alone once it was clear that they would get no response. "The one that I really had trouble with was William Safire," recalls Seymour. "He cut me up in some articles because I wouldn't knuckle under when he threatened me with blackmail. He called and said he would attack me in his column if I didn't return his call by a certain time. I didn't and he made good on his threat."[118]

Alexia Morrison also encountered criticism after the press began to take notice of the Olson case when the constitutional challenge became public. Prior to that time the investigation had been ignored, but after it became apparent that this was the case that would reach the Supreme Court, "people were crawling through the phone wires."[119] The criticism focused on the delays involved in the case and the inability to respond was frustrating for the independent counsel's office. "The answers that the press were seeking were not ones that we could give them in the course of the investigation. So Alexia was getting blasted in the press but couldn't respond. Consequently, relations with the press were sometimes tense and difficult."[120] Olson believed that the press was on his side in this investigation. He characterized the coverage of the case as "sympathetic" and viewed the press as a valuable check on Morrison's power. "The reporters knew the facts and thought that I was getting a raw deal. The existence of a free press was a great source of support for me. They could throw the spotlight on this abusive prosecution. It gave me great comfort to know someone powerful was looking."[121]

The press provides both a source of support for the independent counsel and a means of accountability. With a few exceptions, they have tended to be less of the latter and more of the former. The reason probably lies in the Watergate experience. The press aided the Watergate special prosecutor in getting the public support necessary to stand up to the White House and to remain independent from it.[122] This perception of themselves and the special prosecutor as allies in an adversarial relationship with the executive branch may be at the root of the support the press does provide for the special prosecutor, despite the one-sided nature of the relationship. Their role as a check on the independent counsel exists more in the perceptions of the independent counsel than in the way the press has actually behaved. But the potential to check, because of the links to the public and influential elites, remains important. This role is examined more closely in the next chapter.

CONCLUSIONS

It can be concluded that the creation of an independent prosecutor has been a relatively successful means of removing the influence of the executive branch from the investigation of top executive officials accused of criminal misconduct. The way in which the offices of special prosecutor have operated under the act suggests that while the prosecutors by necessity have had to rely upon the Department of Justice, investigative agencies, and even the White House for resources such as information and expertise, the transfer of these resources has been highly formalized and unilateral in nature.

Congress's role in the process remains essentially the same as it had been before the act: it may use political pressure to influence the decision to request appointment of an independent counsel. Its oversight and investigative functions also encourage it to play a role in the process and can act as restraints on the use of power by the independent counsel. While members of Congress have been willing to defer to the independent counsel in several of these cases, in the Iran-Contra investigation they refused and that decision had a significant impact on the independent counsel's work. The judiciary and defense counsel continue to interact with the independent counsel's office in ways that restrain the independent counsel from abusing power. This occurs because of the linkages that exist between the prosecutors and the legal community within which they must operate and the mutual needs of the two sides in any criminal case.

Perhaps most importantly, these findings point out the impossibility of eliminating the influence of other actors in the prosecutor's discretionary decisions. While some relationships between the special prosecutor and other criminal justice actors were different from those relations in the regular federal justice system, the special prosecutor continued to need certain resources that the other actors controlled. The fact that the independent counsels are removed from the executive branch in the statute does not mean that they are operating in a vacuum. As officers of the court, independent counsel are hardly more "independent" than the U.S. attorneys in their carrying out of the law enforcement function.

What does differ is the degree to which the relations between the special prosecutors and many other actors in the process are more likely to be formal. The provisions of the Ethics Act set out to formalize relations by explicitly removing a specific kind of case, involving particular individuals, from the control of the Department of Justice and giving it to a prosecutor with guaranteed independence from the process. This creates a highly structured set of relations. The statute then mandates the cooperation of the actors in the system and guarantees the special prosecutors the resources they need.

This highly formalized grant of authority has two major consequences for the development of relationships with other political actors. First, it reduces the need for bargaining and diplomacy in obtaining resources on the part of the special prosecutor. Second, it suggests a considerable degree of acceptance of the prosecutor's role. Part of that consensus surely comes from the existence of formal requirements for cooperation and from the relatively limited jurisdiction of the special prosecutor. But there is an informal basis for this agreement as well. The Watergate scandal and its impact on public perceptions of the justice system remain vivid in the institutional memories of the organizations that make up the federal legal process. These memories supplement the formal statute. This consensus helps to explain the willingness of the other organizations to participate in relationships so unilateral in nature.

The formal statutory checks on the special prosecutor are few, but they are not meaningless. On the other hand, the realities of the political and legal processes mean that the office has additional checks, beyond the statutory controls, on its use of power. We have seen in previous chapters that the role of the attorney general in the process and the limitations on the jurisdiction of the independent counsel can act as restraints on the office. In this chapter we have seen that the selection of the individual who will serve as special prosecutor provides a further opportunity for restraint. The primary check noted by the special prosecutors was their own sense of self-restraint. That self-restraint is motivated by two factors. First, the prosecutors are drawn from the private legal community, where they will return at the conclusion of their investigation. Therefore, they are concerned that they not damage their reputations by abusing the immense power granted to them in the statute. Second, and closely tied to the first, is the perception by prosecutors that their work will be closely scrutinized by the press and that they will be judged accordingly by the public. Finally, there are the judges and juries that will scrutinize their work and will make, as they do in all criminal cases, independent judgments about the work of the special prosecutors.

Is this enough? These checks have been sufficient in the investigations carried out thus far. Critics of the arrangement have relied on the wrong evidence to support their argument that the independent counsel is unaccountable. They have focused on the lack of constraints in the language of the statute and the formal removal of the independent counsel from the executive branch. They have ignored the much more complex set of accountability relationships that exist for any actor in the legal process. They have cited examples in which independent counsel have attempted to act in ways that suggest their power is limitless (Morrison's desire to expand her juris-diction, Seymour's attempt to subpoena the Canadian ambassador, and Walsh's efforts to obtain classified documents), but they ignore the fact that in each of these cases the independent counsel's efforts failed or were limited. The evidence presented here indicates that the lack of accountability is exaggerated by its critics. In fact, many of the assumptions about how the office works that are derived from the constitutional debate do not comport with reality. Independence from the executive does not create an unaccountable prosecutor.

Nevertheless, there is reason for concern about the accountability of special prosecutors. Formal and informal checks occasionally break down when complacency sets in. This is true within the established law enforcement arrangements as well as it is with special prosecutors. In fact, given the way the current independent counsel appointment process works, it may be more likely that a person inclined to abuse his or her power would show up in a U.S. attorney's office or in the office of attorney general. Thus far, the powers granted to the special prosecutor have not been abused because the people serving as special prosecutors have been drawn from a group who do not find it in their interests to abuse the power granted them. Should that check break down, one can only speculate at the result. Special prosecutors who find it in their interest to abuse their discretion might be hard to stop in an environment where they have the loyalty of the press and the memory of Watergate behind them. Just as the special prosecutor office was born out of the crisis of Watergate, it may take a similar abuse of power by a special prosecutor to instigate a reexamination of the desirability of having an independent prosecutor's office with so few formal checks on it. However, as long as the memories of Watergate continue to influence the actions of those responsible for creating and implementing the federal special prosecutor, and independent counsel continue to act responsibly, the symbolic value of the position is likely to overshadow these political considerations.

EIGHT

SYMBOLS AND POLITICS: MASS PUBLIC AND ELITE SUPPORT FOR THE SPECIAL PROSECUTOR

Thus far we have examined the relationships that have developed between the various institutions of American government and the independent counsel. Throughout this discussion there has been a recognition that political elites—office holders, their staffs, interest groups, and the media—believe that the special prosecutor arrangement is important because of its symbolic value to the public. Even its opponents express this view. This widespread belief among elites is an intriguing one because much of the literature about American public opinion suggests that the public is not particularly interested in or knowledgeable about politics, especially at the national level. This chapter explores the question of mass and elite support for the special prosecutor arrangement. The argument that the arrangement owes its existence to public demand is far too simplistic and ignores the realities and complexities of the relationship between public opinion, political elites, and public policy. The explanation for the continued use of the special prosecutor provisions lies in a combination of (1) broad-based elite support rooted in the memory of Watergate and in the way the arrangement serves an array of institutional or organizational interests and (2) indirect public support that derives from this elite support. Because the elite is satisfied with the arrangement, it is less likely that that contingent will seek to mobilize public opinion or arouse public concern about these cases of official misconduct.

We might draw two different normative conclusions from these findings. The first is that the symbolic goal of public reassurance is accomplished for positive ends because political stability is maintained through continued public confidence in government. The trauma of another Watergate is avoided. The second, and opposing, conclusion is that symbolic reassurance is accomplished, but with negative implications. Because political elites are reassured by the arrangement, they have little incentive to attempt to arouse the public against a transgressor of the public trust. Consequently, the public remains complacent and uninformed about official misconduct while elites affect the implementation of the arrangement in ways that serve their particular institutional and political concerns.

These conclusions are explored through the use of public opinion data, press coverage of Watergate and Ethics Act cases, and interviews with elites involved in the process. No national polls and none of the arrangement's supporters have attempted to track systematically public confidence in the handling of Ethics Act cases. Public confidence levels in the major institutions of American government have been charted over time[1] but the extent to which changes in these measures are attributable to the 1978 provisions is virtually impossible to assess. Assessment of the extent to which public confidence in the arrangement exists must depend then on inference from the literature on public opinion, general poll data on post-Watergate attitudes, and indirect evidence from news coverage.

PUBLIC OPINION AND PUBLIC POLICY

The literature addressing the questions of how public opinion influences public policy and how the mass media influence public opinion is extensive. In order to summarize this literature, it is useful to look first at the broader question of the connection between policy and opinion and second at the media as an intervening variable in this relationship. From this summary we can begin to draw inferences about the way in which the media, public opinion, and policymakers interact in the case of the federal special prosecutor.

The Distinction between the Elite and the Mass Public

The mass public does not have a significant influence on the day-to-day making of national policy decisions; it cannot because it pays scant attention to ordinary events in Washington. In 1927 Walter Lippmann argued that normally the public "will not be well informed, continuously interested, nonpartisan, creative, or executive." "We must assume," wrote Lippmann, "that a public is inexpert in its curiosity, intermittent, that it discerns only gross distinctions, is slow to be aroused and quickly diverted; that, since it acts by aligning itself, it personalizes whatever it considers, and is interested only when events have been melodramatized as a conflict."[2]

In his less impressionistic study of American public opinion, V. O. Key set forth a similar proposition: that policymakers have broad discretion because of the amorphous nature of public opinion, which tends "toward generality rather than specificity."[3] Key contended that the true shapers of opinion and policy were political activists and elites and that it was in looking at this group's activities that an understanding of American policymaking was to be found. "Mass opinion is not self-generating," Key argued. "In the main it is a response to the cues, the proposals, and the visions propagated by the political activists."[4]

The concept that political activists and elites direct public opinion has been central to an understanding of the influence of public opinion in American politics. Participation by a small group of interested activists helps to explain why a democratic system can continue to function when there is a low level of citizen involvement.[5] The political activists serve as a link between decisionmakers and the inattentive public, for they are engaged in political dialogue with both groups.

W. Russell Neuman argues that the "mass public" is in fact three publics that are distinguished from each other by their sense of civic duty and by their attention to and participation in politics. Approximately 5 percent of the public falls into the activist category, which is characterized by "uniquely high levels of political involvement." The largest group (about 75 percent) falls into a middle category. These people pay little attention to politics and "are mildly cynical about the behavior of politicians" but tend to feel a civic duty to vote "and they do so with fair regularity." The third group is composed of about 20 percent of the public and is an "unabashedly apolitical lot."[6] Neuman suggests that there are important political implications to this breakdown of the public, especially in the separation of the second and third groups from each other. The 75 percent can be mobilized by elites under certain circumstances. Because there is a "tension" between this group's sense of civic duty and its usual political habits, it can be aroused if it perceives that a significant issue is at stake. Thus, the democratic process works despite low public attention and involvement because of "the possibility that at any minute what was once the concern of a tiny group of activists may suddenly crystallize the attention of the mass electorate."[7] Because of this potential for mobilization, "the political elites in this country perceive and act within the constraints of an attentive public. Even for those many obscure and narrowly defined issues which are clearly not in the public eye, the elected and administrative elites have the shared sense that such issues could move into the public eye quite quickly, and they behave accordingly."[8]

Murray Edelman's distinction between the mass public and elites takes a different twist. He argues that "public interest" policy must be understood at two levels. At the level of mass public understanding, this policy is seen as having symbolic importance: that is, certain political actions and out-

comes are symbols that evoke a quiescent mass response because they symbolize a reassurance to the public about some concern with which it feels
emotionally involved. The meaning of these symbols depends very little
upon their objective consequences since the actual acts and consequences
are remote from the public.[9]

Edelman suggests that these symbolic reassurances promise something
much different than what actually occurs. While the public is made quiescent with reassurances that its interests have been considered, smaller organized groups can influence the implementation of the policy to their benefit. "Invisibility" or remoteness of the actual consequences of the act allow
this dichotomy of outcomes to persist.[10]

In Edelman's scenario, the general public sees politics as "a parade of ab-
stractions."[11] During implementation of public interest legislation, administrative activities that will "convey a sense of well-being to the onlooker" are
widely publicized, suggesting that the symbolic ends of the legislation are
being actively pursued. Edelman posits that this publicity, in the form of
press releases, administrative data, and annual reports, in fact shield from
the public eye the true nature of the activity of implementation. In reality
implementation is characterized by "inactivity or protection of the regu-
lated."[12]

Elaborate procedural arrangements are important to fulfillment of this
dual character of public interest legislation. Procedures function to "legiti-
mize what finally is announced by emphasizing the care with which it is related to the agency's symbolic objective." Given the influence of interested
organized groups in the implementation of these laws, Edelman contends
that the result of agency decisionmaking is "foreordained, . . . regardless
of the awesomeness of the procedures."[13]

Edelman takes the position that the consequences for the democratic
process that result from the relationship between the mass public and the
elite are clearly different from those suggested by Key and Neuman. While
Key and Neuman are optimistic about elite responsiveness because of the
potential for mobilization of the mass public, Edelman sees a mass public
lulled into quiescence by symbols while elites pursue their self-interests
through implementation. These alternative views need not be completely in-
compatible in practice. To the extent that the activist public is engaged in
ongoing oversight of the implementation of public interest legislation such
as the Ethics Act, political elites may be forced to act in the spirit of the
symbolic legislation. But, to the extent that the activist public is itself reas-

sured, and thus made quiescent by the symbol, political elites may continue to behave in the way Edelman suggests.

Mass Media and Public Opinion

When considering public attention to government action, it is essential to factor in the way in which that action is presented by the mass media to the public and the way in which the public perceives that presentation. It is only in the recent past that political scientists have begun to address this relationship.[14] Studies of mass media and public opinion tend to confirm and enhance the earlier work on mass publics and elites. Doris Graber suggests that the mass media have greater impact on elites, particularly political decisionmakers, than on the general public because the information provided by the media "relates more directly to their immediate concerns."[15]

Why is it unlikely that the public will be regularly aroused by media exposés and pressure government elites for action? Recognizing that all citizens are overwhelmed by the "flood of news" available to them daily, Graber conducted a panel study of "average citizens" to determine how they process the news and "tame the information tide." She found that people screen out much of the information they receive by employing "schema" through which the information is processed.[16]

In a study of newspaper-reading habits, Graber determined that participants excluded two out of three stories, reading those remaining through reliance on the "inverted pyramid style of reporting," which places most of the important information of the story in the first paragraph. The panelists read only 18 percent of the newspaper stories in full. On the average, only one of fifteen news stories on the nightly television newscasts was retained by the panelists in Graber's study.[17] Participants tended to recall stories given prominent treatment by journalists; in fact, panelists retained only a general understanding of these stories rather than a recollection of specific detail.[18]

Even with major news events, this low level of attention and retention of detail prevails. Edwin Diamond's panel study of the impact of the televised Senate Watergate hearings in the summer of 1973 found that while "middle America" tended to pay close attention to these hearings, it also tended to react to the personalities involved in the scandal rather than to the constitutional and political issues raised by the evidence. Their opinions on Watergate were formed through this personalization process. Thus, former Attorney General John Mitchell was "obviously lying," not because of the evidence against him but because of "his sweaty brow and the way he bites his lip like a fish."[19]

Low levels of news retention by the general public may be explained by that public's relatively low level of interest in politics. Austin Ranney points out:

> Most of the major studies of the attitudes and behavior of mass publics find that a substantial majority of Americans are, most of the time, not very interested in politics. They typically believe that, except in times of great crisis, what presidents and congressmen do or fail to do affects little or not at all the significant aspects of their personal lives—going to school, getting a job, getting married, setting up a home, raising children, staying healthy, watching television, and so on.[20]

It should be noted, however, that the content of the news may have something to do with low retention levels. Neuman points out that even in newspapers, which we tend to believe differ from television because of their focus on news instead of on entertainment, the political content is very low. One study found that about 4 percent of newspaper content is national and international news. While there are many alternative sources for political news, they "are only a small trickle in the broader media tide. To a large extent, only the political elite attend to the political press."[21]

We should also be interested in the content of news in terms of the messages that might be absorbed about politics and politicians. Generally, studies of news gathering and media content demonstrate that where a bias can be detected, it tends to be anti-politician and anti-government. In his study of how news is formulated, Edward Epstein examined the attitudes of journalists and found that they tend to take a "disparaging view" of politicians. He discovered that "The working hypothesis almost universally shared . . . is that politicians are suspect; their public images false, their public statements disingenuous, their moral pronouncements hypocritical, their motives self-serving, and their promises ephemeral."[22]

Reporters' skepticism about the motives of those in power shapes the way in which they perceive their job, and that perception in turn frames the way in which they report the news. Because politicians "are presumed to be deceptive opponents,"[23] journalists view their role as a watchdog and adversary of government. Consequently, Ranney points out, "all journalists, . . . feel their job is, not to make it easier for government to make and carry out its policies, but to probe deeply and tirelessly into what government is really doing so that the people will know."[24]

Finally, we should consider whether the anti-politician content of the news has any impact on public opinion and if so, how that impact is revealed in American politics. The answer to that question is not at all clear. The precipitous decline of public confidence in government in the 1960s and 1970s prompted several political scientists to attempt to discern connections between that decline and negative news coverage. Their findings suggest that there exists some connection. Robinson found that "television journalism does cause frustration, cynicism, self-doubt, and malaise."[25] Miller, Goldenberg, and Ebring assessed the impact of negative criticism of the government in newspaper reporting on the reader's confidence and found a similar association. They concluded that "the public's evaluations of government performance flow rather directly from the image of the political process as seen through the prism of newspaper reporting."[26]

Despite some findings that televising the Watergate hearings was a positive media contribution,[27] Edwin Diamond has suggested that extensive coverage had a different, and negative, impact on public attitudes. Not surprisingly, President Nixon's popularity declined sharply in 1973. But so did the popularity of all politicians. A 1973 Harris poll found that seven out of ten Americans believed that "dirty campaign tactics exist among Democrats and Republicans and the Nixon campaign people were no worse, except that they got caught at it." Diamond argued that the fact that this attitude developed, despite overwhelming evidence to the contrary, demonstrated that television viewers exercise selective perception when processing information they receive. He concluded, "The belief that 'everybody does it' reflects an attitude about politics that, apparently, cannot be eroded by 'information,' no matter how good or how readily available it is."[28]

Whether that public attitude is the result of media content reflecting reporter anti-politician bias or whether that reporter bias is a reflection of American political culture is a question not readily resolved. Perhaps such reporting serves to reinforce the public's existing prejudice. Graber's analysis of how people process the news found that one of the widely shared schema through which people filter the news consists of a negative attitude toward politicians and politics "coupled with a tolerance for their failings and a strong belief that, on balance, the American system is sound."[29] Graber states that this schema had important implications for the political process generally and for the impact of media stories of public corruption specifically. "Such a mixture of beliefs," she argued, "greatly reduces the shock value of media stories so that investigative journalism, which is focused on graphic illustrations of governmental misdeeds, raises little more than eyebrows. It usually fails to spawn 'let's turn the rascals out' political campaigns. In fact, even the news value of many exposes has been comparatively small."[30]

This evidence demonstrates that the relationship between media coverage of government action and public attitudes toward government is more complex and interactive than some contend. Rather than arousing public opinion with exposure of official corruption, an already existing negative view of politicians may simply be reinforced.

What then does this literature suggest to us about the relationship between the mass public, elites, and the media, especially with regard to the special prosecutor issue? We should anticipate low mass public awareness and greater knowledge and understanding among political elites of these cases. Two groups of actors, the mass media and political elites (including officials and activists), are the communication channels between government and the mass public. Ultimately, then, the response of these two groups to the special prosecutor arrangement will determine the extent to which the mass public understands and supports the special prosecutor arrangement.

THE SPECIAL PROSECUTOR AND THE PUBLIC

Some conclusions can be deduced from what has been established about the public opinion-media-policy connection and from some general data that assess public attitudes five and ten years after Watergate. In addition, the impact of Watergate on public attitudes and the role the media played in the exposure and resolution of that crisis have been intensely scrutinized by scholars of politics and communications. Drawing comparisons between these studies and the cases where a statutory prosecutor was used allow us to further assess the possible impact of that law.

Watergate and Public Opinion

Watergate provides an ideal case for studying the nature of public attention to and knowledge of official corruption cases. It involved high-level officials, received extensive media attention, and endured over a period of several years. In retrospect, it seems the classic case in which a vigilant press exposed corruption, aroused public outrage, and consequently triggered major governmental reforms. But it is worth noting that for almost a year following the break-in at the Democratic National Committee headquarters, there was no widespread public concern over the incident. Despite Democratic attempts to the contrary, it was a non-issue in the presidential election of 1972. In fact, for some time public opinion polls indicated that the public had grown weary of the disclosures and believed the press was spending too much time on the story.[31] How then do we explain the general support and acquiescence to Nixon's resignation in 1974, less than two years after winning reelection in a landslide?

Gladys Engel Lang and Kurt Lang provide an answer to this question in their study of the "battle for public opinion" during the two years of the Watergate crisis. They traced the change of public attitudes toward the scandal and what influenced those changes. Seeking to explain the relative lack of public concern about Watergate between June 1972 and the spring of 1973, the Langs examined media coverage and public opinion data during that period. They found that the salience of issues is dependent upon several factors and that the interaction of these factors determines public attention and concern over issues covered by the media.[32]

First, the Langs delineated issues by how they vary along a continuum from low to high threshold. The kind of issues most likely to gain public attention rapidly are low-threshold issues and are characterized by conditions that directly affect the lives of most members of the public (such as energy shortages and high prices). A middle-level category is one in which the impact of the issue is selectively experienced by some group within the general public (such as the military draft or urban congestion). Finally, high-threshold issues are those that are "generally remote from just about everyone." The Langs place the Watergate scandal, and official misconduct cases generally, into this category. Watergate was the kind of issue that required "more than the ordinary amount of news recognition to break through the threshold of inattention."[33]

According to the Langs, Watergate failed to become a major issue on the public agenda in the first stage of the crisis for several reasons, including the language used by the media to describe the incident ("the Watergate caper" and "a third-rate burglary"), the fact that it occurred during an election year and was thus easily written off as "just politics," and the competition in news stories that it faced from such events as the war in Vietnam, the returning POW's, and a troubled economy.[34]

With disclosures mounting and the arrival of a new year, the language employed by the press began to change. Instead of writing about the "bungled burglary" the story had been converted into "a quest for the truth" and a "cover-up" that possibly implicated the president. Indicative of this conversion was the January 1973 *New York Times* editorial calling for the appointment of an independent investigator to get to the bottom of the story. Also in January of that year, the Senate began the process of establishing an investigating committee and by March, media coverage was approaching the "saturation" level.[35]

The Langs argue that saturation coverage of Watergate was necessary before the public's threshold of inattention to the story could be broken. Saturation requires the interacting components of "prominence" and "continuity" to exist in news coverage. These variables are operationalized for newspaper coverage to mean that a story has to receive front-page placement (prominence) on four consecutive days, or five of seven, or six of nine (continuity).[36] Once this occurred with the Watergate story in the spring of 1973, public concern about the issue mounted and the perception that the story was "just politics" declined.[37] Thus, the nature of media coverage was essential to the change in public opinion because "Prominence gives a news item the visibility that facilitates one's attention. Continuity allows for the kind of reiteration and development of news angles that help to fix the basic elements of a story in one's mind. . . . Both are necessary before a high-threshold event like Watergate can break through the barrier of public attention to become a dominant concern."[38]

The Ethics Act Cases

Using the Lang analysis for comparative purposes, we can examine press coverage of cases investigated under the Ethics Act to determine the likelihood of public understanding of them. If press coverage did not reach the level of saturation, as operationalized by the Langs, then it is unlikely that public attention was captured by these cases. If this is true then the belief that public confidence is promoted with the appointment of a special prosecutor is based upon a false assumption about the level of public awareness of these cases.

An analysis of *New York Times*[39] coverage of the Ethics Act cases reveals that news saturation occurred in only two of the nine public cases between 1978 and 1989 (Table 8.1). The clearest case of saturation occurred in the first year of the Iran-Contra case, a scandal with many similarities to Wa-

Table 8.1. *New York Times* Coverage of Ethics Act Cases

	Total Number of stories[a]	Page 1 stories	Months[b]	Days[c]	Saturation?[d]
Jordan	40	6	10	33	No
Kraft	9	3	6.5	6	No
Donovan	79	19	21	63	Some[e]
Meese 1	75	15	7	42	No
Olson	16	2	33	16	No
Deaver	155	23	21	131	No
Iran-Contra	2,058	357	38	633	Yes[f]
Nofziger	45	8	15	43	No
Meese 2	87	14	15	81	No

Source: New York Times Index, 1979–1989.

[a]Includes editorials and op-ed pieces.
[b]From first publication of allegations until subject cleared or convicted of charges.
[c]Actual number of days when story appeared; on some days more than one story related to the case was published.
[d]Page 1 stories on 4 consecutive days, 5 of 7, or 6 of 9.
[e]Only saturation was 9 days from Aug. 27 to Sept. 4, 1982, when investigation reopened and murder of witnesses was revealed.
[f]Saturation occurred during two periods in the first year of the scandal: November 1986–March 1987, when scandal was exposed, and May 1987–August 1987, when Congress conducted its investigation and hearings. After August 1987 no periods of saturation occurred.

tergate. It implicated a number of very highly placed officials, including the president, and involved televised congressional hearings with a complex but dramatic story that gradually unfolded over the course of several months. Even here the saturation pattern suggests less than complete public understanding of the case and the independent counsel's role in it. At the close of the congressional hearings in the summer of 1987, saturation ended. While a fairly consistent pattern of coverage continued, it was most frequently relegated to the later pages of the newspaper. The trials of the indicted officials in the scandal were not given the kind of coverage that the initial allegations or the congressional hearings received during the first year.

The one other case where some saturation occurred was the Donovan case. Here the saturation was not sustained beyond a week. Throughout the former secretary of labor's 1981 confirmation hearings, when the allegations of ties to organized crime surfaced, and during the resurfacing of those allegations and the subsequent special prosecutor investigation, saturation never occurred. It was not until Special Prosecutor Silverman reopened the investigation after having already cleared Donovan and several witnesses were murdered gangland style that saturation coverage occurred, however short-lived. In addition, the headlines and story content during this time had as much to do with organized crime in New York City and New Jersey as it did with a special prosecutor investigation of Secretary Donovan.[40]

This analysis of news saturation suggests that with the exception of the Iran-Contra scandal the cases in which Ethics Act prosecutors were appointed never had the same salience as public issues that the Watergate case eventually gained. Instead, treatment of the cases more closely resembled treatment of the Watergate case in the early stage of that scandal. All of the cases raise issues of official misconduct and thus can be classified as high-threshold issues because of their remoteness from the public. Further, a number of the cases have specific characteristics that make them more likely to be considered high threshold. Six of the nine cases occurred, at least in part, during presidential election years (Jordan, Kraft, Meese 1 and 2, Nofziger, and Iran-Contra). Five of the cases involved a congressional hearing of one sort or another (Donovan, Meese 1, Olson, Deaver, Iran-Contra). Each of these settings is characterized by partisanship; a characteristic the Langs identified as one likely to contribute to low salience. It is interesting to note that during the period of time that the Iran-Contra case overlapped the 1988 presidential election, coverage was at its lowest. In fact, during the months immediately preceding the election there was virtually no meaningful coverage of the scandal. It has been suggested that during the 1988 campaign candidate George Bush was effective at labeling the scandal a partisan issue and that, consequently, reporters backed off from discussing the scandal and the vice president's role in it.[41] Again with the exception of the Iran-Contra case, the cases also tended to last a shorter period of time,[42] implicated a significantly smaller number of people, and were never interpreted as threats to our constitutional system or evidence of a corrupt president.[43] Consequently, the likelihood that the public was aware of the issues in these cases and felt reassured because a judicially appointed independent prosecutor was investigating is minimal.

Public Confidence in Watergate Reforms

Attempts to measure the long-term impact of Watergate on American opinion provide further support for the proposition that the 1978 provisions are unlikely to have had much impact on the public's confidence that "politics" has been removed from the administration of justice. In 1979, five years after Nixon's resignation, and 1982, ten years after the Watergate break-in, polls were conducted that attempted to assess lingering public attitudes toward Richard Nixon and the scandal that brought him down.[44] Opinions on this topic have not changed markedly despite congressional and executive efforts to "clean up government." The polls asked questions that probed attitudes about the probability of another Watergate occurring and that therefore speak directly to our central question of the public's confidence in post-Watergate reforms. Responses both five and ten years later indicate a general lack of faith in the concept that government has been cleaned up since then. For example, in the 1979 poll a plurality of respondents (40 percent) believed it "very likely" that another Watergate-type scandal could happen in the United States. If we add to that 40 percent the 39 percent who believed that possibility to be "somewhat likely," we have a sizeable majority who think it could happen again. The 1982 Newsweek/Gallup poll asked whether the "abuses of presidential power such as were revealed in the Watergate scandal could easily happen again, [or whether] the lessons of Watergate will probably prevent similar abuses of presidential power." Even with this more narrowly drawn question, 53 percent of respondents felt that the abuses "could easily happen again." Furthermore, a 1982 NBC/AP poll found that of those who knew enough about Watergate to have an opinion on it, 68 percent believed that national politics was either equally (56 percent) or more corrupt (12 percent) than it was during Watergate.[45]

The Newsweek poll in 1982 went further and attempted to measure attitudes toward the reforms of the post-Watergate period. Although it did not name specific reforms (i.e. financial disclosure or appointment of special prosecutors), it did ask about the topic areas of relevance to this research. Table 8.2 demonstrates that while about one third of the respondents thought improvements had occurred since Watergate, those who felt things had not changed represented a plurality throughout and, when joined by those who believed things were worse, constituted a clear majority.[46]

When this poll data is combined with the inferences drawn from the literature on public opinion and the findings on press coverage, it seems unlikely that the institutionalization of special prosecutors has had an impact on public confidence in government. The evidence suggests that the public knows little about the arrangement and its use in eight of the nine cases and, whether or not it is aware of the arrangement, has little confidence that post-Watergate reforms have in fact reformed government.

Table 8.2. Opinion Poll Results on Effect of Post-Watergate Reforms on American Government (in percentages)

	Better	Worse	No Change	Don't Know
Presidency	35	16	42	7
Congress	28	15	49	8
News Media	32	24	38	6
Campaigns and Financing	27	22	41	10
Ethical Standards of Government Officials	30	16	43	11

Source: Newsweek/Gallup Poll, June 2–3, 1982. The question read: "Some people believe that the disclosures of Watergate led to positive changes in many of our important democratic institutions; other people believe that some of these changes went too far or made things worse. For each of the following, please tell me if you think there have been changes for the better as the result of Watergate, or if you think changes have made things worse, or if you think there hasn't been any significant change."

SYMBOLIC REASSURANCE AND ELITE SUPPORT

Consideration of elite perceptions of the special prosecutor process yields greater evidence of support and reassurance than was revealed by the focus on the general public. Among elites who pay attention to this issue there is a strong perception that public confidence is maintained through the use of the special prosecutor. In addition, there are other institutional, political, and professional bases for elite support that help explain the continued existence of the arrangement.

The Press

Studies indicate that journalists perceive politicians as adversaries and themselves as the watchdogs of government. Further, this conception seems to have been strengthened by the Watergate experience where the *Washington Post* played a critical role in exposing misconduct.[47] It is not surprising, then, to find that special prosecutors view the press, for the most part, as a potential source of support for their endeavors. While there has been occasional critical coverage, and the *Wall Street Journal* has taken an editorial stance opposing the arrangement, much coverage of the special prosecutors themselves has been positive. Despite the one-sided relationship that usually exists between the investigations and the press, there is little criticism of the prosecutors in the daily press. That which has appeared has tended to focus on the secrecy surrounding the investigations.[48]

We saw earlier that for most of the Ethics Act cases the press has not played the role that it played in Watergate of placing sufficient attention on the cases to make them salient to the general public. A further analysis of press coverage in these cases exposes a pattern indicating that the press itself finds these cases less salient after appointment of an independent prosecutor than before. Journalists may feel less responsible for playing their watchdog role after an independent investigation is begun than they feel prior to that time.

Press coverage of the Ethics Act cases tends to drop off upon appointment of an independent counsel and to stay low unless the official is indicted and goes to trial. In the Jordan, Kraft, Meese 1, and Olson cases, the bulk of coverage occurred between the time that the allegations first surfaced and the appointment of a special prosecutor. From the day after appointment until the day the special prosecutor cleared the official, coverage was significantly reduced, despite the fact that this stage encompassed much longer periods of time. The closest distribution in number of stories before and after appointment occurred in the Olson case, but the extent to which this case follows the pattern becomes more obvious when the length of the investigation is considered. The 56 percent of stories printed prior to the appointment of independent counsel appeared during a five-month period while the 44 percent that appeared after appointment were published over the course of twenty-eight months.

The Donovan and second Meese investigations differ from the other four with no indictment because the pattern of coverage was more consistent after appointment. In each case, new allegations surfaced throughout the investigation. In the Donovan case the probe was closed and then reopened by the special prosecutor, and the story had local and regional interest to *New York Times* reporters in addition to its national importance. Nevertheless there is some similarity to the pattern that suggests more interest in exposure of charges than in the investigation itself. Coverage was high during the secretary of labor's confirmation hearings but dropped to nothing after his confirmation despite the fact that allegations were not resolved at that time. In December 1981, press coverage reached another peak, most of which occurred in the last half of the month, and dropped significantly again after the appointment of Special Prosecutor Silverman in the last week of that year. The next peak in coverage resulted from the combination of Silverman's initial report clearing Donovan and the new allegations that quickly surfaced. Thereafter, coverage dropped again, and while it rose slightly when the investigation resumed and the murders of witnesses were revealed, it never reached the heights that it had previously.

In the second Meese case we see a similar pattern. There was no indictment and yet coverage was more consistent than in the other cases that were not indicted. Again, there are explanations unique to the case that help explain continued interest by the press. This was the second time Meese had been investigated by an independent counsel for allegations of unethical conduct, and this time he was the attorney general of the United States. He had become a controversial figure and was an outspoken critic of the special prosecutor law. Further, some of the allegations against Meese were tied to the larger Wedtech scandal, which implicated a number of prominent politicians. As that investigation and trial progressed in the Southern District of New York, Meese's connections to it were mentioned in a number of articles that were primarily about Wedtech, as opposed to about Meese himself. The renewed coverage at the end of the investigation can be explained by two related incidents. First, the release of the special prosecutor's report, which concluded that Meese had probably violated several laws but stated that the office declined to prosecute, was controversial both with Meese's supporters and detractors.[49] Second, Meese's resignation from office coincided with the release of the report. Despite these various incidents that caused more regular coverage than is usual, we still see lower levels of coverage than occurred up to McKay's appointment.

The investigations that resulted in indictment and trial follow a somewhat different pattern because of the continued news interest that a trial of this sort arouses. In the Deaver, Nofziger, and Iran-Contra cases there was much more consistent coverage (although in the first two at no time was there sufficient front page coverage to produce saturation). There was a drop-off of emphasis in the Iran-Contra case after the congressional hearings. In the Deaver and Nofziger cases, there was a lull in coverage between appointment and indictment and between indictment and conviction.

Even with the variations, analysis of press coverage suggests that appointment of a special prosecutor reassures the press, so it places less emphasis on the story. The pattern also gives an indication of why officials one would expect, from an institutional standpoint, to be hostile to the arrangement are in fact at times its supporters. We will return to this point after examining the views of elites more naturally supportive of the special prosecutor.

Interest Groups

There are two groups in particular that have focused their attention on the creation and implementation of the special prosecutor provisions and that have an ongoing interest in maintaining the arrangement. Earlier chapters outlined the participation of the American Bar Association and Common Cause in the creation of the device. This section looks more closely at the nature of the interests that motivate them to stay involved with the issue and to support its maintenance.

The American Bar Association. The ABA can be considered to be the genesis of the special prosecutor arrangement in its present form. It was a special committee of the organization, established in 1974, that devised and recommended to Congress a method by which a special prosecutor could be judicially appointed. In addition, representatives of the organization appeared before every congressional hearing on the issue and in each case urged the creation of an independent arrangement.[50] This critical role in the formation of the arrangement may in itself be sufficient explanation for the ABA's continued interest in and support of the special prosecutor. However, there are other reasons for this interest. The nature of the organization's mission generally and the impact of the Watergate scandal on the legal profession provide additional motivation.

From the time of its founding in 1878 the ABA saw as one of its central missions the responsibility to work toward political and legal reforms. Its founder, Simeon Baldwin, considered the promotion of "the administration of justice and uniformity of legislation throughout the union" as one of the new organization's key objectives. Other lawyers responded to Baldwin's call for the national association with enthusiastic support, writing that "such an association . . . would be conducive of much good . . . in inaugurating and carrying forward such true reforms as are in harmony with the progressive spirit of the age" and that "important advantages might be secured . . . in improving the law and legislation of our country."[51]

The ABA continues to view as a part of its mission its active role in legislation affecting criminal law and the legal profession. Among other things, a lawyer is considered to have a "special responsibility for the quality of justice."[52] The ABA's *Model Rules of Professional Conduct* encourages lawyers to fulfill this responsibility. It reads: "A lawyer should seek improvement of the law, the administration of justice and the quality of service rendered by the legal profession. As a member of a learned profession, a lawyer should . . . employ that knowledge in reform of the law . . . [and] should be mindful of deficiencies in the administration of justice. . . . A lawyer should aid the legal profession in pursuing these objectives and should help the bar regulate itself in the public interest."[53]

The bar association places great importance upon its ability to govern itself or to regulate itself, especially given "the close relationship between the profession and the processes of government and law enforcement."[54] Self-regulation in order to ensure continued self-government is of critical importance to the legal profession. The ability to remain independent of government is seen as an essential element of the bar's mission of legal reform because "an independent legal profession is an important force in preserving government under law, for abuse of legal authority is more readily challenged by a profession whose members are not dependent on government for the right to practice."[55]

The Watergate scandal had a profound impact on many in the legal profession and was of particular concern to the national bar association. It quickly became involved in searching for a solution to the politicization of justice that was at the root of the scandal. Robert Evans, director of the Washington office of the ABA, stated that the Watergate revelations forced some self-examination by the association and raised questions about the implications of the scandal for the legal profession. "Why were so many lawyers involved in the scandal? Should we be concerned about this? How does it look for so many in this profession to be implicated?"[56]

In setting up the special committee that came up with the idea of the "triggering process" for independent appointment of a special prosecutor, the organization was taking the lead in an area particularly well suited to its mission.[57] The issues of politics and justice and the implications for needed reform that emanated from Watergate were ideal for the ABA's involvement given its objectives and long history of concern about reforming the legal process and regulating the legal profession. Given its concerns about self-regulation and independence, it is not at all surprising that it viewed the appointment of an independent prosecutor drawn from the private sector as the answer to the problem of prosecuting public officials. Such a scheme fits well with the aforementioned view that an independent legal profession can act as a check on abuses of government power. In addition, its interest in self-regulation of the profession goes a long way in explaining its focus upon the Department of Justice and other federal law enforcement agencies that are government entities composed primarily of members of the profession.

Since passage of the special prosecutor legislation, the ABA's Washington office has taken responsibility for monitoring the act, albeit inconsistently and somewhat superficially. Evans explained: "Once the House of Delegates accepted the recommendations of the Special Committee, the attention of the bar as a whole has not been focused on these issues because they are not perceived as bread and butter issues. After the Act was passed in 1978, Spann [Chair of the Committee], Miller [Committee consultant], and I were involved in the implementation only in that we followed the initial couple of cases, got the final reports and sent them to other members of the Committee."[58]

The ABA also participated in the reauthorization hearings and filed amicus curiae briefs in the constitutional challenges to the law. It is the official position of the association that the office of special prosecutor has worked effectively and does not require significant change. The association did have some problems with the increased discretion granted to the attorney general in the 1982 amendments and lobbied for more restricted discretion in 1987. Evans believes that the arrangement has fulfilled its purpose of enhancing public confidence in the investigation of high-level officials because "the findings of the special prosecutor have been accepted by the media and the public as being honest, fair assessments."[59]

Common Cause. The "citizen's lobby" Common Cause was founded in 1970 at the time when public opinion polls reflected declining public confidence in government. Its founder, John W. Gardner, felt that that decline indicated a deep-seated desire in the American public for reform of its government, and he formed the public interest group in order to tap those concerns.[60] Initially, the organization focused its efforts on lobbying Congress in opposition to American involvement in Vietnam. In 1973 it shifted its focus to "structure and process issues": those that deal with government reform. These continue to be the central issues for which the group lobbies.[61]

Gardner believed that Common Cause was needed "to restore the confidence of our people in their institutions. That means . . . making the institutions worthy of their confidence."[62] He argued that institutions of self-government should be characterized by "effectiveness, access, responsiveness, and accountability."[63] Therefore, Common Cause's mission was to use lobbying tactics to work, in the public interest, for reform of government.

The period of time in which Common Cause was formed had great impact on its mission. It was barely two years old when Watergate occurred, and that scandal became a rallying point for the fledgling organization. In 1973, Gardner wrote, "Watergate demonstrated much that Common Cause has been saying since 1970 about the root problems of the political process."[64]

Several of Common Cause's early successes were Watergate related. In 1973 it successfully sued the Committee to Re-elect the President, forcing it to disclose contributors to the campaign coffers. It expended much energy in lobbying for the Federal Election Campaign Amendments of 1974. In 1975 it was the primary interest group supporting the government in the sunshine law passed that year. And it put great effort into pushing for passage of the Ethics in Government Act of 1978. While its primary interest in the act was in its financial disclosure provisions, it also strongly supported and committed a "modest amount of resources" to lobbying for the special prosecutor provisions.[65] In the 1980s it has remained active in this area, although in this decade its efforts are directed toward sustaining the reforms it supported in the 1970s. The Reagan administration's public criticism of many of the post-Watergate reforms has provided the organization with a new angle on the old issues that mobilize its members.[66]

Since passage of the Ethics Act, Common Cause has, like the ABA, conducted some limited monitoring of implementation of the act. That effort has been "more haphazard than organized" and has consisted primarily of contacts with the subcommittees responsible for oversight of the provisions. The organization does watch more closely the Office of Government Ethics, an agency created by the Ethics Act to oversee the disclosure provisions of the act.[67] Jay Hedlund, a former legislative director for the national office, explained that Common Cause's monitoring of the provisions often is in the form of watching for warning signals in the media. "Our political antennae went up when Reagan came in and started criticizing the legislation. We keep an eye on the news and when questions come up in the press, we increase our watchdog role."[68]

An early and important act of oversight by Common Cause was its filing of an amicus brief in the *Kraft v. Gallinghouse* suit brought by Timothy Kraft against the special prosecutor. The Justice Department refused to aid Gallinghouse in the case and Common Cause offered its help. Hedlund called this action on Gallinghouse's behalf "a typical example of us using the courts to protect changes we've been able to make through legislation. It was part of our general oversight function."[69] The group also filed briefs in support of the special prosecutor in the *Morrison v. Olson* case.[70]

Common Cause's views were sought by the oversight subcommittees during both reauthorizations of the special prosecutor provisions. The organization was basically satisfied with the form of the 1978 law, although it recognized that the Jordan and Kraft cases may have tainted the act "because they raised fuzzier questions than the basic integrity questions for which the Act was designed."[71] Nevertheless, Common Cause took the position that the triggering process did not need to be changed. It believed that with more experience, the triggering of the special prosecutor appointment would become more neutral; that the "more automatic the trigger, the more neutral the environment will be."[72] Consequently, Common Cause was opposed to any efforts to increase the discretion of the attorney general in triggering the act. During the 1987 hearings it urged renewed limits on the attorney general's discretion.[73] But Common Cause continues to believe that the act adequately limits the attorney general, that the threshold for appointment is still fairly low, and that the provisions have fulfilled their central goal of assuring public confidence in the fairness and integrity of investigations of high-level officials.[74]

As a demonstration of its continued support, Common Cause is prepared to fight any further efforts to dismantle the independent arrangement. In fact, such a battle is at the core of the group's mission:

> The Act doesn't have any outside organized traditional groups ready to march if something is done to it. But if the Reagan Administration tried anything, it would be playing with fire. Common Cause's best battles are in these white hat issues where we are clearly on the side of right. It is an issue that taps into public expectations of fairness and impartiality. . . . This is a battle that we cannot fight in subtle ways. When they say they are only making "technical changes" we have to show them for what they are and show the stakes clearly.[75]

Common Cause and the ABA are clearly the predominant organized interests working to support the special prosecutor arrangement. Their interest is based upon their sense of their organizational missions. The concept of a prosecutor who is independent, born out of the scandal of Watergate, is an institutional arrangement worthy of protection by these groups.

Congress

The Ethics Act is part of a package of laws passed by a resurgent Congress in the 1970s which attempted to restrain presidential power. This explains, in part, why it has been protective of the act. Naturally, all members of Congress are not equally involved in the oversight of the special prosecutor provisions. As we saw in Chapter 4 the Senate Subcommittee on Oversight of Government Management of the Committee on Government Operations and the House Subcommittee on Administrative Law and Governmental Relations of the Committee on the Judiciary are responsible for oversight of the Ethics Act. Oversight is infrequent and reactive, focusing on reauthorization every five years and on allegations that receive attention in the media.[76] The key senators and representatives on this issue are ones who have a particular policy interest: Senators Cohen and Levin and Congressman Barney Frank.[77] These three and their staffs have worked to maintain support for the provisions and have resisted efforts to alter significantly or to repeal them. The question of possible repeal has never been considered seriously because these leaders have convinced most members of Congress that the act serves the important functions of avoiding conflict of interest and building public confidence in the administration of justice.[78]

The other group in Congress with an occasional active interest in the existence of the statutory special prosecutor is made up of members of the "out" party: Republicans during the Carter administration and Democrats during the Reagan administration. Congress's statutory role in the process is structured along partisan lines. The act permits a majority of either party of either judiciary committee to request that the attorney general seek the appointment of a special prosecutor. The attorney general is not obligated to fill the congressional request but must explain a negative decision.[79] During the Carter administration, Republican congressmen led the calls for appointment of a special prosecutor, and during the Reagan administration, Democrats initiated those calls. The chance to embarrass the other party with a highly publicized special prosecutor appointment is not easy to back away from. In each of the cases, the "in" party has accused the "outs" of using the arrangement for partisan purposes and for leaking allegations obtained through congressional investigations to the press. Critics claim that the provisions for congressional involvement further politicize the process because "calls for the special prosecutor are useful to the opposition party."[80]

The Department of Justice

The interaction between the Department of Justice and the special prosecutors has been examined in depth in previous chapters. For the purposes of this discussion, it is worth a moment to reiterate some of the points established previously about the department's views on and participation in the process. For obvious reasons, the department views the special prosecutor arrangement as a usurpation of its power and has been consistently opposed to the temporary appointment of the prosecutors by a panel of judges. It has complied with the statute but has interpreted the language of the act to channel its opposition into changes in the arrangement that make it less offensive. On several occasions it has had the chance to defend its organizational prerogatives with regard to the statute. To the extent that it has been an effective actor in the implementation of the process, the department has played a role similar to that suggested by Edelman: it has been able to affect implementation in its interest and contrary to the symbolic image presented to the public. The department has been a key actor in assuring itself a continued and critical role in a process that is supposed to symbolize independence from that same department.

Nonetheless, there is reason to believe that the department, or at least parts of it, does not always see the arrangement as undesirable. Former Attorney General Meese himself requested appointment of an independent counsel in the Iran-Contra case very quickly and without the usual prolonged preliminary investigation. He clearly saw the value of using the arrangement when the breadth of the scandal became apparent. There are also some career officials in the department who see value in the arrangement because it relieves them of the burden of investigating and prosecuting their colleagues and superiors.[81] In addition, several past and present department officials acknowledge that the appearance of independence is important to public confidence and that, consequently, there are some cases where the arrangement's use is desirable. For example, a Department of Justice official from the Carter administration said, "The Jordan case was ridiculous. But it would have been much harder for me to dismiss it than for a special prosecutor. I would have had to worry about the appearance of favoritism if I had stuck to the principal that we shouldn't prosecute for the private activity of a public official unless we would do the same for a regular person."[82] While arguing that the law should give the attorney general greater discretion than it does, the official believed that the concept itself was not flawed. "Partisan politics is just too strong," he said. "People just wouldn't trust the administration with cases involving central figures. We can create trust in the remaining areas that the Department handles. In cases like this that are always so full of doubt it is much better to knock it off and give it to someone else so that it doesn't affect everything we do."[83]

An official within the Public Integrity Section argued that while the department is capable of conducting impartial investigations, "Appearances are important and that's what the act is all about."[84] The section chief sees some advantages to the statute as well. While acknowledging that it devalues the department, he suggested that many in the department have learned to live with it and recognize its benefits: "Given the ambiguity of many of the statutes we are asked to enforce, if the Department declined to prosecute people would not credit it with doing a thorough enough job. The independent counsel has more of a sense of legitimacy. Since Watergate, the climate is such that suspicion of the Department's decisions lingers. The statute does take the process away from the politicization of Department decisions that has occurred since Watergate."[85]

Thus, while its public position has been opposition to the special prosecutor arrangement, there are some in the department who believe that the arrangement does serve some institutional interests, especially in post-Watergate Washington. This view has also been demonstrated by the White House on some occasions.

The White House

During his two terms of office Ronald Reagan took the public position that the special prosecutor arrangement was an unconstitutional usurpation of executive power. Nonetheless, there were several occasions where the arrangement proved useful to the White House, and it was not above using it despite the philosophical objections. The use of a special prosecutor in the first Meese case clearly aided the president in the confirmation of his nominee for attorney general. A Department of Justice investigation into the allegations against Meese had already concluded that Meese had violated no criminal laws. However, extensive press coverage of the confirmation hearings and the allegations had put "terrific heat" on the nomination. An assistant special prosecutor in the case said, "It was a real smart move on Garment's [Meese's lawyer] part to request a special prosecutor. The effect of the appointment was to remove the Senate Judiciary Committee's jurisdiction by invoking the special prosecutor act and therefore diffusing the heat. It was a very good tactical move on their part."[86] The result was a sharp decline in press coverage and a lengthy delay in the confirmation hearings while the investigation was conducted. Following the 1984 landslide re-election of Reagan, Meese's nomination was resubmitted. In the interim the special prosecutor had cleared Meese of any criminal wrongdoing. While Democratic opponents of Meese's nomination attempted to point out the difference between criminal and ethical wrongdoing, the distinction was lost on many in the Senate and Meese was confirmed. In the aftermath one commentator wondered whether the special prosecutor may not have become a "special protector."[87]

The early experience with the arrangement lent support to the idea that the provisions could actually serve the White House's interests if used properly. In each of the early cases two things had happened. Press coverage dropped considerably during the investigation, and the target of the investigation was cleared of criminal charges. This sense that independent counsel investigations might be preferable to departmental investigations because of the secrecy and reduced press coverage was apparently widespread. One of Theodore Olson's defense attorneys noted, "There was a feeling at the time that it was a good way to clear your name. The previous investigations had been relatively short and the experience so far had not been that bad."[88]

The other examples that demonstrate White House ambivalence about the arrangement are the two reauthorization bills that Reagan signed and his rapid decision to seek appointment of a special prosecutor in the Iran-Contra case. Each example illustrates the perception that the arrangement is an important way to assure public confidence in the handling of official misconduct cases.

This review of elite support for the arrangement delineates two bases for that support. On the one hand, there are organizational or institutional interests that are served by the arrangement. On the other hand, all of these elites, whether more or less supportive for organizational reasons, believe that the arrangement serves an important symbolic function. Even its most vigorous political opponents in the executive branch perceive this to be its central value.

CONCLUSIONS

In *The Phantom Public* Lippmann argued that American government generally operates without regular substantive direction from the public. The public, he believed, becomes involved and concerned when crises occur and its involvement is predicated upon the desire to have the crises ended. In these situations Lippmann contended that public opinion aligns men "in such a way as to favor the action of individuals who may be able to compose the crisis." In Lippmann's scheme, public opinion acts as a "reserve of force" for use by those who represent the rule of law against those who represent the abuse of power. Consequently, public opinion cannot "make the law. But by canceling lawless power it may establish the condition under which law can be made."[89]

Lippmann's scenario has great applicability to both the Watergate case and to public corruption cases generally. It suggests that when the traditional bargaining and accommodation among the various decisionmakers in American government breaks down, when one branch abuses its powers or oversteps its bounds, the ensuing interbranch conflict will become a crisis in American politics to which the public will respond. Its support for those battling the abuse of power will aid in the resolution of the crisis and a return to the equilibrium among the branches that the separation of powers scheme envisions.

The Langs' study of the battle for public opinion during Watergate provides a remarkably accurate confirmation of Lippmann's theory. It demonstrates clearly the importance of this interaction between elite action and public opinion in times of crisis in American politics. For example, in their view the Saturday Night Massacre was a critical juncture in the resolution of the crisis because it brought together public opinion and elites opposing Nixon. When Archibald Cox called a press conference shortly before he was fired, he spoke not only to reporters and the wider public but also to Congress, Judge Sirica, Attorney General Richardson, and the White House: elites "in whose hands the crucial decisions lay, and . . . whose next step depended on what he would do."[90] The Langs conclude that the firing of Cox started the alignment of public opinion with the forces against Nixon. "If Nixon's action had only affected his standing with the public, . . . he probably could have survived; but after October 20th his reputation in the government was irrevocably damaged."[91]

In the months following the Saturday Night Massacre, the battle for public opinion was waged between Nixon and his opponents. It was a "period during which the adversaries maneuvered for mass support that neither side could take for granted but each felt it needed to put an end to Watergate."[92] The unfolding of Watergate is thus seen as a series of plays and counterplays by elite opponents who recognize that victory lies in the ability to convince the mass public that their cause is right. The alignment of mass opinion became the essential ingredient in the resolution of the crisis.

Lippmann and Edelman both suggest that in times of crisis, when the "sleeping giant" of public opinion is aroused, the public seeks reassurance and an end to feelings of insecurity and uncertainty generated by the crisis. Lippmann asserts that public opinion aligns itself with the group that represents the rule of law against that group representing the "brute assertion" of power.[93] Edelman's propositions on the symbolic uses of politics dovetail well with Lippmann's contentions and the Langs' explanation of Watergate. Edelman argues that the public tends to ignore the details of daily governance "until political actions and speeches make them symbolically threatening or reassuring, and it then responds to the cues furnished by the actions and the speeches, not to the direct knowledge of the facts."[94]

As long as Watergate was viewed as a partisan dispute, as it was in the months immediately following the break-in, it remained a "high-threshold" issue that was unlikely to be viewed as out of the ordinary by the public. Watergate engaged public attention and led to a crisis of confidence "only after it came to stand for something much more serious, for Presidential complicity in a political scandal and a continuing effort to cover-up that complicity. With Watergate now a symbolic issue involving the integrity of the Presidency and the democratic values of governance, it could no longer be settled to almost everyone's satisfaction through the usual political bargaining."[95]

Thus, elite conflict brought on by intense dispute between the branches of government entered the realm of public concern when the elites framed their positions in symbolic terms. When the scandal was presented as a battle between "the rule of law" and "the abuse of power," the sides were clearly drawn and the public aligned itself with the former. The Langs assert that a major scandal like Watergate "overrides at least temporarily the normal political divisions, [and] the symbolic issue dominates."[96]

Special prosecutors are useful and functional "symbols of justice" when major political scandals occur in American politics. When allegations of public corruption reveal widespread wrongdoing, implicate the revered presidency, and pit Congress against the executive, the public perception of the problem changes. Rather than seeing the allegations as mere political shenanigans, the scandal threatens the confidence of the public in the system. At these times the evocation of the symbol of impartial justice and the rule of law, which an independent prosecutor represents, becomes necessary in order to allay these fears. The appointment of a special prosecutor becomes essentially an effort to frame the conflict in such a way that the public is able to identify and to align itself with the forces that represent the rule of law.

When we endow the special prosecutor with this function, it becomes clear that except for the Iran-Contra scandal none of the Ethics Act cases meets the conditions that demand resort to such a symbol. The cases implicate only one or two public officials and focus on fairly narrow legal issues. Analysis of press coverage, or the lack thereof, suggests that the media perceive the cases as relatively unimportant. Diminished press coverage in turn suggests a failure by elites to become aroused about the case. Therefore the mass public will remain unaware of the cases and of the way in which they are handled by the special prosecutors. In the end, the "sleeping giant" is not awakened.

How is it that an institution almost universally lauded by elites as a symbol of reassurance to the public can be characterized by so little public awareness and understanding? The answer lies in the dynamics of the process of elite reassurance by the symbol. It is evident from interviewing the elites who have been involved in this process that the Watergate crisis had a profound and lasting impact on the collective mind of Washington, D.C. The aftershocks still resonate in the day to day politics of the capital city. They can be seen in the way the executive and legislative branches deal with each other and in the way that elites outside of government feel about those in governmental positions. Post-Watergate politics are characterized both by an underlying sense of distrust and a deeply felt sense of regret for what was lost because of the scandal. It may be that elite confidence in government was more profoundly and permanently shaken than was that of the general public.

In addition, there seems to be a renewed sense of, or fear of, the potential power of public opinion. The public's acquiescence in the resignation of a president who just two years before had been returned to office by an overwhelming margin and its punishment of that president's party in the 1974 and 1976 elections were acutely noticed by observant elites. The trauma of Watergate may well have faded in the public memory but it remains clear in the minds of Washington elites, and it has important implications for the politics of special prosecutors.

The institutionalization of the special prosecutor and its broad-based support among elites is testament to the fact that Watergate changed the face of how these elites treat each other. The feelings of distrust are institutionalized through this mechanism. Because Congress and nongovernmental elites (the press, interest groups) lack confidence in the ability of the executive to investigate itself, they support an institution that removes their own responsibility to act on that distrust. And because the Department of Justice and the White House distrust Congress and the press, they too frequently see the value of a special prosecutor. The investigation can be "depoliticized," removed from the hands of elites who have this profound distrust for each other and given to an investigator able to make an impartial judgment about the allegations.

Coupled with this sense of mutual distrust is a sense of loss for a now almost mythical pre-Watergate era where consensus was more easily built, where partisanship was less sharply divisive, where politics was a gentlemen's game, and where ethics was a course some took in college, not a topic for intricate and ambiguous legislation. Finally, there is a lingering sense of fear. In this confusing post-Watergate era, where the old politics-as-usual can become tomorrow's front page ethical violations, no one seems safe for long. A public cynicism about the motives of those in power is easily fed by a similarly cynical press. Voters may not "throw the rascals out" very often, but Watergate made it apparent that it is possible. The post-Watergate elite, then, exhibit a combination of distrust, regret, and fear. As a result, an institution like the special prosecutor acts as a symbol, not so much for the general public (which is only vaguely aware of it) but much more so for elites who want, above all else, to avoid another crisis of confidence of the magnitude of Watergate.

This attitude explains much of the support for the special prosecutor arrangement. The more easily it is triggered, the sooner an independent investigator steps in, the more likely it is that a prolonged struggle between elites will be avoided and a cynical press will turn its attention elsewhere. The public will not be forced to take sides or be reminded of the potential for misconduct that exists among its chosen officials.

It was suggested at the opening of this chapter that one might draw two different and potentially conflicting conclusions from this finding of elite reassurance that breeds low public awareness of the cases. We might conclude that the politics of special prosecutors in the post-Watergate era is a positive development. It institutionalizes the rule of law, avoids another Watergate, and maintains, however indirectly, public confidence in government. Elites resort to and support the use of special prosecutors because they are conscious of the potential for mobilization of public opinion on these issues. The special prosecutor arrangement is a more efficient and more stabilizing way to provide for the triumph of the rule of law. In this view, the provisions are examples of policy made and implemented by responsive elites who recognize the threat to public confidence that exists in these cases.

While there is some truth to this conclusion, this study provides some evidence that there are more self-interested motives at work here as well. Re-election concerns may be at the forefront of this concern about public confidence. We have seen also that the Department of Justice continues to have an important and influential role in the implementation of the provisions, despite appearances. The White House has seen the arrangement as useful for reducing attention to charges of misconduct by executive branch officials. Once an independent counsel is appointed, the executive can continue to assert certain constitutional prerogatives (i.e. foreign affairs powers, classification of documents, executive privilege) that can undermine in significant but often invisible ways the work of the independent counsel. Members of Congress can use it to avoid difficult political decisions about confirmation of controversial nominees or the direction of public policy. To what extent do these self-interested motives drive the politics of special prosecutors? Edelman's scenario seems a realistic one to describe the arrangement and why it endures. While the public remains essentially unaware of the arrangement and its actual operation, interested elites may use the device in self-interested ways that thwart its stated goals.

The relative invisibility of the issue to the public makes it difficult to conclude that the public is reassured by the arrangement. This invisibility occurs because the watchdogs in the connection between the mass public and public officials—the press and political activists—are themselves reassured by the appointment of an independent counsel. Once an independent counsel is appointed, activists regain confidence in the system and attention to the case drops off. The crisis is resolved. The rule of law has won.

Such an arrangement is not without its costs. The lack of ongoing oversight by interested nongovernmental elites creates the potential for several democratically troublesome results. One is that the public is kept in the dark about charges of official misconduct against its governmental representatives. To the extent that it is informed, the public is aware of information about the charges against officials rather than the resolution of those charges. Further, in the turning over of government power to an official outside the established institutions of American government, these institutions are able to avoid some of the democratic responsibility they have in the system, whether it be to make thoughtful advice and consent decisions or to be held accountable for the nomination of responsible and ethical persons to appointed positions. Finally, elite reassurance may result in the ability of other interested elites to affect implementation of the provisions in ways that promote their narrow interest rather than the public interest.

The more likely the press and political activists are to be reassured by the symbol of justice that the special prosecutor represents, the less likely they are to pay attention to what happens after appointment, and the more likely it is that these negative results will occur.

NINE

ON "THE NECESSITY OF AUXILIARY PRECAUTIONS"

In a 1981 speech on post-Watergate reforms, former Attorney General Benjamin Civiletti warned his audience about the possibility of unintended consequences from well-intentioned reform. "We cannot be complacent," he said, "We cannot be content to congratulate ourselves on the purity of our original legislative intentions, the soundness of our values, the beauty of our policies in theory. We must find out how our policies actually work. We must acquaint ourselves with facts. We must be pragmatists."[1] This study of the use of special prosecutors in American politics is designed to follow Civiletti's advice. The literature heretofore on special prosecutors has centered on an abstract constitutional debate about the theory of separation of powers. Is the special prosecutor constitutional? May Congress vest appointment of a special prosecutor in a court of law? Does judicial appointment usurp fundamental executive power? Is the separation of powers a flexible arrangement permitting adaptation and innovation or a more tightly structured command for separate functions?

While the Supreme Court's response to this debate in *Morrison v. Olson* has by no means settled these questions for everyone,[2] its greatest value may lie in encouraging us to look beyond these questions to the actual consequences of adopting the arrangement. While the arrangement has now been determined to be constitutional we must still discern whether it is good public policy. Making that determination requires that we address a different set of questions. What is it that we hope to accomplish by adopting an arrangement for independent investigation and prosecution? How well does the arrangement serve these ends? Are there any unintended consequences of adopting such an arrangement? What are the costs and benefits of its use for American politics?

To understand the strengths and weaknesses of the special prosecutor, it is necessary to move out of the rarefied air of constitutional theory and to try to distance ourselves from the almost mythological proportions that the institution took on after Watergate. Constitutional theory should guide us in our final normative judgments about the arrangement's worth. The profound impact of the Watergate experience on American politics makes it impossible to disregard the scandal when evaluating its progeny. But to conclude that the arrangement is bad because it intrudes on traditional executive power, or good because it is within Congress's power to create such an arrangement, or bad because it is an overreaction to Watergate, or good because it ensures no future Watergates will occur, is to oversimplify vastly the issues. This study reveals that the implementation of the special prosecutor provisions of the Ethics Act has resulted in an arrangement that is neither so dangerous as its critics suggest nor so beneficial as its supporters contend.

Both sides of the debate about the independent counsel have missed much by their focus on the constitutional issues. The arrangement is flawed in that it removes only the appearance of conflict of interest by the attorney general but does little to disarm the potential for actual conflict; it has an overly sensitive trigger that makes it likely that independent prosecutors will be appointed for reasons other than actual existence of conflict of interest or that there is a likelihood that the target has actually committed a crime; it is not needed if we accept the argument that in cases implicating the president and/or attorney general political pressure and public confidence concerns will force the appointment of an independent investigator; and, finally, it raises false expectations about what an independent prosecutor can accomplish in a system of dispersed power that encourages institutional competition. On the other hand, the dangers of a special prosecutor have been exaggerated by its opponents. The special prosecutors are not loose cannons with no accountability because they are not, and cannot be, truly independent from the legal and political systems. The statute does not emasculate the executive because it permits significant executive influence in the early, less visible, stages of the process and permits continued exercise of important executive prerogatives during the investigation. Finally, while the targets of special prosecutor investigations are no doubt harmed by such investigations, we must ask whether the alternative would cause less harm. It is difficult to see how that would be possible. The appointment of a special prosecutor diminishes, and in some cases virtually eliminates, press interest in the case. Rather than being tried in the unreliable and unpredictable court of public opinion (which is overseen by the press) the target is investigated, and in some cases prosecuted, by officers of the court and provided all of the protections guaranteed by the legal process. In the end, if subjects of preliminary investigations are not indicted, they are reimbursed for at least a portion of their attorneys' fees, a protection that would not be in force if the Department of Justice were to conduct the investigation. In most cases, the length of the investigations and the methods used are little different than they would be if they were carried out by the Department of Justice.[3] Further, the deep distrust of the department on the part of many elites would taint any final conclusions about the target's innocence in a way that does not happen with the special prosecutor.

IRAN-CONTRA AND
THE LIMITS OF LEGALISM

A weighing of the costs and benefits that inhere in the special prosecutor arrangement can aid in a final assessment of its value. We can look to the Iran-Contra investigation, certainly the most important case arising under the provisions, for evidence of both the strengths and weaknesses of the Ethics Act provisions.

The Case for the Special Prosecutor

The strength of elite support for the institution of the special prosecutor is perhaps the arrangement's greatest contribution to American politics. Even among those who believe that the resolution of the Watergate scandal demonstrated that "the system worked," there is a deep-seated anxiety about the potential of another crisis of those proportions. The system may have worked, but how many shocks of this magnitude can it endure before it fails to work? For a younger and more skeptical set of elites, the potential for another Watergate lies just below the surface of the choppy waters of present day politics. Distrust and suspicion of each other and anxiety about the "sleeping giant" of public opinion create a climate in Washington that challenges the traditional self-policing mechanisms of American government. Divided government has intensified partisan competition. Policy disputes are easily transformed into charges and countercharges of unethical, and sometimes criminal, behavior.

Confidence of elites in the impartiality of independent counsel investigations helps to defuse the animosities and limit the conflict between the branches and the parties in American politics. While calls for the appointment of special prosecutors may sometimes be prompted by the less admirable motivations of congressional politicians or the press, the acquiescence, and sometimes initiative, of the executive branch in seeking special prosecutors demonstrates that there is more to the use of this institution than partisan punishment. It is, at the least, an implicit recognition by both sides of the inability or undesirability of trying to resolve these cases through traditional mechanisms. Neither side trusts the other to do that in anything other than a self-interested way.

Given this political climate, the special prosecutor arrangement serves an important function in American politics. It does not completely remove official misconduct cases from this political environment, but it does create some distance from it, which, in the end, is probably better for the targets of the investigation and for the institutions of government. Appointment may be politically motivated, but the investigation and results will not be. This result may be the most that can be hoped for in post-Watergate politics.

It is also true that in an indirect way this confidence on the part of political elites helps to promote public confidence. Because every allegation of misconduct does not turn into a struggle among the various branches of government or the factions among the elite for public support, the public is not constantly required to choose sides, to decide which side represents the rule of law and which the forces of evil in the way Lippmann described. Although there is some reason to believe that the arrangement may work to lull the unsuspecting public into an unfounded complacency, it hardly seems desirable to have the opposite sort of reaction either. All allegations of misconduct are not equal either in breadth or depth and not all require a Lippmannesque solution. The special prosecutor mechanism works to sort out these cases in a relatively invisible way. The truly serious issues do make their way to public consciousness as was demonstrated by the Watergate and Iran-Contra cases.

Because the allegations implicated the president and the attorney general and held the threat to public confidence that they did, the Iran-Contra case presented the textbook opportunity for resort to independent counsel. The fact that the White House moved so quickly in announcing its intent to seek an appointment and that the Department of Justice offered a parallel appointment to Walsh when the constitutionality of the provisions was challenged demonstrates the widespread belief that the Ethics Act arrangement was tailor-made for the occasion. Apparently, everyone wanted to avoid "another Watergate." The senators on the Iran-Contra investigating committee "were urgently hoping to avoid a crisis."[4] A congressional staff member for the Senate subcommittee that oversees the Ethics Act noted that Iran-Contra was much less traumatic than it might have been had there been no independent counsel arrangement.[5] But the problems that the investigation has encountered since its inception tell us much about the limits and costs of choosing this route in official misconduct cases.

The Case against the Special Prosecutor

One of the strongest arguments against the special prosecutor arrangement is that it adds little to our ability to resolve official misconduct cases. While *Morrison v. Olson* settled, at least temporarily, the theoretical constitutional dispute about the special prosecutor arrangement, it did not address other issues concerning the separation of powers with practical implications for the operation of the independent office. We know that the fears of too much independence and lack of accountability are overdrawn because the special prosecutor still must interact with the other actors in the political and legal systems. The darker side to this finding is that this reduced independence can interfere with special prosecutor investigations in significant ways.

The structural impediments to criminal investigation and prosecution of official misconduct charges are easily overlooked. The dispersion of power and the competing institutional interests at play impact on these cases whether they are pursued by an independent counsel or through traditional channels. An "independent" investigation can no more extricate itself from this web of competing forces than a regular prosecutor can. A particular weakness of the special prosecutor arrangement, however, is that we expect it to be able to overcome these barriers because of its special nature. We may even believe that because we are blinded by its symbolic independence and fail to see that true independence is impossible. This perception creates a problem of false expectations that is dangerous to the extent that it causes us to believe that the special prosecutor will resolve problems that, in fact, he cannot.

The competing institutional interests of Congress and the special prosecutor in the Iran-Contra case provide a prime example of the the way in which dispersed power can hamper investigation. The special prosecutor may not answer to Congress, but neither does the Congress answer to the special prosecutor. In its desire to pursue the political issues that were raised by Iran-Contra, Congress chose to publicize its hearings and immunize key witnesses in a manner that negatively impacted the ability of Lawrence Walsh to pursue his criminal cases. Walsh was forced to speed up his investigation in order to develop his case prior to the grants of immunity. Because Congress, the administration, and the defendants were anxious to get the scandal over with as quickly as possible, the needs of the prosecution took a back seat to the needs of these other actors. During the early 1987 negotiations between Walsh and the congressional committees over when to grant immunity, a *New York Times* editorial, entitled "Don't Wallow in the Iran Scandal," urged the sides to compromise. But it concluded that "if many more weeks pass, Congress will have to choose between informing itself and the public, and preserving Mr. Walsh's prosecution options. At that point, having already given him four months or more, it will have to choose the informing function of open hearings."[6]

Attorneys for the defendants saw advantages to their clients in having both a congressional investigation and a criminal investigation. One attorney told a *Washington Post* reporter, "With parallel proceedings you have an opportunity to confuse things. You can take advantage of the different interests, the obvious conflict between the independent counsel not wanting immunity and the Hill wanting to hear from these guys now."[7] In fact, it has been suggested that North's initial suit challenging the constitutionality of the independent counsel statute was designed to take advantage of this situation. The further delays that would result might "give that wavering congressman or senator a push."[8]

The decision to grant immunity to North and Poindexter affected Walsh's work not just initially but throughout the trials as well. It caused substantial delays in getting to trial, disruptions during the conduct of the trial, and, ultimately, has called into question the whole point of the lengthy and expensive criminal investigation. The decision by the D.C. Court of Appeals requiring Walsh to demonstrate that there was no use of immunized testimony at all, even with witnesses whose memories might have been refreshed in watching the televised hearings, imposes a standard that Walsh may well not be able to meet.[9]

As we have seen in earlier chapters, Congress was not the only institution in conflict with the independent counsel in the Iran-Contra case. Walsh was also engaged in a battle with the executive branch over classified documents. The prosecutor's case, notes Harold Koh, "degenerated into the case of the United States versus itself. . . . The Justice Department, the congressional committees, the White House, and the intelligence agencies all subsequently threw major roadblocks into the independent counsel's path."[10] Given the institutional competition surrounding this case, it is remarkable that the North and Poindexter cases ever made it through trials. What is clear is that this competition created a situation in which the criminal investigation and prosecution ended up being relatively meaningless.

The ambiguity of the extent of constitutional powers creates further problems for the investigation and prosecution of official misconduct cases. Both the Iran-Contra case and the investigation of Theodore Olson were, at least in part, about power struggles between the president and Congress. This is not to suggest that these cases were "merely" constitutional struggles[11] but rather that the constitutional struggle at the root of each case complicated it and made it more difficult to determine whether or not the behaviors involved were in fact prosecutable.

In the Olson case, involving conspiracy to withhold evidence from Congress in its 1982 investigation of the EPA, the constitutional issue was the use of executive privilege. Congress and the president had sharp differences over the use of the privilege and an assessment of the behavior of Olson had to rest in part on an interpretation of the legitimacy of the executive privilege claims originally made. Whether or not criminal intent existed in this case would rest upon whether one believed that Olson was exercising the constitutional prerogative of the president to withhold sensitive enforcement information or whether he set out to deceive Congress in order to hide information damaging to the White House.

The Iran-Contra case points out two other problematic areas of ambiguity in constitutional powers: (1) the extent of executive power in foreign affairs and (2) the difficulty of locating responsibility in a system where power is dispersed. The extent of the president's powers in foreign affairs and national security has prompted heated debate among scholars and between the legislative and executive branches of government. The political debate about power in foreign affairs was at the core of the Iran-Contra case and explains Congress's willingness to jeopardize the criminal prosecutions of key witnesses in order to have them testify in public hearings.[12] They also explain the dropping by the independent counsel of a number of the charges of which these witnesses were initially accused.[13]

Finally, the modern system of separated powers makes the location of responsibility for misconduct a difficult one. The dispersion of power and accountability makes "it difficult even in principle to identify who is morally responsible for political outcomes."[14] The "problem of many hands"[15] was clearly at work in efforts to unravel the Iran-Contra affair. In fact, it became a part of North's defense of his actions, for he argued that he was following the directions of others or was acting within a larger policy framework that dictated that he take certain actions. The jury apparently accepted that argument for it declined to convict him on some charges for which his defense was that he had been authorized by his superiors to act. And, in refusing to sentence North to prison, Judge Gesell also indicated his unwillingness to force North to bear the brunt of the responsibility for these actions. Gesell said in his comments at sentencing, "I do not think

. . . you were a leader at all, but really a low-ranking subordinate working to carry out initiatives of a few cynical superiors. You came to be a point man in a very complex power play developed by higher ups."[16] If the North and Poindexter convictions are negated because of the immunized testimony, no one may be held legally accountable for the events of Iran-Contra.

The incompatibility of political disputes with criminal investigations has been made clear in the Iran-Contra case. Choosing a legalistic approach to resolve disputes that at their core are political can thwart the very purpose of using a special prosecutor. Theodore Draper has suggested that the demands of the criminal justice process have resulted in a dissatisfying resolution to the Iran-Contra case. The special prosecutor was forced to frame narrowly the charges against North and Poindexter in order to maximize the likelihood of conviction. The problem with focusing the cases on the charges of misleading Congress is that, while serious, "it is only a small part of the larger story."[17] About the 1990 trial of John Poindexter, Draper writes:

Like its predecessors, it was an exercise in public relations more than a serious examination of the forces that brought about the breach of trust on the highest levels of government. At a time of the Reagan Administration's greatest crises, the independent counsel was appointed to stave off a potential threat of impeachment and to appease public dismay. Once launched, the legal process took on a life of its own and became excessively "legal" in order to get convictions on any grounds that could stand up in court.[18]

Consequently, Draper concludes, the "main offenses against responsible constitutional government—offenses that were part of the operations themselves" have been subordinated to peripheral allegations more easily prosecutable.[19] The legalistic approach then can divert our attention from profound constitutionally important questions that underlie these cases but that are not easily accessible through the legal process.

The problems inherent in the legalistic approach can also be found in efforts to deal with the gray area of unethical but not criminal behavior. Experience with the Ethics Act suggests that with allegations of ambiguous ethical violations, appointment of an independent counsel may in the end do little to uphold ethical standards for public officials. By turning such allegations over to an officer whose jurisdiction is restricted to criminal matters, a full and open debate about the behavior is stifled. The central question of "ethical fitness" is lost to a discussion of whether the target is a criminal or not. If the goal of the ethics legislation is to raise, or at least to maintain, the standards to which we hold our public officials, adopting a standard of "criminal/not criminal" as opposed to "ethical/not ethical" is a step in the wrong direction. The criminal standard may be the easier solution to legislate but far more careful thought ought to go into the consequences of criminalization before this lower standard is adopted.

THE INSTITUTIONALIZATION OF DISTRUST

The special prosecutor is a reflection of the distrust among elites in post-Watergate Washington. At the root of the special prosecutor arrangement lies a distrust of the political process as it traditionally operates. It assumes that in cases involving officials of the executive branch the traditional operations of government will not suffice to handle the case. There are several dangers in this approach that can have far-reaching implications for American politics. It institutionalizes distrust of the Department of Justice, and most particularly, the attorney general, the chief law enforcement officer in the land. It suggests that the agency charged with the enforcement of the laws of the land cannot be trusted to enforce those laws against its colleagues. The spillover effect of such an assumption cannot be measured but surely exists. To what extent can we trust this individual and his agency in other areas of law enforcement?

The arrangement also institutionalizes irresponsibility on the part of the president and the Senate in the process of nomination and confirmation of attorneys general. What difference does it make who the attorney general is if we are going to begin with the assumption that he or she cannot be trusted? With a special prosecutor mechanism in place, poor choices will matter less because there is a way to remove these cases from the attorney general's jurisdiction. This creates a vicious cycle wherein poor choices for attorney general (and other executive appointments as well) make it more likely that a special prosecutor will be needed which in turn reinforces the idea that one is always needed, and so on. Over a period of time in which frequent resort to a special prosecutor occurs, the existence of the arrangement could do more to undermine public confidence in government than to build it. In the meantime, the Senate and the president avoid responsibility for making thoughtful choices in nomination and confirmation. The special prosecutor is there to clean up the mistakes.

The institutionalization of distrust and irresponsibility leads to the overuse of an independent counsel. There are few cases in which an independent investigation is demanded. In those few cases, it is highly likely that an independent investigator would be appointed, even without a statutory requirement. The existence of a statutory requirement encourages a habit of resort to special prosecutions that only further aggravates distrust of the department.

SUGGESTIONS FOR REFORM

This accounting of the strengths and weaknesses of the special prosecutor arrangement suggests that it is an occasionally useful, but overused, approach to dealing with allegations of official misconduct. In the next reauthorization the provisions should be reformed in a way that reduces the likelihood of their use but makes them available for those few cases where the situation demands independent investigation. Reform of this type should follow three avenues. First, there should be an effort to define the categories of cases where a special prosecutor is clearly needed. Second, the attorney general should be given greater discretion to decline appointment of special prosecutors but with added accountability measures so that that decisionmaking process is on the record. Finally, the oversight and reauthorization provisions in the legislation should be maintained.

Categories of Coverage

There are two changes that ought to be made in the coverage of the special prosecutor provisions. The number of executive branch officers covered and the types of behavior requiring investigation should be reduced. The result should be a reduction in the likelihood that the mechanism will be triggered.

Covered Officials. There are two groups of officials who should be covered under a statutory special prosecutor arrangement. Their inclusion is based upon their relationship to the officers in the Department of Justice who would be charged with investigating and prosecuting them or upon their relationship to the president or attorney general. In this sense, this recommended change would both narrow and broaden the reach of the statute. It would narrow it in the sense that it would eliminate many of the executive officers now covered by the act. It would broaden coverage in the sense that it might include persons not presently covered because of their official status inside or outside of government.

The first category of covered officials should be those who bear ultimate responsibility for law enforcement and to whom department investigators must ultimately answer. This would include the president, the vice president, and the attorney general and his immediate subordinates who are politically appointed. It would be extremely difficult for lower level career officials in the department to investigate, and perhaps prosecute, these officials. There is the greatest likelihood of real conflict of interest in these cases and of endangering public confidence by keeping investigation within the department. As the Watergate case revealed, in the rare cases where there is real criminal misconduct by one of these officials there is also the greatest opportunity for the use of power to obstruct justice. This category would eliminate other cabinet officials and their political appointees except in those cases where they fall into the next category.

A second category of coverage should include individuals both inside and outside of government who have close personal relationships with the covered officials listed above. This category will in all likelihood cover many of the top White House aides who have worked with the president during his campaign and in many cases through most of his career. It might in some cases include members of the president's family. It should include those officials or private individuals who have relationships with the president, vice president, or attorney general that are so close as to make it very difficult for the executive branch law enforcement agencies to investigate or prosecute with impartiality. The danger of adding this category is that it might encourage greater, less responsible use of the arrangement. Consequently, it is important that the behaviors covered also be narrowed and that the attorney general be granted increased discretion in triggering.

A further reform frequently advocated is to include Congress in the coverage of the act. When we consider the purposes of the provisions and the problems with their usage with those now covered, it makes little sense to argue that coverage should be extended to Congress. It would be very difficult to make the argument that a conflict of interest, either real or apparent, exists when the executive branch investigates the legislative branch. History suggests that the Department of Justice has been able to do so with much success. In addition, it is ironic that the calls for extended coverage come from opponents of the act.[20] If the act is flawed, it does not make sense to create opportunities for increased use. The call for congressional coverage is more likely motivated by the belief that if Congress were subjected to the act, it would not last long. If so, this is a disingenuous and contradictory approach to abolishing the provisions.

Covered Behaviors. There are several categories of official misconduct, and not all of them require criminal investigation and prosecution. Although the act only requires appointment for allegations of violations of the criminal law, all four of these categories can be found among the allegations that prompted appointment of Ethics Act prosecutors. There are significant differences among the cases both in terms of the kinds of behavior in question and in the "victims" of that behavior. The four categories can be labeled institutional boundary struggles, traditional public corruption cases, unethical but not criminal behavior, and ordinary crimes. Consideration of appointment of a special prosecutor should depend upon (1) whether or not the official is covered in the two categories listed above and (2) whether or not the behavior involves allegations best suited to resolution through the process of criminal investigation and prosecution. When these categories of officials converge with this category of behaviors, it is likely that independent investigation will be needed both to remove conflict of interest and to reassure the public and elites that impartial investigation will occur. In the other categories, there are alternative mechanisms to sanction the wrongdoer without encountering the problems identified in the case against the special prosecutor. In particular, alternative sanctioning mechanisms can reduce the problems of competing institutional interests, the institutionalization of distrust, and the costs inherent in a legalistic approach to official misconduct.

Cases arising out of struggles between the separate institutions of American government are the most problematic for the labeling of criminal behavior, and consequently, for effective investigation and prosecution. Further, the category of institutional boundary struggles raises provocative questions of how to identify the victim of such constitutional struggles. When the boundaries of a particular branch's powers are ambiguous, as they clearly are in our constitutional system, it becomes extremely difficult to identify certain actions taken by one of the branches (or its representatives acting in their official capacity) as "criminal." In a system as open to interpretation as ours, criminalizing boundary struggles may well have the undesirable effect of imposing rigidity on a relatively flexible system. To the extent that we value that flexibility and find the ambiguity useful for adaptation, we should avoid rigid codification of the powers of each branch in order to punish official misconduct of this type. There are alternative mechanisms for resolving these struggles that are embodied in the system of checks and balances.

In fact, these means of resolution are suggested by identification of the primary victim of this kind of misconduct. The most immediate harm in abuse of constitutional power is done to the opposing institution whose powers are encroached upon. Making use of the institutional means available for resisting that encroachment, or appeal to the Supreme Court as the referee of these disputes, seems the more desirable solution to these conflicts. The public is harmed to the extent that constitutional principles are violated, but this harm is extremely diffuse in cases where the dispute is over the proper interpretation of those constitutional principles. The appointment of an independent investigator whose powers are limited to criminal investigation and prosecution hardly seems the appropriate remedy. Full public exposure and debate, best gained through such means as congressional or special commission hearings, are more desirable ways to air differences over the use of powers in the political system. Essentially political problems are best solved with political means.

Traditional public corruption laws (including those against bribery, fraud, perjury, and obstruction of justice by public officials), while by no means easy to enforce,[21] have existed long enough to have a tradition that ensures that prosecutors are not entering uncharted waters. This category involves actions taken while in the capacity of public official but for private gain or advantage. Studies suggest that there is a fairly widespread consensus that actions of this type should be treated as criminal.[22] The victim of such crimes, the public, justifies sanction by the government, and when the case involves the officials listed above, independent investigation and prosecution. Criminalizing this behavior and prosecuting it in a way that insures public confidence in the outcome serves important values in a democratic society. In addition to serving the ideal of equal justice under law, "criminal punishment is both specific and severe in condemning, on behalf of the democratic community, the violation of shared standards of public office."[23]

The line between traditional public corruption and unethical but not criminal behavior is not a clear one. The blurring occurs in efforts to find intent to commit crimes prohibited under traditional public corruption statutes, and particularly in the emerging area of regulating conflict of interest.[24] Consequently, an independent investigation may be triggered because there is potentially criminal behavior involved, but the investigation concludes that the actions do not meet the strict requirements of the relevant criminal statute. This situation is most likely to occur in efforts to enforce ethics legislation that is relatively new, lacks clearly defined categories of misconduct, and lacks a well-developed interpretation that comes with experience in enforcement. In this instance the costs of triggering a special prosecutor, both to the government and the defendant, should be weighed against the values to be gained or vindicated. The costs of such an investigation have been discussed previously. Most significant here is the lowering of the standards to which we hold our public officials. The fact that they are not criminals does not necessarily mean that they are ethically fit to hold public office, and criminal investigation encourages us to focus on the first question instead of the second.

Further, there is a lack of consensus on whether certain behaviors are indeed "wrong" and thus require vindication of the public trust. The difficulty of identifying the harm and the victim of such behavior contributes to this lack of consensus. For example, it appears that the public is more likely to disapprove of actions that cause physical rather than economic harm.[25] It has also been asserted that the American political economy and culture encourage, or at least condone, certain misconduct that may have negative economic or political consequences.[26] Some unethical political behavior is even more problematic in this regard because the harm done to public confidence and to democratic ideals is so difficult to identify and to measure. Because the lines are so difficult to draw, independent counsel investigations for ethical violations should be rare. When the criminality of such actions is unclear, appointment can have the undesirable effect of removing the potential for political "punishment" through the electorate or institutional sanctions such as refusal to confirm, forced resignation, or impeachment. The Office of Government Ethics, an independent executive agency created by the Ethics in Government Act, should be encouraged to play a greater role in checking for compliance with ethical standards and for sanctioning in administrative ways those who deviate from those standards.

"Ordinary Crimes" are encompassed in another category. These behaviors are usually the least difficult to identify, investigate, and prosecute for their definition is well established in American law. They also involve misconduct not related to the role of those accused as public servants or are not committed in an official capacity. For example, the allegations of cocaine use against Jordan and Kraft and the alleged organized crime activity of Donovan fall into this category. These cases should not prompt special prosecutor investigations. They should be handled through traditional law enforcement mechanisms and be subjected to the same treatment they would receive if an ordinary member of the public were the accused. The Jordan, Kraft, and Donovan cases illustrate why this is the most desirable approach. In the first two the targets were subjected to six-month grand jury investigations for allegations that would have been dropped without investigation had they been made against an average citizen. But once special prosecutors were appointed they felt that they had to conduct exhaustive investigations because of public expectations. Special prosecutor investigations in these kinds of cases create the clearest example of the dual standard of justice the provisions' opponents complain about. The goal of the legislation is supposed to be to ensure equal justice not stricter standards for public officials. The Donovan case illustrates other problems. The Department of Justice has a well-established division with experienced attorneys who deal exclusively with organized crime cases. They know who the players are and the way in which different cases interrelate. They make decisions all the time about which organized crime figures are worth pursuing and which are secondary players who might be useful as witnesses but who are not targets for prosecution. Interjecting into that ongoing investigative process an independent prosecutor with little experience in the investigation and prosecution of organized crime creates significant problems for the ongoing investigations and for the immediate special prosecutor investigation. Given these costs plus that fact that "ordinary crimes" usually do not involve violations of the public trust and are not committed by the person when acting in his or her official capacity, a special prosecutor investigation is not warranted.

Separating out the various kinds of official misconduct has several benefits. It can help to explain the problems encountered in the past by special prosecutors. It also demonstrates the way in which structural and definitional barriers can limit the effectiveness of criminal investigation and prosecution as a means to handle official misconduct allegations. Finally, a typology of official misconduct can aid in thinking about when an independent criminal investigation is a "necessary auxiliary precaution" in the political system and when alternative sanctioning mechanisms are more suitable. If we were to apply these new rules of coverage to the cases studied here, the number of cases would be reduced significantly and the focus of the Iran-Contra investigation would have been somewhat different. The Jordan, Kraft, Donovan, Olson, and first Meese cases would not have triggered the appointment of special prosecutors. The limitation on categories of behaviors covered would have simplified the Iran-Contra prosecutor's job. An insider's account of the investigation suggests that the criminal case against North on the obstruction of a congressional investigation was indictable prior to his public immunized testimony. The Office of Independent Counsel delayed the indictment in order to pursue the more difficult conspiracy charge (the criminality of which was far more ambiguous), thus risking what ultimately came to pass: the setting aside of the verdict because of the failure to show no use of immunized testimony.[27] While North, Secord, and Hakim do not per se fall into the group of covered officials, the case taken as a whole would nonetheless have triggered appointment of a special prosecutor because at least initially, the president, vice president, and attorney general were implicated. Once the potential parameters of the case indicate appointment of independent counsel, it makes sense to include other key actors subsumed in the case.

Attorney General's Discretion

Combined with the revision of coverage and categories of behavior should come a revision of the discretion given the attorney general. The attorney general should be empowered to make the decision about which of the above categories he believes are implicated in the allegations and to decline to seek appointment unless the case falls into the very narrow set of cases identified above. Congress should reconsider its decision to deny the department the power to subpoena witnesses in the initial investigation of the allegations. The department already has a significant "screening" role and the compulsory process would permit it to dispose of more cases without appointment of an independent counsel. It would help to avoid situations like the Jordan case where witnesses refused to speak to department investigators because they could not be forced to do so and because they anticipated an independent investigation. Since Congress has already made the decision to permit the department a substantial role in the triggering process, it makes sense to give the department the tools to make informed decisions about when an independent counsel is truly needed. It would protect the targets of investigations as well and save the money spent on unnecessary independent investigations.

However, should it expand the attorney general's role in the process, Congress should carefully review the implications of the court opinions declaring the attorney general's discretion to be unreviewable. The decisions are based, in part, on the reading of the legislative history that suggests Congress intended for no judicial review. Some limited judicial review should be considered for those few cases where a real conflict of interest may exist for the attorney general but in which he refuses to recuse himself or the department. With increased discretion should come increased accountability. The attorney general need not trigger the appointment as often, but he must be held accountable for that decision.

The frequency of appointment could still be reduced if Congress were to follow another course of action that requires no legislation. During the first years after the Watergate affair and in early consideration of reform in response to the scandal, there was much discussion of the need to depoliticize the Department of Justice and especially the position of attorney general. There was regular reference to the problem of presidents selecting close personal advisers or campaign officials for the post and the consequences of this for public and elite confidence in the department. The Senate can act on that concern by raising the standards by which it evaluates nominees for attorney general. The chief law enforcement officer in the country has at least as much impact on the development of the law as an individual justice on the Supreme Court, and yet the Senate treats nominees for the position with no more seriousness than it does nominees for other cabinet offices. It should reconsider this approach. A vote for confirmation of a nominee for attorney general should be a vote of confidence in the integrity of that person. It should be an implicit statement that the Senate trusts this person to take care that the laws are faithfully executed and to remove himself from cases where he or the department has a conflict of interest. If the Senate is not confident of that, then it ought not to confirm the nominee. Presidents, too, should see it as in the interest of their administration to nominate individuals with a reputation for integrity in the legal profession. It is possible to find people who are both ideologically compatible (so that one's policy direction will be pursued) and have a reputation that will inspire confidence among partisan opponents. This kind of responsible appointment process, already permitted and expected under the Constitution, would go a long way toward reducing the pressure for use of the special prosecutor mechanism.

Maintaining Oversight Provisions

During the 1987 reauthorization process, some supporters of the provisions argued that the statute should be permanently authorized rather than being subjected to review every five years. The reauthorization process should continue; it has been the major impetus for study of the effectiveness of the provisions, for the airing of problems in implementation, and for oversight of the Department of Justice's enforcement of the act. Congressional overseers and outside interest groups admit that their oversight activities have hinged on that process. Removing the reauthorization requirement reduces significantly the likelihood of any meaningful oversight of the provisions and would have at least three negative consequences. It would reduce one of the few formal checks on the powers of both the special prosecutor and the attorney general. It would make less likely the correction of any problems in implementation that might arise. For example, the first reauthorization process corrected the triggering mechanism that resulted in the appointment of special prosecutors in the Jordan and Kraft cases. Finally, it would be far less likely that the arrangement will ever be abolished. As the memory of Watergate fades from the collective memory of those in government, an arrangement of this type may no longer be needed. If it outlives its usefulness, it should be eliminated. Regular reauthorization encourages regular reassessment of its importance. That sort of consideration ought to be encouraged.

CONCLUSIONS

In his famous justification for the Constitution's system of separation of powers, James Madison wrote: "It may be a reflection on human nature that such devices should be necessary to control the abuses of government. But what is government itself but the greatest of all reflections on human nature? . . . A dependence on the people is, no doubt, the primary control on the government; but experience has taught mankind the necessity of auxiliary precautions."[28]

The wisdom of this statement still resonates today. It is no coincidence that supporters of the provisions referred to this statement in their endorsement of the special prosecutor mechanism. It provides for us a useful way to close this study of the use of special prosecutors because the issues it raises are at the core of the debate about the arrangement. Is it a necessary "auxiliary precaution" in a world where men are not angels and where the people are not always a sufficient check against the abuse of power by those in government? Or is it rather an unnecessary device that ignores the "auxiliary precautions" already embodied in the structure of government? Experience with the use of special prosecutors suggests that there is some truth to both contentions, although the latter is closest to the truth.

The checks and balances of the American system are in most cases adequate for the exposure and disposal of official misconduct cases. The competing institutional interests, the dispersal of power, the influence of nongovernmental elites, a free press, and the potential power of public opinion all work to ensure that the abuse of power by public officials will not go unnoticed for long. In this sense, Watergate and its resolution appears as the classic Madisonian event. The Congress, the press, political activists, and ultimately, the public, joined forces to end the abuse of power. The Watergate special prosecutor, a product of this system, served as the symbol of the rule of law, the value to be upheld in this constitutional crisis.

In the end, "the system worked." But it worked at great cost, especially to the psyche of Washington's elite both inside and outside of government. The problem with these checking mechanisms of American government is that they can take a long time to work, they can be messy, and they require a level of responsible action by the various players that seems increasingly difficult to sustain in modern American politics. It is for these reasons that we have resorted to the use of a new "auxiliary precaution." It is neater, faster, and less difficult for government officials, nongovernmental elites, and the public to resort to this arrangement. But it is not the panacea for our problems nor is it without costs. In the final evaluation of its usage, it is important that both the costs and benefits be recognized. When we do that we should see that we have relied far too frequently on the special prosecutor and far too infrequently on auxiliary precautions already available for the resolution of official misconduct cases.

NOTES

CHAPTER I. THE SPECIAL PROSECUTOR
AND THE SEPARATION OF POWERS

1. James Madison, Alexander Hamilton, and John Jay, *The Federalist Papers* (New York: New American Library, 1961), p. 322.

2. Ibid.

3. 28 U.S.C. 591-598 (Public Law 95-521) (1978). See U.S., Congress, Senate, Committee on Governmental Affairs, *The Ethics in Government Act of 1978*. S. Rept. 95-170, March 16, 1977, reprinted in *U.S. Code Congressional and Administrative News*, 95th Cong., 2d sess., 1978 (St. Paul, Minn.: West Publishing Co., 1979), p. 4220, for reference to Madison.

4. The provisions permit the judicial panel responsible for appointment to determine whether or not the request for appointment, the appointment itself, and/or the final report should be made public. 28 U.S.C. 593(b)(4); 594(h)(2)(1987). There have been at least two cases in which an appointment was not made public. Interview with Judge George E. MacKinnon, Washington, D.C., July 17, 1989; U.S., Congress, Senate, Committee on Governmental Affairs, *Independent Counsel Reauthorization Act of 1987*, S. Rept. 100-123, 100th Cong., 1 sess., July 24, 1987, p. 7.

5. Herbert Jacob, *Law and Politics in the United States* (Boston: Little, Brown, 1986), p. 1.

6. Ibid.

7. George F. Cole, *The American System of Criminal Justice*, 4th ed. (Monterey, Calif.: Brooks Cole, 1986), p. 27.

8. Ibid.

9. Studies of the operation of prosecutors' offices that note the way in which prosecutorial decisionmaking is influenced by other actors in the legal and political systems include James Eisenstein, *Counsel for the United States: U.S. Attorneys in the Political and Legal Systems* (Baltimore: Johns Hopkins University Press, 1978); and George F. Cole, "The Decision to Prosecute," *Law and Society Review* 4 (1970): 313-43.

10. C. Vann Woodward, ed., *Responses of the Presidents to Charges of Misconduct* (New York: Delacorte Press, 1974).

11. "The Special Prosecutor in the Federal System: A Proposal," *American Criminal Law Review* 11 (Spring 1977): 577-638.

12. There are a number of books on Dewey's career. See Barry Beyer, *Thomas E. Dewey, 1937-1947: A Study in Political Leadership* (New York: Garland, 1979); Richard Norton Smith, *Thomas E. Dewey and His Times* (New York: Simon and Schuster, 1982); and Stanley Walker, *Dewey, An American of This Century* (New York: McGraw-Hill, 1944).

13. Maurice H. Nadjari, "New York State's Office of Special Prosecutor: A Creation Born of Necessity," *Hofstra Law Review* 2 (1974): 97-124.

14. "Special Prosecutor's Office Is Topic of Continuing Debate in Maryland," *Washington Post*, April 15, 1984, p. C1.

15. Burt Noggle, *Teapot Dome: Oil and Politics in the 1920's* (Baton Rouge: Louisiana State University Press, 1962), pp. 80–115; C. Vann Woodward, ed., *Responses of the Presidents*, pp. 279–84.

16. Woodward, *Responses of the Presidents*, pp. 339–41; Newbold Morris, *Let the Chips Fall: My Battles with Corruption* (New York: Appleton-Century-Crofts, 1955).

17. Arthur Christy, *Report of the Special Prosecutor on Alleged Possession of Cocaine by Hamilton Jordan in Violation of 21 U.S.C. Sec. 844(a)*, New York, May 28, 1980; Gerald Gallinghouse, *In Re Investigations of Allegations Concerning Timothy E. Kraft: Report of Special Prosecutor in Compliance with 28 U.S.C. 595(b)*, New Orleans, January 15, 1982.

18. Interview with Leon Silverman, New York, September 25, 1984; Leon Silverman, *Report of the Special Prosecutor*, Washington, D.C., June 25, 1982.

19. In the first amendments to the provisions the name was changed to "independent counsel." However, the position is still commonly referred to as the "special prosecutor." The names are used interchangeably throughout this work.

20. Telephone interview with Jacob Stein, Washington, D.C., May 2, 1985; Jacob Stein, *Report of Independent Counsel Concerning Edwin Meese III*, Washington, D.C., September 20, 1984; Nadine Cohadas, "Meese Is Confirmed by Senate in Unusual Saturday Session," *Congressional Quarterly Weekly Report* 43 (March 2, 1985): 385.

21. Interviews with James McKay and Carol Bruce (deputy independent counsel), Washington, D.C., July 13, 1989; James McKay, *Report of Independent Counsel in Re Edwin Meese III*, Washington, D.C., July 5, 1988.

22. U.S., Congress, House, Committee on the Judiciary, *Report on the Investigation of the Role of the Department of Justice in the Withholding of Environmental Protection Agency Documents from Congress in 1982–1983*, 98th Cong., 1st sess., 1985.

23. *Morrison v. Olson*, 487 U.S. 654 (1988).

24. Interview with Alexia Morrison, Washington, D.C., July 14, 1989; Alexia Morrison, *In Re Theodore B. Olson and Robert M. Perry: Report of the Independent Counsel* (Washington, D.C.: December 27, 1988).

25. Telephone interview with Whitney North Seymour, November 30, 1989.

26. *Report of the Congressional Committees Investigating the Iran-Contra Affair*, abridged ed. (New York: Times Books, 1988). See especially pp. 266–68 for discussion of Meese's inquiry.

27. Office of Independent Counsel, *Fact Sheet*, September 1989; Lawrence Walsh, *Independent Counsel's Report to the Subcommittee on Legislation of the Permanent Select Committee on Intelligence of the U.S. House of Representatives*, September 19, 1989 (photocopies of each obtained from Office of Independent Counsel). In this testimony Walsh explains the effect of national security concerns on his ability to pursue some of the charges involved in the scandal.

28. *United States v. North*, 910 F.2d 843 (D.C. Cir. 1990).

29. Interview with McKay and Bruce; *United States v. Nofziger*, 878 F.2d 442 (D.C. Cir. 1989).

30. Jill Zuckerman, "Former HUD Secretary Pierce Faces Special Prosecutor," *Congressional Quarterly Weekly Report* 48 February 3, 1990: 331.

31. Justice Scalia, dissenting in *Morrison v. Olson*, 487 U.S. 654 (1988), makes this argument (pp. 697–734). See also the opinion of former Attorney General William French Smith in the first reauthorization hearings (U.S., Congress, Senate, Committee on Governmental Affairs, *Special Prosecutor Provisions of the Ethics in*

Government Act of 1978, Hearing Before the Subcommittee on Oversight of Government Management, 97th Congress, 1st sess., 1981, p. 3). This argument was also used in opposition to the original provisions. See for example Howard H. Baker, "The Proposed Judicially Appointed Independent Office of Public Attorney: Some Constitutional Objections and an Alternative," *Southwestern Law Journal* 29 (1975): 671-83.

32. See for example, U.S., Congress, Senate, Committee on Governmental Affairs, *Ethics in Government Act Amendments of 1982, Hearings before the Subcommittee on Oversight of Government Management*, 97th Congress, 2d sess., 1982, pp. 63-85; and Donald J. Simon, "The Constitutionality of the Special Prosecutor Law," *University of Michigan Journal of Law Reform* 16 (1982): 45-73.

33. Senate, *Special Prosecutor Provisions (1981)*, pp. 6-9; William French Smith, "Independent Counsel Provisions of the Ethics in Government Act," in L. Gordon Crovitz and Jeremy A. Radkin, eds., *The Fettered Presidency: Legal Constraints on the Executive Branch*, p. 257 (Washington, D.C.: American Enterprise Institute, 1989); interview with Theodore Olson, Washington, D.C., October 15, 1990.

34. Senate, *Special Prosecutor Provisions* (1981), p. 6-9; Smith, "Independent Counsel Provisions," pp. 257-59.

35. Smith, "Independent Counsel Provisions," p. 254; "Caught in a Web of Politics, Power," *Insight*, June 5, 1989, p. 13; *Sen. Report 100-123*, pp. 34-35.

36. Senate, *Independent Counsel Reauthorization Act of 1987*, pp. 33-34; Smith, "Independent Counsel Provisions," p. 253; Olson interview. Several defense attorneys in independent counsel investigations discussed what they perceived as the lack of constraints on the independent counsel. Some prefer to remain anonymous. Others include E. Lawrence Barcella and Robert Plotkin (attorneys for Lynn Nofziger), Washington, D.C., June 30, 1989.

37. Nadine Cohodas, "The Special Prosecutor as Special Protector," *Congressional Quarterly Weekly Report* 43 (March 2, 1985): 423.

38. Mark Bertozzi, "The Federal Special Prosecutor: Too Special?" *Federal Bar News and Journal* 29 (1982): 222-30.

39. Senate, *Special Prosecutor Provisions* (1981); Senate, *Independent Counsel Reauthorization Act of 1987*, p. 5; interview with Robert Evans, Washington, D.C., June 27, 1989; interview with Marcy Frosh and Mike Mawby, Common Cause, October 17, 1989.

40. Interviews with Evans, Frosh, and Mawby; interviews with Elise Bean and Mary Gerwin, Subcommittee on Oversight of Government Management, Washington, D.C., July 14 and 17, 1989.

41. Ibid. This argument was also made by a number of the independent counsel and their staff.

42. Clinton Rossiter, "Introduction," to *The Federalist Papers* (New York: New American Library, 1961), pp. xiv-xv. These arguments are most concisely represented in Federalist papers No. 10 and No. 51.

43. Ibid., p. 325.

44. All of Louis Fisher's books have the concept of shared powers as a central thesis. See especially *The Politics of Shared Power: Congress and the Executive* , 2d ed. (Washington, D.C.: Congressional Quarterly Press, 1987).

45. Fisher, *Shared Power*; Ann Stuart Anderson, "A 1787 Perspective on Separation of Powers," in Robert A. Goldwin and Art Kaufman, eds., *Separation of Powers—Does It Still Work?* (Washington, D.C.: American Enterprise Institute, 1986), pp. 138-67.

46. Anderson, "A 1787 Perspective," p. 156.

47. See for example the majority opinions in *INS v. Chadha*, 462 U.S. 919 (1983), and *Bowsher v. Synar*, 478 U.S. 714 (1986), and Scalia's dissent in *Morrison v. Olson*. See also Crovitz and Rabkin, *The Fettered Presidency*, and Gordon S. Jones and John A. Marini, eds., *The Imperial Congress: Crisis in the Separation of Powers* (New York: Pharos Books, 1988), pp. 239-67. These collections of essays have as their theme (with several exceptions) this more formalistic view of the doctrine.

48. When we examine the bulk of the Court's opinions regarding separation of powers this more flexible view is clearly dominant causing *Chadha* and *Bowsher* to appear to be aberrations in doctrinal development. See for example *Humphrey's Executor v. United States*, 295 U.S. 602 (1935); *Youngstown Sheet and Tube v. Sawyer*, 343 U.S. 579 (1952); *United States v. Nixon*, 418 U.S. 683 (1974); *Morrison v. Olson*; and *Mistretta v. United States*, 488 U.S. 361 (1989).

49. See for example Louis Fisher, *President and Congress* (New York: Free Press, 1972); *Shared Power; Constitutional Conflicts between Congress and the President*, 3d ed., revised (Lawrence: University Press of Kansas, 1991); *Constitutional Dialogues* (Princeton, N.J.: Princeton University Press, 1988); and Henry Merry, *Five Branch Government* (Urbana: University of Illinois Press, 1980).

50. *McCulloch v. Maryland*, 17 U.S. (4 Wheat) 315 (1819).

51. Fisher, *Shared Power* and *Constitutional Conflicts*.

52. Stephen L. Carter, "The Beast that Might Not Exist: Some Speculations on the Constitution and the Independent Regulatory Agencies," in Burke Marshall, ed., *A Workable Government? The Constitution After 200 Years* (New York: W.W. Norton, 1987), p. 76. Carter discusses the impact of the New Deal, particularly the vast expansion of the administrative state, on the formal doctrine of separation of powers. It should be noted that Carter does not view this fundamental transformation as a positive development.

53. Fisher, *Shared Power*, p. ix.

54. Ibid., p. 18.

55. In addition to the attention paid the constitutional debate in the previously cited hearings, it has received extensive coverage in legal literature. See for example Baker, "Constitutional Objections," (1975); "Special Prosecutor in the Federal System"; "Removing Politics from the Justice Department: Constitutional Problems with Institutional Reform," *New York University Law Review* 50 (1975): 366-435; Lloyd Cutler, "A Proposal for a Continuing Public Prosecutor," *Hastings Constitutional Law Quarterly* 2 (1975): 21-25; Frank M. Tuerkheimer, "The Executive Investigates Itself," *California Law Review* 65 (1977): 597-635; Victor Kramer and Louis P. Smith, "The Special Prosecutor Act: Proposals for 1983," *Minnesota Law Review* 66 (1982): 963-96; Constance O'Keefe and Peter Safirstein, "Fallen Angels, Separation of Powers, and the Saturday Night Massacre: An Examination of the Practical, Constitutional, and Political Tensions in the Special Prosecutor Provisions of the Ethics in Government Act," *Brooklyn Law Review* 49 (Fall 1982): 113-47; Simon, "Constitutionality of the Special Prosecutor Law," (1982); Charles Tiefer, "The Constitutionality of Independent Officers as Checks on Abuses of Executive Power," *Boston University Law Review* 63 (January 1983): 59-103; and Carl Levin, "The Independent Counsel Statute: A Matter of Public Confidence and Constitutional Balance," *Hofstra Law Review* 16 (Fall 1987): 11-22.

CHAPTER 2. AD HOC APPOINTMENT OF SPECIAL PROSECUTORS

1. Morton Keller, "Corruption in America: Continuity and Change," in *Before Watergate: Problems of Corruption in American Society*, ed. Abraham S. Eisen-

stadt, Ari Hoogenboom, and Hans L. Trefousse (New York: Brooklyn College Press, 1978), pp. 7-34; and Larry L. Berg, Harlan Hahn, and John R. Schmidhauser, *Corruption in the American Political System* (Morristown, N.J.: General Learning Press, 1976), pp. 1-30.

2. See for example C. Vann Woodward, ed., *Responses of the Presidents to Charges of Misconduct* (New York: Delacorte Press, 1974); and Blair Bolles, *Men of Good Intentions: Crisis of the American Presidency* (Garden City, N.Y.: Doubleday, 1960).

3. Berg, Hahn, and Schmidhauser, *Corruption*; Eisenstadt, Hoogenboom and Trefousse, *Before Watergate*; Jarol B. Manheim, *Déjà Vu: American Political Problems in Historical Perspective* (New York: St. Martin's Press, 1976); Jack D. Douglas and John M. Johnson, eds., *Official Deviance: Readings in Malfeasance, Misfeasance, and Other Forms of Corruption* (Philadelphia: J. B. Lippincott, 1977).

4. In each of the three ad hoc appointments there was a congressional request, in some form, made to the president for a special prosecutor investigation. However, the president was not legally required to grant that request.

5. Burt Noggle, *Teapot Dome: Oil and Politics in the 1920's* (Baton Rouge: Louisiana State University Press, 1962), p. 22.

6. Ibid., pp. 42-49. *Senate Resolution 282*, 67th Cong., 2d sess., 29 April 1922, and *Senate Resolution 294*, 67th Cong., 2d sess. The first resolution requested information on the leases and authorized the committee to investigate those leases. The second amended the first, authorizing the committee to subpoena witnesses, require production of documents, employ counsel and expert help, and cite noncooperating witnesses with contempt. Atlee Pomerene Papers, Teapot Dome files, Box 1, National Archives, Washington, D.C.

7. Noggle, *Teapot Dome*, pp. 51-63.

8. Ibid., p. 91.

9. Ibid., pp. 91-115.

10. Ibid., pp. 117-27, 210-11. See also Pomerene Papers, Owen Roberts Papers, Teapot Domes files, National Archives; and Department of Justice files (Box 107), in Teapot Dome files. U.S., Congress, Senate, Committee on Public Lands and Surveys, *Leases Upon Naval Oil Reserves*, 68th Cong., 1st sess., 1923.

11. U.S., Congress, House, Ways and Means Committee, *Final Report of the Subcommittee on Administration of Revenue Laws*, 82d Cong., 2d sess., 1952; Committee on the Judiciary, *Investigation of the Department of Justice: Hearings before the Special Subcommittee to Investigate the Justice Department*, 82d Cong., 2d sess., 1952.

12. See Harold F. Gosnell, *Truman's Crises: A Political Biography of Harry S. Truman* (Westport, Conn.: Greenwood Press, 1980), pp. 498-499; Robert H. Ferrell, *Harry S. Truman and the Modern American Presidency* (Boston: Little, Brown, 1983), pp. 143-44.

13. Ferrell, *Truman and the Modern Presidency*, p. 144.

14. Robert J. Donovan, *Tumultuous Years: The Presidency of Harry S. Truman, 1949-1953* (New York: W. W. Norton, 1982), p. 377.

15. Gosnell, *Truman's Crises*, p. 501; Newbold Morris, *Let the Chips Fall: My Battles with Corruption* (New York: Appleton-Century Crofts, 1955), pp. 14-15. A copy of the questionnaire can be found in the back of Morris's book, pp. 297-308.

16. Ferrell, *Truman and the Modern Presidency*, p. 144.

17. See Watergate Special Prosecution Force (WSPF), *Report* (Washington, D.C., 1975), pp. 155-66.

18. Richard Ben-Veniste and George Frampton, Jr., *Stonewall: The Real Story of the Watergate Prosecution* (New York: Simon and Schuster, 1977); Charles Colson, *Born Again* (Old Tappan, N.J.: Chosen Books, 1976); Samual Dash, *Chief Counsel: Inside the Ervin Committee—The Untold Story of Watergate* (New York: Random House, 1976); John W. Dean, *Blind Ambition: The White House Years* (New York: Simon and Schuster, 1976); Maureen Dean, *"Mo": A Woman's View of Watergate* (New York: Simon and Schuster, 1975); James Doyle, *Not above the Law: The Battles of Watergate Prosecutors Cox and Jaworski* (New York: William Morrow, 1977); John Erlichman, *Witness to Power: the Nixon Years* (New York: Simon and Schuster, 1982); Samuel Ervin, *The Whole Truth: The Watergate Conspiracy* (New York: Random House, 1980); H. R. Haldeman, *The Ends of Power* (New York: Times Books, 1978); Leon Jaworski, *The Right and the Power: The Prosecution of Watergate* (New York: Readers Digest Press, 1976); G. Gordon Liddy, *Will: The Autobiography of G. Gordon Liddy* (New York: St. Martin's Press, 1980); Jeb Stuart McGruder, *An American Life: One Man's Road to Watergate* (New York: Atheneum, 1974); James McCord, *A Piece of Tape: The Watergate Story, Fact and Fiction* (Rockville, Md.: Washington Media Sources, 1974); Richard Nixon, *RN: Memoirs of Richard Nixon* (New York: Grosset and Dunlap, 1978); John J. Sirica, *To Set the Record Straight: The Break-in, the Tapes, the Pardon* (New York: W. W. Norton, 1979); Fred Thompson, *At That Point in Time: The Inside Story of the Watergate Committee* (New York: Quadrangle/New York Times Books, 1975).

19. There are far too many books to list here. The most recent history of the scandal relies on documents not available in early accounts. See Stanley I. Kutler, *The Wars of Watergate* (New York: Alfred A. Knopf, 1990).

20. For day-by-day detailing of events throughout the Watergate affair see *Watergate and the White House: June 1972–July 1973*, Vol. 1 (1973); *July–December 1973*, Vol. 2 (1974); and *January–September 1974*, Vol. 3 (1974); all published by Facts on File in New York.

21. The account of the reporters' uncovering of the Watergate story is told in Carl Bernstein and Bob Woodward, *All the President's Men* (New York: Simon and Schuster, 1974).

22. Gladys Engel Lang and Kurt Lang, *The Battle for Public Opinion: The President, the Press, and the Polls during Watergate* (New York: Columbia University Press, 1983), pp. 26–43.

23. Ibid., pp. 96–109.

24. Jaworski had been offered the appointment in May when Richardson first sought a special prosecutor but he refused it, believing at that time that there was insufficient guarantee of independence. Leon Jaworski, "Oral Interviews with Leon Jaworski," typed transcript of a videotaped series of interviews conducted by Thomas L. Charlton (Waco, Tex.: Baylor University, 1982), pp. 448-52. See also Jaworski, *The Right and the Power*, pp. 1-7.

25. *United States v. Nixon*, 418 U.S. 683 (1974).

26. WSPF, *Report*, pp. 166–70.

27. "Establishing the Office of Watergate Special Prosecution Force," Executive Order No. 517-73, 38 Federal Register 14, 688 (1973); "Remarks of Acting Attorney General Robert Bork Announcing His Appointment of Leon Jaworski," *Weekly Compilation of Presidential Documents.* 9 (November 1, 1973): 1303; Executive Order No. 551-73, 38 Federal Register 30, 738 (1973) as amended by Executive Order No. 554-73, 38 Federal Register 32 805 (1973) (re-establishing the WSPF).

28. Ben-Veniste and Frampton, *Stonewall*, p. 16. See also note 24.

29. Interview with Archibald Cox, Cambridge, Mass., February 5, 1985.

30. WSPF, *Report*, p. 195.
31. Ibid., pp. 196–200.
32. Ibid., pp. 201–2.
33. Ibid.
34. Ibid., pp. 202–4.
35. Jaworski, *The Right and the Power*, pp. 5–6; Letter from Robert H. Bork, acting attorney general, to Leon Jaworski, November 21, 1973, Leon Jaworski Papers, Box 5, Texas Collection, Baylor University, Waco, Texas; letter of resignation to Attorney General Saxbe from Leon Jaworski, October 12, 1974, Jaworski Papers, Correspondence File 1.
36. WSPF, *Report*, p. 204.
37. Ibid., pp. 196, 201–2.
38. Ibid., pp. 190–94; Ben-Veniste and Frampton, *Stonewall*, pp. 24–31.
39. Jaworski, *The Right and the Power*; Ben-Veniste and Frampton, *Stonewall*; and Doyle, *Not above the Law*, provide the best evidence of these relationships. Additionally, the WSPF *Report*, as if anticipating such an analysis, devoted several sections to describing relationships with the U.S. attorneys' offices, the attorney general, the White House, the Congressional committees, the investigative agencies, and the press.
40. WSPF, *Report*, pp. 166–70.
41. Sirica, *To Set the Record Straight*, pp. 56–70.
42. Ibid., pp. 143–60.
43. *Nixon v. Sirica*, 487 F.2d 700 (D.C. Cir. 1973).
44. *United States v. Nixon*, 418 U.S. 683 (1974). See also WSPF, *Report*, pp. 92–115.
45. Sirica, *To Set the Record Straight*, p. 173.
46. Ibid., p. 176.
47. Jaworski, "Oral Interviews," p. 604.
48. Lang and Lang, *Battle for Public Opinion*, pp. 62–93; Edwin Diamond, "The Folks in the Boondocks: Challenging the Journalistic Myth," *Columbia Journalism Review* (November–December 1973): 58–59.
49. Dash, *Chief Counsel*, pp. 142–44.
50. Ibid., p. 124.
51. WSPF, *Report*, pp. 6–7.
52. Ibid., p. 205.
53. Ibid., p. 211.
54. Dash, *Chief Counsel*, p. 227.
55. U.S., Congress, Senate, Select Committee on Presidential Campaign Activities, *Final Report*, 93d Cong., 2d sess., 1974.
56. WSPF, *Report*, pp. 211–12.
57. Jaworski, "Oral Interviews," p. 559.
58. U.S., Congress, Senate Committee on the Judiciary, *Nomination of Elliot Richardson to be Attorney General*, 93d Cong., 1st sess., 1973, pp. 4, 146–60.
59. Elliot Richardson, "The Saturday Night Massacre," *Atlantic Monthly*, March 1976, p. 71.
60. WSPF, *Report*, p. 213.
61. Ibid.
62. Jaworski, *The Right and the Power*, pp. 124–25; A series of letters exchanged between Jaworski and St. Clair over this dispute can be found in Jaworski Papers, Box 5.

63. Letter from Leon Jaworski to James O. Eastland, May 20, 1974, Jaworski Papers, Box 5.

64. Letter from James O. Eastland to Attorney General William Saxbe, May 21, 1974, Jaworski Papers, Box 5.

65. WSPF, *Report*, p. 124.

66. Ibid., pp. 126–28; Jaworski, *The Right and the Power*, pp. 99–104; Jaworski, "Oral Interviews," pp. 624–27; Watergate Task Force, Prosecutive Report, January 7, 1974, Jaworski Papers, Box 6. A handwritten note on the table of contents of this report identifies it as the "Report of Grand Jury to be transmitted to the House Jud. Committee considering Articles of Impeachment." The report outlines Nixon's involvement in the cover-up.

67. Jaworski, "Oral Interviews," p. 559.

68. Ibid., p. 560.

69. Ibid.

70. Ibid., p. 1123.

71. Ibid., p. 561.

72. Jaworski, *The Right and the Power*, p. 42.

73. Ibid., pp. 42–43.

74. Jaworski, "Oral Interviews," p. 467.

75. Jaworski, *The Right and the Power*, p. 22.

76. Ibid., p. 43.

77. Ben-Veniste and Frampton, *Stonewall*, pp. 86–87.

78. Ibid., p. 89.

79. WSPF, *Report*, pp. 87–95.

80. Ben-Veniste and Frampton, *Stonewall*, p. 92.

81. Cox interview.

82. Jaworski, "Oral Interviews," p. 685.

83. Interview with George Frampton, Washington, D.C., October 19, 1984. Frampton, an assistant special prosecutor who worked on the Watergate cover-up case, recalls in a comparison of Cox and Jaworski, "There were differences in their personal style. Cox made no great effort to keep his own counsel. . . . But then, he didn't know at that time that he had the President. Jaworski did, and he tended to hold his cards closer to his chest."

84. Ben-Veniste and Frampton, *Stonewall*, p. 197.

85. Jaworski, "Oral Interviews," pp. 706–7. Jaworski pointed out, "Al Haig was not liked by a single member of my staff. There were several who would have liked to have found something to pin on Haig."

86. Jaworski, *The Right and the Power*, p. 4.

87. Ibid., pp. 5–7.

88. Ibid., pp. 23–25.

89. Jaworski refers twenty different times in his memoirs to meetings and phone calls between himself and Haig between the time of his appointment and Nixon's resignation. Several of these references are to regular and multiple contacts. It becomes obvious from reading *The Right and the Power* that the two were in regular contact throughout Jaworski's tenure.

90. Ibid., pp. 81–82.

91. Handwritten note, Jaworski Papers, Box 5.

92. Jaworski, *The Right and the Power*, pp. 129–32.

93. Ben-Veniste and Frampton, *Stonewall*, pp. 275–76.

94. Jaworski, *The Right and the Power*, p. 206.

95. Ibid., pp. 217–19.

96. Ben-Veniste and Frampton, *Stonewall*, pp. 291–96; Seymour M. Hersch, "The Pardon: Nixon, Ford, Haig, and the Transfer of Power," *The Atlantic*, August 1983, pp. 68–69.

97. Jaworski, *The Right and the Power*, pp. 217–19, 240–41; "Oral Interviews," pp. 1092–93.

98. See Lang and Lang, *Battle for Public Opinion* generally, and chapter 4, particularly pp. 44–61.

99. One of the best participant accounts of the operation of the WSPF, and especially of its press relations is Public Affairs Officer James Doyle's *Not above the Law*.

100. Jaworski Papers, Box 5 and Box 6.

101. WSPF, *Report*, pp. 227.

102. Ibid., pp. 228–29.

103. Ben-Veniste and Frampton, *Stonewall*, p. 44.

104. Ibid., pp. 86–87.

105. Cox interview.

106. Jaworski, "Oral Interviews," pp. 583–90.

107. Ibid., p. 587.

108. Ibid., pp. 585–86 (N.Y.T.), and pp. 597–98 (Safire).

109. WSPF, *Report*, p. 134.

CHAPTER 3. A WATERGATE LEGACY

1. John W. Kingdon, *Congressmen's Voting Decisions*, 2d ed. (New York: Harper and Row, 1981), p. 285. Kingdon says, "Once a matter is in the congressman's attention field, events may take place which have a powerful focusing effect."

2. "Opinion Roundup," *Public Opinion* (June–July 1981): 34.

3. James L. Sundquist, *The Decline and Resurgence of Congress* (Washington, D.C.: Brookings Institution, 1981).

4. This analysis is guided in particular by Kingdon, *Voting Decisions*; Randall B. Ripley, *Congress: Process and Policy*, 4th ed. (New York: W. W. Norton, 1988); and David R. Mayhew, *Congress: The Electoral Connection* (New Haven, Conn.: Yale University Press, 1974).

5. See for example Elliot Richardson, "The Saturday Night Massacre," *Atlantic*, March 1976, pp. 40–71; James Doyle, *Not above the Law: The Battles of Watergate Prosecutors Cox and Jaworski* (New York: William Morrow, 1977), pp. 163–223; Richard Ben-Veniste and George Frampton, Jr., *Stonewall: The Real Story of the Watergate Prosecution* (New York: Simon and Schuster, 1977); and Harvard Law School Program on the Legal Profession, *The Saturday Night Massacre* (Cambridge, Mass.: Harvard Law School, 1977).

6. "Statement by the President Announcing Resignations and Appointments, Together with Assignment of Responsibilities Regarding the Watergate Investigation," *Weekly Compilation of Presidential Documents* 9 (April 30, 1973): 431.

7. "Watergate Chronology of 1973," *Congressional Quarterly Almanac 1973* (Washington, D.C.: Congressional Quarterly, 1974), pp. 1014–43.

8. U.S., Congress, Senate, Committee on the Judiciary, *Nomination of Elliot Richardson to Be Attorney General*, 93d Cong., 1st sess., 1973, p. 4 (Richardson statement of intent to accept Senate Judiciary Committee approval of special prose-

cutor), and pp. 146–60 (Cox testimony). Richardson was confirmed by the Senate on May 23, 1973, by a vote of 82 to 3. *Congressional Record*, May 23, 1973, pp. 16749–56.

9. "Establishing the Office of Watergate Special Prosecution Force," *Attorney General Order No. 517-573*, May 31, 1973.

10. *Nixon v. Sirica*, 487 F.2d 700 (D.C. Cir. 1973).

11. The "Stennis Compromise," offered by Nixon, would have permitted Sen. John Stennis, an esteemed but aging and hard-of-hearing Democrat, to review the tapes, aided by transcripts prepared by the White House.

12. The WSPF was dissolved as an independent entity by Acting Attorney General Robert Bork. "Abolition of Office of Watergate Special Prosecution Force," *Attorney General Order No. 546-73*, October 23, 1973.

13. Ben-Veniste and Frampton, *Stonewall*, p. 150.

14. U.S., Congress, House, Committee on the Judiciary, *Special Prosecutor and Watergate Grand Jury Legislation, Hearings before the Subcommittee on Criminal Justice*, 93d Cong., 1st sess., 1973; and Senate, Committee on the Judiciary, *Special Prosecutor*, 93d Cong., 1st sess., 1973. House hearings were held between October 29 and November 8, 1973. Senate hearings began October 29 and ran until November 20, 1973.

15. *Congressional Record*, October 23, 1973, p. 34872.

16. Prepared statement of Rep. John C. Culver, House, Committee on the Judiciary, *Special Prosecutor and Grand Jury*, pp. 66–67.

17. Statement of Birch Bayh, *Congressional Record*, October 26, 1973, p. 35076.

18. "Remarks of Acting Attorney General Robert Bork Announcing His Appointment of Leon Jaworski," *Weekly Compilation of Presidential Documents* 9 (November 1, 1973): 1303.

19. Statement of Leon Jaworski, Senate, Committee on the Judiciary, *Special Prosecutor*, pp. 569–613; and House, Committee on the Judiciary, *Special Prosecutor and Grand Jury*, pp. 443–62. The WSPF was re-established by *Attorney General Order No. 551-73*, November 19, 1973.

20. Figure cited in U.S., Congress, Senate, Committee on the Judiciary, *Removing Politics from the Administration of Justice. Hearings before the Subcommittee on the Separation of Powers*. 93d Cong., 2d sess., 1974, p. 234.

21. Gladys Engel Lang and Kurt Lang, *The Battle for Public Opinion: The President, the Press, and the Polls during Watergate* (New York: Columbia University Press, 1983), pp. 241–46.

22. "Opinion Roundup," *Public Opinion* (June–July 1981): 34.

23. "More Confidence in Leadership," *Current Opinion* 5 (1977): 37. Data from a Harris survey conducted February 1–7, 1977, with a national sample of 1,522.

24. "Rating of Congress at All-Time Low," *Current Opinion* 2 (March 1974): 32. Data from a Harris survey conducted January 1974 with a national sample of 1594.

25. "Increase in Approval of Congress," *Current Opinion* 2 (October 1974): 119. Data from Gallup poll conducted August 16–19, 1974, with a national sample of 1,435.

26. "Congress's Popularity Lower than Ford's," *Current Opinion* 3 (April 1975): 34. Data from Gallup poll conducted February 28–March 3, 1975, with a national sample of 1,576.

27. "Priorities for New Congress," *Current Opinion* 4 (December 1976): 128. Data from Harris survey conducted August 1976 with a national sample of 1,532.

28. Sundquist, *Decline and Resurgence of Congress.*

29. Ibid., p. 2.

30. Ibid., p. 5.

31. Statement of John C. Anderson, *Congressional Record,* June 19, 1974, p. 19854. Sundquist mentions this speech in *Decline and Resurgence of Congress,* p. 6, note 19.

32. Ibid., p. 345. For in-depth discussion of each of these areas of resurgence see the following specific chapters in Sundquist: "War Powers," pp. 238-72; "Budget and Impoundment," pp. 199-237; "Foreign Policy," pp. 273-314; "Oversight," pp. 315-43; and "Legislative Veto," pp. 344-66.

33. Ripley, *Congress.*

34. See for example, Louis Fisher, *The Politics of Shared Power: Congress and the Executive* (Washington, D.C.: Congressional Quarterly, 1987), and *Constitutional Conflicts between Congress and the President* (Lawrence: University Press of Kansas, 1991).

35. This view was especially prevalent in the early hearings by the House and Senate judiciary committees following the Saturday Night Massacre. Sirica's refusal to believe that the Watergate burglars were telling the whole story contributed to the unraveling of the cover-up. See John Sirica, *To Set the Record Straight* (New York: W. W. Norton, 1979).

36. These arguments appeared in the hearings and in a number of law review articles published during consideration of the act. These include "The Special Prosecutor in the Federal System: A Proposal," *American Criminal Law Review* 11 (Spring 1973): 577-638; and "Removing Politics from the Justice Department: Constitutional Problems with Institutional Reform," *New York University Law Review* 50 (1975): 366-435.

37. Senate, Committee on the Judiciary, *Special Prosecutor,* p. 72.

38. Ibid., p. 73.

39. *In the Matter of Hennan,* 38 U.S. 230 (1834); *Ex Parte Siebold,* 100 U.S. 371 (1897); *United States v. Solomon,* 216 F.Supp. 835 (S.D.N.Y. 1963); *Hobson v. Hansen,* 265 F.Supp. 902 (D.D.C. 1967).

40. Senate, Committee on the Judiciary, *Removing Politics,* p. 84. Law review articles making the argument for executive power also appeared during congressional consideration. Luis Kutner, "Nixon v. Cox: Due Process of Executive Authority," *St. John's Law Review* 48 (March 1974): 441-60; Howard H. Baker, "The Proposed Judicially Appointed Independent Office of Public Attorney: Some Constitutional Objections and an Alternative," *Southwestern Law Journal* 29 (1975): 671-83; and Frank M. Tuerkheimer, "The Executive Investigates Itself," *California Law Review* 65 (1977): 597-635.

41. *Ponzi v. Fessenden,* 258 U.S. 244, (1922); *Springer v. Philippines,* 277 U.S. 189, (1928); *United States v. Cox,* 342 F.2d 167, 171 (5th Cir. 1965); *Newman v. United States,* 382 F.2d 479, (D.C. Cir. 1967). But see *Ex Parte Siebold,* and Louis Fisher, "Statutory History of Supervisors and U.S. Commissioners Responsible for Federal Elections (1870-1897)," Congressional Research Service memo to Michael Davidson, Senate Legal Counsel, February 25, 1988 (photocopy).

42. See Senate, Committee on the Judiciary, *Special Prosecutor,* pp. 37-38; Baker, "Proposed Public Attorney," pp. 679-81; Kutner, "Nixon v. Cox," pp. 451-56; and *United States v. Marzano,* 149 F.2d 923, 926 (2d Cir. 1945), which says, in part, that prosecution and judgment "are separate functions" that "must not merge." This case was cited by Judge Gesell in *Nader v. Bork,* 366 F.Supp. 104, 109 (D.D.C. 1973), the suit that challenged the firing of Cox. Gesell said that sugges-

tions that the judiciary appoint the special prosecutor were unfortunate because, "The Courts must remain neutral. Their duties are not prosecutorial."

43. Proposals ranged from terms of three years to fifteen years. Appointment schemes varied, some permitting presidential appointment and others requiring judicial appointment. All contained removal restrictions.

44. These views were particularly evident in testimony during hearings on the Watergate Reorganization and Reform Act of 1975, which proposed the establishment of a permanent office of public attorney. U.S., Congress, Senate, Committee on Government Operations, *Watergate Reorganization and Reform Act of 1975, Part I*, 94th Cong., 1st sess., 1975. See for example the statements of Senator Weicker, pp. 4–5; Senator Mondale, p. 5; Sam Dash, p. 86; and a letter from James Sundquist, p. 297.

45. Ibid., statements of Leon Jaworski, pp. 103–5; Henry Ruth, pp. 120–21; and letter from Peter Dingman, p. 219.

46. Interview with Robert Evans, Washington Office of the American Bar Association, Washington, D.C., October 16, 1984. See also Special Committee to Study Federal Law Enforcement Agencies, *Preventing Improper Influence on Federal Law Enforcement Agencies*, (Washington, D.C.: American Bar Association, 1976), pp. 18–20.

47. *Humphrey's Executor v. United States*, 295 U.S. 602 (1935).

48. *Myer's v. United States*, 272 U.S. 52 (1926).

49. Mayhew, *Electoral Connection*.

50. Ibid., p. 115.

51. Ibid., pp. 61–62.

52. Ibid., p. 71.

53. *Congress and the Nation*, Vol. 4 (Washington, D.C.: Congressional Quarterly, 1977), p. 8.

54. Ibid., p. 9.

55. Gerald Pomper et al., *The Election of 1976: Reports and Interpretations* (New York: David McKay, 1977), p. 87.

56. Ibid.

57. Statement by Senator Ervin, *Congressional Record*, December 11, 1974, pp. 39011–12.

58. U.S., Congress, Senate, Select Committee on Presidential Campaign Activities, *Final Report*, S. Rpt. 93–981, June 1974.

59. S. 495, reprinted in *Watergate Reorganization and Reform Act, Part I*, p. 161.

60. Ibid., statement by Weicker, p. 4.

61. Ibid.

62. Ibid.

63. Ibid., prepared statement by Rooney, p. 335.

64. Ibid., statements of Javits, p. 3; Percy, p. 3; and Baker, pp. 21–24.

65. Ibid., statement by Percy, p. 3.

66. Amendment to S. 495, ibid., reprinted in pp. 310–14.

67. Ibid., see especially Baker testimony, pp. 22–24.

68. Ibid., statement of Glenn, p. 5.

69. Kingdon, *Voting Decisions*, pp. 82–85.

70. Richard F. Fenno, Jr., *Congressmen in Committees* (Boston: Little, Brown, 1973).

71. Senate, Committee on Government Operations, *Watergate Reorganization*

and Reform Act of 1975, Part II, testimony of ABA representative Spann, pp. 162–63.

72. Mary Link, "Senate Prepares to Debate Watergate Reform Measure," *Congressional Quarterly Weekly Report* 34 (July 17, 1976): 1903-04.

73. Mary Link, "Senate Passes Watergate Reform Measure with Administration's Changes," *Congressional Quarterly Weekly Report* 34 (July 24, 1976): 1953-54.

74. Ibid. See also *Congressional Record*, July 21, 1976, p. 23075.

75. U.S., Congress, House, Committee on the Judiciary, *Provision for Special Prosecutor, Hearings before the Subcommittee on Criminal Justice*, 94th Cong., 2d sess., 1976.

76. Ibid., testimony of Ribicoff, p. 5.

77. Ibid., testimony of Weicker, p. 10.

78. Ibid., testimony of Kennedy, p. 11.

79. Ibid., testimony of Percy, p. 12.

80. Ibid., statement by Holtzman, pp. 7-8.

81. Ibid., statement by Wiggins, pp. 5-6.

82. Ibid., statement by Hyde, pp. 15-16.

83. Ibid., testimony of Levi, pp. 32-36.

84. Ibid., testimony of Dash, pp. 125-30.

85. Ibid., statement by Hyde, p. 148.

86. Ibid., p. 178.

87. The House Judiciary Committee and the Senate Governmental Affairs Committees are classified as policy committees, their members' main goal being to make good public policy. Steven S. Smith and Christopher J. Deering, *Committees in Congress* (Washington, D.C.: Congressional Quarterly Press, 1984), pp. 90, 112.

88. U.S., Congress, Senate, Committee on Governmental Affairs, *Public Officials Integrity Act of 1977, Blind Trusts, and Other Conflict of Interest Matters*, 95th Cong., 1st sess., 1977, p. 1.

89. Ibid., statement by Chiles, p. 3.

90. Ibid.

91. Ibid., statement by Weicker, p. 5.

92. "The President's Message to Congress Urging Enactment of the Proposed Ethics in Government Act of 1977 and Special Prosecutor Legislation," *Weekly Compilation of Presidential Documents* 13 (May 3, 1977): 647-50.

93. Senate, *Public Integrity Act*, statement of John Harmon, Office of Legal Counsel (OLC), p. 9. The OLC is responsible for preparing constitutional analyses for the president and attorney general.

94. "New Senate Watergate Bill Allows Special Prosecutor, Sets Financial Disclosure," *Congressional Quarterly Weekly Report* 35 (June 18, 1977): 1235-36. *Congressional Record*, June 27, 1977, p. 21007.

95. Ann Cooper, "Watergate-Inspired Bill May Force Vote on Korea Probe Issue, *Congressional Quarterly Weekly Report*, 36 (March 18, 1978): 683.

96. The House committees with jurisdiction over some aspect of the Ethics Act included the Select Ethics Committee, the Judiciary Committee (with two separate bills, one for the special prosecutor and the other for the more general ethics provisions), Armed Services, and Post Office and Civil Service. *Congress and the Nation*, Vol. 5 (Washington, D.C.: Congressional Quarterly, 1981), p. 825.

97. Cooper, "Korea Probe," p. 684.

98. U.S., Congress, House, Committee on the Judiciary, *Special Prosecutor Act*

of 1978, H. R. 95-1307, June 19, 1978. Additional remarks and dissents on pp. 21–24.

99. *Congressional Record*, October 7, 1978, p. 34526 (Senate vote on conference report); *Congressional Record*, October 12, 1978, p. 36469 (House vote on conference report); "Remarks on the Signing of S. 555 into Law," *Weekly Compilation of Presidential Documents* 14 (October 26, 1978): 1854–56.

100. Kingdon, *Voting Decisions*, p. 149.

101. Ripley, *Congress*, pp. 256, 262–63.

102. Kingdon, *Voting Decisions*, pp. 154–58.

103. ABA Special Committee to Study Federal Law Enforcement Agencies, *Preventing Improper Influence*.

104. Ripley found that public interest groups such as Public Citizen and Common Cause were "highly visible and quite effective" in the seventies. Their influence diminished in the eighties. Ripley, *Congress*, p. 265.

105. Special Committee to Study Law Enforcement Agencies, *Removing Political Influence from Federal Law Enforcement Agencies (A Preliminary Report)* (American Bar Association, 1975), p. 1.

106. ABA Special Committee, *Preventing Improper Influence*.

107. *Watergate Reorganization and Reform Act, Part II*, p. 163.

108. ABA Special Committee, *Preventing Improper Influence*, pp. 18–19.

109. House, Committee on the Judiciary, *Provision for Special Prosecutor*, pp. 51–71.

110. *Watergate Reorganization and Reform Act, Part II*, testimony of David Cohen, p. 64.

111. Nelson Polsby, "The Washington Community, 1960–1980," in Thomas E. Mann and Norman J. Ornstein, eds., *The New Congress* (Washington, D.C.: American Enterprise Institute, 1981), p. 14. See also Douglas Cater, *Power in Washington* (New York: Random House, 1964).

112. *Watergate Reorganization and Reform Act, Part I*, letter from Clark Clifford, pp. 203–5; Erwin Griswold, pp. 227–55; Philip Lacovara, pp. 259–80; Elliot Richardson, pp. 284–86, and Harold Seidman, pp. 288–89, reprinted in hearing record.

113. Ibid., Griswold letter, p. 234.

114. Ibid., Clifford letter, p. 203.

115. Ibid., Lacovara letter, p. 261.

116. Ibid., Seidman letter, p. 288.

117. Ibid., Berger letter, p. 199.

118. Ibid., Sundquist letter, p. 297.

119. Ibid., Dingman letter, pp. 218–20; J. Clay Smith letter, pp. 290–91.

120. Ibid., Burns letter, p. 202; Cutler letter, p. 206; and Mosher letter, pp. 281–82.

121. Interview with Lloyd Cutler, Washington, D.C., October 15, 1984.

122. *Watergate Reorganization and Reform Act, Part I*, Cutler letter, p. 206.

123. Ibid., p. 210.

124. *Watergate Reorganization and Reform Act, Part II*, Cutler testimony, p. 38.

125. Ibid., pp. 40–41.

126. *Watergate Reorganization and Reform Act, Part I*, Dash testimony, pp. 89–91.

127. Ibid., Jaworski testimony, pp. 104–8; Ruth testimony, pp. 120–22.

128. Watergate Special Prosecution Force, *Report* (Washington, D.C., October 1975), pp. 136–40.

129. Nelson Polsby, *Congress and the Presidency*, 4th ed. (Englewood Cliffs, N.J.: Prentice-Hall, 1986).

130. Kingdon, *Voting Decisions*, p. 180.

131. Ibid., p. 179; see also Fisher, *Shared Power* and *Constitutional Conflicts*.

132. Kingdon found that when congressmen appear to vote against constituent views they find the need to explain their votes in order to justify this vote. *Voting Decisions*, p. 216.

133. *Watergate Reorganization and Reform Act, Part II*, statement by Weicker, pp. 28–29.

134. Ibid., statement by Percy, pp. 31-32.

135. Ibid., letter from Assistant Attorney General Uhlmann to Senator Ribicoff, January 23, 1976, reprinted pp. 555–57.

136. 28 U.S.C. 591 (1978).

137. 28 U.S.C. 592 (a)(1) and (2) (1978).

138. 28 U.S.C. 592 (c)(1) (1978).

139. 28 U.S.C. 592 (b)(1) and (2) (1978).

140. 28 U.S.C. 49.

141. 28 U.S.C. 593 (b) and (c), and 595 (b) (3) (1978).

142. 28 U.S.C. 596 (a) (1978).

143. 28 U.S.C. 592 (f) (1978).

CHAPTER 4. IMPLEMENTATION AND CONGRESSIONAL OVERSIGHT

1. See David Mayhew, *Congress: The Electoral Connection* (New Haven, Conn.: Yale University Press, 1974), pp. 116, 132–34; and James Sundquist, *The Decline and Resurgence of Congress* (Washington, D.C.: Brookings Institution, 1981), pp. 329–39.

2. Morris Ogul, *Congress Oversees the Bureaucracy* (Pittsburgh: University of Pittsburgh Press, 1976), pp. 11–20.

3. Ibid., pp. 22–23.

4. U.S., Congress, Senate, Committee on Governmental Affairs, *Special Prosecutor Provisions of the Ethics in Government Act of 1978, Hearings before the Subcommittee on Oversight of Government Management*, 97th Cong., 1st sess., 1981; *Ethics in Government Act Amendments of 1982, Hearings before the Subcommittee on Oversight of Government Management*, 97th Cong., 2d sess., 1982; House, Committee on the Judiciary, *Amendment of the Special Prosecutor Provisions of Title 28, Hearings before the Subcommittee on Administrative Law and Governmental Relations*, 97th Cong., 2d sess., 1982.

5. 28 U.S.C. 595 (congressional oversight); 28 U.S.C. 599 (sunset provision) (1987).

6. Senators Cohen and Levin and staff members Mary Gerwin and Elise Bean are generally acknowledged to be the key individuals with interest in this issue by outside groups and by others within Congress. Rep. Barney Frank (D.-Mass.), chair of the House subcommittee with jurisdiction, is identified as being an interested supporter but one more interested in the broader question of ethics in government.

7. Arthur Christy, *Report of the Special Prosecutor on Alleged Possession of*

Cocaine by Hamilton Jordan in Violation of 21 U.S.C., sec. 844(a), New York, May 28, 1980; Gerald Gallinghouse, *In Re Investigation of Allegations Concerning Timothy Kraft: Report of the Special Prosecutor in Compliance with 28 U.S.C. 595(b)*, New Orleans, January 15, 1982.

8. The Jordan investigation cost $259,588. (Senate, *Special Prosecutor Provisions*). The Kraft case has been estimated at $3,348.00 and the Donovan investigation at $326,443.00 (*Washington Post*, April 4, 1984, p. A21). These amounts are significantly lower than subsequent investigations. "The Cost of Counsels," *Insight*, June 5, 1989, p. 13.

9. Interview with Benjamin Civiletti, Washington, D.C., October 19, 1984. Senate, *Special Prosecutor Provisions*, testimony of Benjamin Civiletti, pp. 8-9.

10. Memorandum of Points and Authorities in Support of Plaintiff's Motion for a Preliminary Injunction, *Kraft v. Gallinghouse*, CA No. 80-2952 (filed D.D.C. November 19, 1980).

11. Ibid., p. 2.

12. Ibid., pp. 8-14.

13. Memorandum of Common Cause as *Amicus Curiae* in Support of the Constitutionality of the Special Prosecutor Law, *Kraft v. Gallinghouse*, CA No. 80-2952 (filed D.D.C. January 15, 1981), p. 28.

14. Joint Motion to Dismiss and Order of Dismissal, *Kraft v. Gallinghouse*, CA No. 80-2952 (filed D.D.C. March 24, 1981).

15. The memorandum of each side appears in Senate, *Special Prosecutor Provisions*.

16. Letter to Senate Legal Counsel Michael Davidson from Attorney General William French Smith, April 17, 1981, reprinted in Senate, *Special Prosecutor Provisions*, pp. 249-250.

17. Interview with Mary Gerwin, counsel, Senate Subcommittee for Oversight of Government Management, Washington, D.C., October 16, 1984; and interview with William Shattuck, counsel, House Subcommittee on Administrative Law and Governmental Relations, Washington, D.C., July 1, 1985.

18. 28 U.S.C. 592 (a) (1) (A) and (B) (1983).

19. 28 U.S.C. 596 (a) (1) (1983).

20. 28 U.S.C. 594 (f) (1983).

21. Interview with Robert Evans, Washington, D.C., October 16, 1984. See also American Bar Association, Section on Criminal Justice, *Report to the House of Delegates* (American Bar Association, August 1987), p. 8.

22. Interview with Marcy Frosh and Mike Mawby, Common Cause, Washington, D.C., October 17, 1989; interview with Jay Hedlund, Common Cause, Washington, D.C., October 17, 1984.

23. 28 U.S.C. 593 (f). The statute allows reimbursement of "any reasonable expense" of unindicted targets. The special court panel that appoints the independent counsel is charged with determining to what extent the target can be reimbursed. Few targets can expect complete reimbursement. In a 1985 ruling on attorneys' fees for Raymond Donovan the court panel wrote that "Inquiries into the awarding of attorney's fees under the Act have focused on two elements: 1)whether the fees would have been incurred 'but for' the Act and 2)whether such fees are 'reasonable.' *In Re: Raymond J. Donovan*, Division No. 85-1, filed June 9, 1989 (slip opinion). Judge MacKinnon notes that the term *reasonable* has been construed strictly by the court panel. Interview with Judge George E. MacKinnon, Washington, D.C., July 17, 1989.

24. *Deaver v. Seymour*, 656 F.Supp 900 (D.D.C. 1987); *North v. Walsh*, 656 F.Supp 414 (D.D.C.1987); *In Re Sealed Case*, 665 F.Supp 56 (D.D.C. 1987).

25. See for example Bruce Fein, "Is Walsh's 'Independent Counsel' Appointment Constitutional?" *Human Events*, January 31, 1987, p. 12; Carl Levin and William S. Cohen, "The Deaver-North Challenge," *New York Times*, March 2, 1987, p. 19; Anthony Lewis, "It Means What It Says," *New York Times*, March 2, 1987; "Symposium on Special Prosecutors and the Role of Independent Counsel," *Hofstra Law Review* 16 (Fall 1987).

26. Interview with Alexia Morrison, Independent Counsel in Olson case, Washington, D.C., July 21, 1989.

27. Staff members confirm the importance of the cases to congressional deliberation. Interview with Elise Bean, Washington, D.C., July 14, 1989; interview with Mary Gerwin, July 17, 1989.

28. *Nathan v. Attorney General*, 557 F.Supp. 1186 (D.D.C. 1983).

29. Ibid., 1190.

30. *Nathan v. Attorney General*, 563 F.Supp. 815, 817 (D.D.C. 1983).

31. *Nathan v. Attorney General*, 737 F.2d. 1069, 1070-72 (D.C. Cir. 1984).

32. Ibid., 1077.

33. In fact, previous versions of the bill that contained a private right of action were rejected as too controversial. Ibid., 1080-81.

34. Ibid., 1079.

35. Ibid., 1080.

36. *Dellums v. Smith*, 573 F.Supp. 1489 (N.D.Cal. 1983).

37. Ibid., 1496, 1504.

38. *Dellums v. Smith*, 577 F.Supp 1449, 1452 (N.D. Cal. 1984).

39. Ibid. At the same time, the court also rejected the department's motion for a stay of judgment pending appeal. *Dellums v. Smith*, 577 F.Supp. 1456 (N.D.Cal. 1984).

40. *Dellums v. Smith*, 797 F.2d 817 (9th Cir., 1986).

41. *Banzhaf v. Smith*, 588 F.Supp. 1489 (D.D.C. 1984).

42. Interview with Judge Robert Richter, former member of Public Integrity Section of Department of Justice, Washington, D.C., July 1, 1985.

43. *Banzhaf v. Smith* , 1495.

44. Ibid.

45. Ibid., 1498.

46. *Banzhaf v. Smith*, 588 F.Supp 1498 (D.D.C. 1984).

47. *Banzhaf v. Smith*, 737 F.2d 1167 (D.C. Cir. 1984).

48. In addition to the evidence in the legislative history cited by the court, this position was confirmed by staff interviews. Interviews with Gerwin (1984), Bean, and Shattuck.

49. Interviews with Bean and Gerwin (1989).

50. Gerwin interview (1989).

51. Ronald D. Elving and Janet Hook, "The Reagan Presidency Fades into the Twilight," *Congressional Quarterly Weekly Report* 45 (October 17, 1987): 2499-2503.

52. Bean interview.

53. U.S. Senate, Committee on Governmental Affairs, *Independent Counsel Reauthorization Act of 1987*, *S. Rept. 100-123*, 100th Cong., 1st sess., 1987, p. 7.

54. Ibid., pp. 11-13.

55. Ibid. See also testimony of John R. Bolton, assistant attorney general for legislative affairs, in 1987 Senate subcommittee hearings, pp. 8-37. For example, the

requirement for attorney general recusal in cases where there was a conflict of interest had been interpreted to mean that there was a presumption against recusal because the attorney general is the department official named throughout the act as having primary responsibility for implementation. The department believed that the attorney general could remove the independent counsel for "good cause" if the counsel disobeyed a "lawful presidential order, even an order which seeks to compromise the very independence of the proceedings under the statute." Finally, the department believed that independent counsel and their staff were technically members of the Department of Justice and that they were therefore subject to all the conflict of interest regulations applicable to regular department employees.

56. Senate, Committee on Governmental Affairs, *Oversight of the Independent Counsel Statute, Hearings before the Subcommittee on Oversight and Government Management*, 100th Cong., 1st sess., 1907, p. 2.

57. Senate, *Independent Counsel Reauthorization Act of 1987*, pp. 13–14.

58. *1987 Sen. Hearings*, p. 25.

59. Ibid.

60. *Statement of Irvin B. Nathan, on Behalf of the American Bar Association before the Subcommittee on Oversight of Government Management of the Committee on Governmental Affairs on the Subject of Independent Counsel Provisions of the Ethics in Government Act*, March 19, 1987, p. 2 (copy obtained from ABA Governmental Affairs Office).

61. *Testimony of Archibald Cox, Chairman of Common Cause, on the Independent Counsel Provisions of the Ethics in Government Act before the Subcommittee on Administrative Law and Governmental Relations of the House Judiciary Committee*, April 23, 1987, p. 1 (copy obtained from Common Cause).

62. "Additional Views of Mr. Rudman," in Senate, *Independent Counsel Reauthorization Act of 1987*, p. 33.

63. "House Votes to Renew Special-Prosecutor Law," *Congressional Quarterly Weekly Report*, October 24, 1987, p. 2604. The proposed amendments and the votes on each were (1) apply provisions to Congress, 169 to 243; (2) reauthorize for only one year, 171 to 245; and (3) limit the length of independent counsel investigations to one year, 185 to 231.

64. Nadine Cohodas, "Senate Votes to Extend Special Prosecutor Law," *Congressional Quarterly Weekly Report* 45 (November 7, 1987): 2751. For example, an amendment to apply the provisions to Congress was rejected by a much closer vote of 49 to 46. Supporters of the Act called this a "killer" amendment, designed to diminish support for the provisions in Congress. Interview with Frosh and Mawby; interview with Bean.

65. Interviews with Bean, Frosh, and Mawby.

66. *Congressional Record*, November 3, 1987, S.15642.

67. Richard Cowan, "Independent Prosecutor Bill Pulled from House Schedule," *Congressional Quarterly Weekly Report* 45 (October 3, 1987): 2388.

68. See Senate debate on this issue in *Congressional Record*, November 3, 1987, S.15632–15642.

69. "Senate Votes," *Congressional Quarterly Weekly Report* 45 (November 7, 1987): 2751. The article opens, "The Justice Department may be setting President Reagan up for another confrontation with Congress that he can't win."

70. Mark Willen, "Balky Reagan Signs Extension of Independent Counsel Law," *Congressional Quarterly Weekly Report* 45 (December 19, 1987): 3166.

71. Ibid. See also *Weekly Compilation of Presidential Documents* 23 (December 15, 1987).

72. Statement by Congressman Barney Frank, quoted in "House Votes," *Congressional Quarterly Weekly Report* 45 (October 24, 1987): 2604.

73. 28 U.S.C. 591(d)(1) (1987).

74. 28 U.S.C. 591(d)(2) and 592(a)(1) (1987).

75. 28 U.S.C. 591(e) (1987).

76. 28 U.S.C. 592(a)(2)(B) (1987).

77. *INS V. Chadha*, 462 U.S. 919 (1983)(legislative veto unconstitutional); and *Bowsher v. Synar*, 478 U.S. 714 (1986) (Gramm-Rudman unconstitutional).

78. 28 U.S.C. 593(c)(1987).

79. Interview with Gerwin (1989).

80. 28 U.S.C. 594(h)(1)(A) (1987).

81. 28 U.S.C. 593(b)(2) (1987).

82. Interview with Gerwin (1989).

83. Ibid.

84. Lawrence Walsh, *Independent Counsel's Report to the Subcommittee on Legislation of the Permanent Select Committee on Intelligence of the U.S. House of Representatives*, September 19, 1989 (photocopy from Office of Independent Counsel).

85. Interview with Bean.

CHAPTER 5. IS THE SPECIAL PROSECUTOR CONSTITUTIONAL?

1. *Kraft v. Gallinghouse*, CA No. 80-2952 (D.D.C. 1980).

2. *Banzhaf v. Smith*, 588 F.Supp 1498 (D.D.C. 1984).

3. *Nathan v. Attorney General*, 737 F.2d 1069, 1079 (D.C. Cir. 1984).

4. *Deaver v. Seymour*, 656 F.Supp. 900 (D.D.C. 1987).

5. Ibid., 901-2.

6. *North v. Walsh*, 656 F.Supp. 414 (D.D.C. 1987).

7. 52 Fed. Reg. 7270 (March 10, 1987); 28 CFR Parts 600–601.

8. *North v. Walsh*, 419.

9. Ibid., 420.

10. Ibid., 420–21, notes 9 and 10.

11. *In Re Sealed Case*, 827 F.2d 776 (D.C. Cir. 1987) (per curiam).

12. *In Re Sealed Case*, 666 F.Supp 231 (D.D.C. 1987), *affd.* 829 F.2d 50 (D.C. Cir, 1987).

13. See for example, Bruce Fein, "Is Walsh's 'Independent Counsel' Appointment Legal?" *Human Events*, January 31, 1987, p. 12; "Look Who's Charging Impropriety," *New York Times*, February 26, 1987, p. 26; Carl Levin and William S. Cohen, "The Deaver-North Challenge," *New York Times*, March 2, 1987, p. 19; Anthony Lewis, "It Means What It Says," *New York Times*, March 3, 1987, p. 23; Laurence Tribe, "Damn the Torpedoes, Full Speed Ahead," *Washington Post National Weekly Edition*, March 16, 1987, pp. 24–25.

14. Congress held the director of the EPA, Anne Gorsuch, in contempt for refusal to turn over certain documents. The Department of Justice filed suit requesting the district court to uphold the executive privilege claim. In *United States v. House of Representatives*, 556 F.Supp. 150 (D.C.C. 1983), the court dismissed the suit, urging the two sides to come to a political accommodation. This eventually occurred.

15. U.S., Congress, House, Committee on the Judiciary, *Report on the Investigation of the Role of the Department of Justice in the Withholding of Environmental Protection Agency Documents from Congress in 1982–83*, 98th Cong., 1st sess., 1985.

16. Public Integrity Section Memo of April 4, 1986, cited in Alexia Morrison, *In Re Theodore B. Olson and Robert M. Perry. Report of the Independent Counsel* (Washington, D.C.: December 27, 1988), p. 11.

17. Ibid., pp. 10–15.

18. Interview with Earl Dudley, Jr., deputy independent counsel, Arlington, Va., July 13, 1989. The independent counsel report also discusses this concern, pp. 17–18.

19. Morrison, *Report of Independent Counsel*, p. 21.

20. *In Re Olson*, 818 F.2d 34 (D.C.Cir. 1987).

21. *In Re Sealed Case*, 665 F.Supp. 56, 62 (D.C.C. 1987).

22. Ibid., 58–60.

23. *United States v. Nixon*, 418 U.S. 683 (1974); *Humphrey's Executor v. United States*, 295 U.S. 602 (1935); *Weiner v. United States*, 357 U.S. 349 (1958).

24. *In Re Sealed Case*, 838 F.2d 476, 477 (D.C.Cir. 1988).

25. Interview with Alexia Morrison, independent counsel, Washington, D.C., July 21, 1989. Interview with Dudley.

26. *In Re Sealed Case*, 838 F.2d 476 (D.C.Cir. 1988).

27. Ibid., 480.

28. Ibid., 484.

29. Ibid., 486–87.

30. Ibid., 488–89.

31. Ibid., 490.

32. *Myers v. United States*, 272 U.S. 52 (1926).

33. *In Re Sealed Case*, 497–99.

34. Ibid., 502–3.

35. Ibid., 504–8

36. Ibid., 511–15

37. Ibid., 518–36.

38. Eugene Grossman, "A Symposium on Special Prosecutors and the Role of the Independent Counsel: Introduction," *Hofstra Law Review* 16 (Fall 1987): 9.

39. Morton Rosenberg, "Congressional Prerogative over Agencies and Agency Decisionmakers: The Rise and Demise of the Reagan Administration's Theory of the Unitary Executive," *George Washington Law Review* 57 (January 1989): 627–703.

40. Grossman, "Introduction," p. 9.

41. *INS v. Chadha*, 462 U.S. 919 (1983).

42. *Bowsher v. Synar*, 478 U.S. 714 (1986).

43. See Justice White's dissent in *INS v. Chadha*, 462 U.S. 919, 968 (1983).

44. *INS v. Chadha*, at 944.

45. Ibid., 951.

46. Ibid., 972.

47. Ibid., 978.

48. Ibid., 1002. Silberman refers to White's remark in *In Re Sealed Case*, 838 F.2d 476 (D.C. Cir. 1988). Earl Dudley, Jr., suggests that Silberman cited White in order to encourage that justice to join a majority in striking down the independent

counsel statute. "Morrison v. Olson: A Modest Assessment," *American University Law Review* 38 (Winter 1989): 271n.90.

49. Grossman, "Introduction," p. 8.

50. The briefs for each side are reprinted in the symposium on independent counsel in *Hofstra Law Review* 16: 66-130.

51. Interviews with Morrison and Dudley.

52. Nadine Cohodas, "Court Moves toward Ruling on Special Prosecutor Law," *Congressional Quarterly Weekly Report* 46 (April 30, 1988), p. 1161.

53. Nadine Cohodas, "Court Rules Against Reagan in Power Clash," *Congressional Quarterly Weekly Report* 46 (July 2, 1988): 1791. (statements by Congressman Barney Frank and Sen. Carl Levin.)

54. Ibid., p. 1794.

55. See for example, Stephen L. Carter, "Comment: The Independent Counsel Mess," *Harvard Law Review* 102: (1988): 105; and Terry Eastland, *Ethics, Politics, and The Independent Counsel* (Washington, D.C.: National Legal Center for the Public Interest, 1989).

56. *Morrison v. Olson*, 487 U.S. 654, 670-77 (1988).

57. Ibid., 677-80, note 18.

58. Ibid., 680-81.

59. Ibid., 682-83.

60. Ibid., 683-84.

61. Ibid., 684.

62. Ibid., 684-85.

63. Ibid., 685-91.

64. Ibid., 691-93.

65. Ibid., 693-96.

66. Scalia overlooks the fact that on three different occasions presidents had had the opportunity to veto the provisions but had failed to do so.

67. Ibid., 698-99.

68. Ibid., 699-702.

69. Ibid., 703-07.

70. Ibid., 710-13.

71. Ibid., 715-27.

72. Ibid., 727-33.

73. Dudley, "Modest Assessment," p. 265; Carter, "Independent Counsel Mess."

74. Gary Goodpaster, "Rules of the Game: Comments on Three Views of the Independent Prosecutor Case," *American University Law Review* 38 (Winter 1989): 393.

75. Dudley, "Modest Assessment," p. 271.

76. Harold Krent, "Separating the Strands in Separation of Powers Controversies," *Virginia Law Review* 74 (1988): 1256.

77. Ibid.

78. Dudley, "Modest Assessment," p. 265.

79. Ibid., 1257.

80. *Mistretta v. United States*, 488 U.S. 361 (1989).

81. Ibid.

82. Goodpaster, "Rules of the Game," p. 393. "As a ruling in the great, ongoing game of governmental power, *Morrison* puts the ball back in play."

CHAPTER 6. THE ATTORNEY GENERAL
AND CONFLICT OF INTEREST

1. 28 U.S.C. 591-598 (1987).
2. Lloyd N. Cutler, "Conflicts of Interest," *Emory Law Journal* 30 (1981): 1017.
3. Frank M. Tuerkheimer, "The Executive Investigates Itself," *California Law Review* 65 (1977): 597.
4. Special Committee to Study Federal Law Enforcement Agencies, *Preventing Improper Influence on Federal Law Enforcement Agencies* (Washington, D.C.: American Bar Association, 1976), p. 34.
5. Victor Navasky, *Kennedy Justice* (New York: Atheneum, 1971), p. 379.
6. Luther A. Huston, *The Department of Justice* (New York: Frederick A. Praeger, 1967), p. 3.
7. Frederick C. Mosher, *Watergate: Implications for Responsible Government* (New York: Basic Books, 1974), p. 45.
8. Arthur S. Miller, "The Attorney General as the President's Lawyer," in *Roles of the Attorney General of the United States* (Washington, D.C.: American Enterprise Institute, 1968), p. 41.
9. Ibid., p. 60.
10. Homer Cummings and Carl McFarland, *Federal Justice* (New York: Macmillan, 1937), pp. 221-22.
11. William S. McFeely, *Grant: A Biography* (New York: W. W. Norton, 1981), pp. 404-16.
12. Special Committee, *Preventing Influence*, p. 38.
13. U.S., Congress, Senate, Committee on the Judiciary, *Removing Politics from the Administration of Justice, Hearings before the Subcommittee on the Separation of Powers*, 93d Cong., 2d sess., 1974, p. 234.
14. Cutler, "Conflicts of Interest," p. 1020. See also Donald J. Simon, "The Constitutionality of the Special Prosecutor Law," *University of Michigan Journal of Law Reform* 16 (1982): 45-73. Simon argues that Watergate "revealed that if public confidence in government was to be restored and maintained, remedying the actual conflict of interest in Justice Department prosecution of high officials was not enough; the appearance of impropriety had to be removed as well" (p. 51).
15. Mark Bertozzi, "The Federal Special Prosecutor: Too Special?" *Federal Bar News and Journal* 29 (1982): 224-26.
16. *Principles of Federal Prosecution* (Washington, D.C.: U.S. Department of Justice, 1980), p. 1.
17. Ibid., p. 3.
18. Kenneth Culp Davis, *Discretionary Justice: A Preliminary Inquiry* (Baton Rouge: Louisiana State University Press, 1969), p. 25.
19. Robert Palmer, "The Confrontation of the Legislative and Executive Branches: An Examination of the Constitutional Balance of Power and the Role of the Attorney General," *Pepperdine Law Review* 11 (1984): 353. See also *Principles of Federal Prosecution*, p. 1; and Howard H. Baker Jr., "The Proposed Judicially Appointed Independent Office of Public Attorney: Some Constitutional Objections and an Alternative," *Southwestern Law Journal* 29 (1975): 675.
20. *The Confiscation Cases*, 74 U.S. (7 Wall.) 458 (1868); *United States v. San Jacinto Tin Co.*, 125 U.S. 279 (1887); *Ponzi v. Fessenden*, 258 U.S. 262 (1922).
21. *Milliken v. Stone*, 7 F.2d 397, 399 (S.D.N.Y. 1925).

22. *Pugach v. Klein*, 193 F.Supp 630, 634–35 (S.D.N.Y. 1961); *Moses v. Kennedy*, 219 F.Supp. 762, 764 (D.C.C. 1963); *United States v. Cox*, 342 F.2d 167, 177 (5th Cir. 1965); *Powell v. Katzenbach*, 359 F.2d 234 (D.C.Cir. 1965); *Newman v. United States*, 382 F.2d 479, 480 (D.C.Cir. 1967).

23. *Boyd v. United States*, 345 F.Supp. 790, 792–93 (E.D.N.Y. 1972).

24. Davis, *Discretionary Justice*, p. 25.

25. Palmer, "Confrontation of the Legislative and Executive," pp. 353–54.

26. "Removing Politics from the Justice Department: Constitutional Problems with Institutional Reform," *New York University Law Review* 50 (1975): 397.

27. *Nathan v. Attorney General*, 737 F.2d 1069 (D.C.Cir. 1984); *Banzhaf v. Smith*, 737 F.2d 1167 (D.C.Cir. 1984); *Dellums v. Smith*, 797 F.2d 817 (9th Cir. 1986).

28. *In Re Olson*, 818 F.2d 34 (D.C.Cir. 1987).

29. *Morrison v. Olson*, 487 U.S. 654 (1988).

30. Interview with Judge Robert Richter, Washington, D.C., July 1, 1985. The Senate subcommittee report on the 1987 reauthorization states that between 1978 and 1982 there were twelve preliminary investigations of covered officials, leading to three requests for independent counsel. U.S. Congress, Senate, Committee on Governmental Affairs, *Independent Counsel Reauthorization Act of 1987*, S. Rept. 100–123, 100th Cong., 1st sess., 1987, p. 7.

31. Senate, *Independent Counsel Reauthorization Act of 1987*, pp. 6–7.

32. "Carter Warehouse Files are Examined," *Washington Post*, January 27, 1979, p. A3.

33. Fred Barbash and Charles R. Babcock, "Justice Department Seeks People, Methods for Inquiry into Carter Family Business," *Washington Post*, March 20, 1979, p. A8.

34. Charles Babcock and Ted Gup, "Special Counsel Is Appointed in Carter Warehouse Probe," *Washington Post*, March 21, 1979, p. A1.

35. Ibid.

36. John F. Berry and Ted Gup, "Independence Guarantee Urged for Special Counsel," *Washington Post*, March 22, 1979, p. A16.

37. Interview with Paul Curran, New York City, January 25, 1985.

38. Charles R. Babcock, "Special Counsel Given Watergate-Style Power," *Washington Post*, March 24, 1979, A1.

39. John F. Berry and Ted Gup, "Inquiry Clears Carter Family's Peanut Business," *Washington Post*, October 17, 1979, p. A1; and Paul J. Curran, *Investigation of Carter's Warehouse and the National Bank of Georgia, Report to the Congress of the United States*, October 1979. A separate report was submitted to the attorney general which detailed protected grand jury testimony.

40. "The Special Counsel's Report," *Washington Post*, October 18, 1979, p. A18.

41. "The Peanut Money," *Washington Post*, March 24, 1979, p. A14.

42. "A Secret White House Meeting: Carter's Fat Cats," *New York*, November 13, 1978.

43. *Report of the Attorney General Pursuant to 28 U.S.C. sec. 592(b)*, filed with the United States Court of Appeals for the District of Columbia Circuit, Special Prosecutor Division, February 1, 1979.

44. *Motion of the Attorney General for Leave to Disclose Report Pursuant to 28 U.S.C. 592 (d)(2)*, filed with the United States Court of Appeals for the District of Columbia Circuit, Special Prosecutor Division, February 1, 1979.

45. *Report of the Attorney General*, February 1, 1979.

46. Interview with Philip Heymann, Harvard Law School, Cambridge, Mass., March 26, 1985.

47. Ibid.

48. Ibid.

49. Interview with Marshall Jarret, Public Integrity Section, Department of Justice, Washington, D.C., June 27, 1985.

50. Lee Lescaze and Patrick E. Tyler, "Allen Accepted Interviewers' Two Watches, Japanese Paper Says," *Washington Post*, November 21, 1981, p. A2.

51. *Report of the Attorney General Pursuant to 28 U.S.C. 592(b), Subject: Assistant to the President for National Security Affairs Richard Allen*, filed with the United States Court of Appeals for the District of Columbia Circuit, Special Prosecutor Division, December 22, 1981, p. 6.

52. Ibid., pp. 5–6.

53. *Washington Post*, November 24, 1981.

54. *Report of the Department of Justice Regarding Richard V. Allen's Ethics in Government Act Disclosure Report*, December 22, 1981, p. 8.

55. Ibid., pp. 9–10.

56. Interview with Mary Gerwin, Subcommittee on Oversight of Government Management, Washington, D.C., October 16, 1984. Gerwin said, "We consider the triggering standard to be stricter than does the Department of Justice and have had some problems with their interpretation. We believe that if there is any doubt in the mind of the Attorney General as to whether or not to trigger, he should request appointment."

57. American Bar Association, Section on Criminal Justice, *Report to the House of Delegates* (Washington, D.C.: American Bar Association, August 1987), p. 13.

58. Ibid., pp. 13–14. See also Testimony of Archibald Cox, chairman of Common Cause, on The Independent Counsel Provisions of the Ethics in Government Act, before the Subcommittee on Administrative Law and Governmental Relations of the House Judiciary Committee, April 23, 1987 (copy obtained from Common Cause), p. 14.

59. Cox testimony, p. 14. See also Senate, *Independent Counsel Reauthorization Act of 1987*, p. 9.

60. Congressional staff members identify this process as the one most likely to trigger oversight inquiries from their office during times when reauthorization is not on the agenda. Interview with Mary Gerwin, July 17, 1989; interview with Elise Bean, Staff Counsel for Senate Subcommittee, Washington, D.C., July 14, 1989.

61. Senate, *Independent Counsel Reauthorization Act of 1987*, pp. 6–7.

62. Ibid., p. 9.

63. Ibid.

64. Cited in Cox testimony, p. 18.

65. Ibid., p. 19.

66. Gerwin interview (1989).

67. Alexia Morrison, *In Re Theodore B. Olson and Robert M. Perry: Report of the Independent Counsel* (December 27, 1988), p. 11.

68. *In Re Olson*, 818 F.2d 34 (D.C.Cir. 1987).

69. Interview with Earl Dudley, Jr., Arlington, Va., July 13, 1989.

70. Interview with Alexia Morrison, Washington, D.C., July 21, 1989.

71. Senate, *Independent Counsel Reauthorization Act of 1987*, pp. 10–11.

72. When the problems of the use of classified documents became apparent, there was much speculation about whether or not the case could be tried at all. See, for example, Glen Craney, "Classified Data, Immunity Pose Delay in Iran-Contra

Case," *Congressional Quarterly Weekly Report* 46 (April 16, 1988): 997; and Ann Pelham, "Can North Be Tried? Who's to Be Trusted?" *Legal Times*, February 20, 1989, p. 1.

73. See also Glen Craney, "Access to Secret Papers Snarls Iran Contra Case," *Congressional Quarterly Weekly Report* 46 (April 30, 1988): 1157–58; Craney, "Judge Won't Derail North's Iran-Contra Trial," *Congressional Quarterly Weekly Report* 46 (November 26, 1988): 3403; "Secrecy Spat Jeopardizes Iran-Contra Trial," *Congressional Quarterly Weekly Report* 46 (December 3, 1988): 3455; and Ann Pelham, "Walsh Clashes with Justice Department over Secrets," *Legal Times*, July 31, 1989, p. 2.

74. Public Law No. 96–456, 94 Stat. 2025 (codified at 18 U.S.C. app.).

75. 18 U.S.C. app. sec. 5(a).

76. 18 U.S.C. app. sec. 6.

77. Brian Z. Tamanaha, "A Critical Review of the Classified Information Procedures Act," *American Journal of Criminal Law* (Summer 1986) 13: 280.

78. Pelham, "Can North Be Tried?" p. 11.

79. Harold Hongju Koh, *The National Security Constitution* (New Haven, Conn.: Yale University Press, 1990), p. 31.

80. Craney, "Judge Won't Derail," p. 3403.

81. "Secrecy Spat," p. 3455.

82. Glen Craney, "Iran-Contra Case May Drop Two Counts," *Congressional Quarterly Weekly Report* 47 (January 7, 1989): 28–29; and "Two Iran-Contra Charges against North Dismissed," *Congressional Quarterly Weekly Report* 47 (January 14, 1989): p. 99.

83. Koh, *National Security Constitution*, p. 26.

84. Pelham, "Can North Be Tried?" p. 11.

85. Gerwin interview, (1984); interview with William Shattuck, counsel for House Subcommittee on Administrative Law and Governmental Relations, Washington, D.C., July 1, 1985; Richter interview; *Banzhaf v. Smith*, 737 F.2d 1167 at 1169.

86. Pelham, "Can North Be Tried?" p. 11.

CHAPTER 7. ACCOUNTABILITY, INDEPENDENCE, AND THE SPECIAL PROSECUTOR

1. *Morrison v. Olson*, 487 U.S. 654, 716-723 (1988) (Scalia dissenting).

2. U.S., Congress, House, *Independent Counsel Reauthorization Act of 1987*, Conference Report 100–452, 100th Cong., 1st. sess., November 1987, p. 37.

3. This statement was made with the understanding that it was not for attribution.

4. Interview with Theodore Olson, Washington, D.C., October 15, 1990.

5. Olson interview. Interview with E. Lawrence Barcella and Robert Plotkin, Washington, D.C., June 30, 1989.

6. George F. Cole, "The Decision to Prosecute," *Law and Society Review* 4 (February 1970): 342; James Eisenstein and Herbert Jacob, *Felony Justice: An Organizational Analysis of Criminal Courts* (Boston: Little, Brown, 1977); Milton Heumann, *Plea Bargaining: The Experiences of Prosecutors, Judges, and Defense Attorneys* (Chicago: University of Chicago Press, 1978); Albert Alschuler, "The

Prosecutor's Role in Plea Bargaining," *University of Chicago Law Review* 36 (1968): 50–112; and "The Defense Attorney's Role in Plea Bargaining," *Yale Law Journal* 84 (1975): 1179–1314; and James Eisenstein, *Counsel for the United States: U.S. Attorneys in the Political and Legal Systems* (Baltimore: Johns Hopkins University Press, 1978).

7. 28 U.S.C. 49, sec. 593.

8. 28 U.S.C. 594(a) (1987).

9. 28 U.S.C. 594(c) (1987).

10. 28 U.S.C. 593(b)(2) (1987).

11. 28 U.S.C. 597(a) (1987).

12. 28 U.S.C. 592(1987).

13. 28 U.S.C. 594(a)(10)(1987).

14. 28 U.S.C. 594(d)(1987).

15. 28 U.S.C. 594(f)(1987).

16. 28 U.S.C. 594(g)(1987).

17. 28 U.S.C. 596(a)(1)(1987).

18. Interview with Philip Heymann, Harvard Law School, Cambridge, Mass., March 26, 1985.

19. Interview with Gerald McDowell, Public Integrity Section Chief, Department of Justice, Washington, D.C., June 28, 1989.

20. Telephone interview with Whitney North Seymour, independent counsel in Deaver case, November 30, 1989; interview with Alexia Morrison, independent counsel in Olson case, Washington, D.C., July 21, 1989.

21. Interview with Benjamin Civiletti, Washington, D.C., October 19, 1984; interview with Gregory P. Joseph, New York City, September 25, 1984; Arthur Christy, *Report of the Special Prosecutor on Alleged Possession of Cocaine by Hamilton Jordan in Violation of 21 U.S.C. sec. 844(a)*, Washington, D.C., May 28, 1980, p. 52.;Seymour interview.

22. Interview with Arthur Nealon, New York City, September 21, 1984.

23. Interview with Arthur Christy, New York City, September 17, 1984.

24. Joseph interview.

25. Interview with Leon Silverman, New York City, September 25, 1984.

26. Jacob A. Stein, *Report of the Independent Counsel Concerning Edwin Meese III*, Washington, D.C., September 20, 1984, p. 7.

27. Morrison interview.

28. Interview with James McKay and Carol Bruce, Washington, D.C., July 13, 1989.

29. Interviews with Civiletti, Heymann, McDowell; interview with Edward Dennis, deputy attorney general, Washington, D.C., June 29, 1989.

30. Interview with Rudolf Giuliani, New York City, January 24, 1985.

31. Charles R. Babcock, "Civiletti and Justice Staff Find Themselves on the Defense," *Washington Post*, September 3, 1979, p. A31.

32. McDowell interview. Interview with Marshall Jarret, Public Integrity Section, Washington, D.C., June 27, 1985.

33. Memorandum of Points and Authorities in Support of Plaintiff's Motion for a Preliminary Injunction, *Kraft v. Gallinghouse*, CA No. 80-2952 (filed D.D.C., November 19, 1980).

34. Telephone interview with Gerald Gallinghouse, New Orleans, La., October 28, 1985.

35. Civiletti interview.

36. Memorandum of Common Cause as *Amicus Curiae* in Support of the Con-

stitutionality of the Special Prosecutor Law, *Kraft v. Gallinghouse*, CA No. 2952 (filed D.D.C., January 15, 1981).

37. Joint Motion to Dismiss and Order of Dismissal F.R.C.P. Rule 41 (a)(2), *Kraft v. Gallinghouse*, CA No. 80-2952 (filed D.D.C., March 24, 1981).

38. *Dellums v. Smith*, 797 F.2d 817 (9th Cir. 1986); *Nathan v. Attorney General*, 563 F.Supp. 815 (D.D.C. 1983), *reversed* 737 F.2d 1069 (D.C. Cir. 1984); *Banzhaf v. Smith*, 588 F.Supp. 1498 (D.D.C. 1984), *vacated* 737 F.2d 1167 (D.C.Cir. 1984); *In Re Theodore Olson*, 818 F.2d 34 (D.C. Cir. 1987).

39. Interview with Judge MacKinnon, D.C. Circuit Court of Appeals, Washington, D.C., July 17, 1989.

40. Ibid. See also U.S., Congress, Committee on Governmental Affairs, *Independent Counsel Reauthorization Act of 1987*, S. Rept. 100-123, 100th Cong., 1st sess., 1987, p. 13.

41. Ibid.

42. Seymour interview.

43. "Independent Counsels Win Reprieve," *National Washington Post Weekly Edition*, April 27, 1987, p. 38. See also 28 U.S.C. sec. 594(i).

44. Interview with Bart Schwartz, New York City, January 24, 1985.

45. Christy interview; Silverman interview; telephone interview with Jacob Stein, Washington, D.C., May 2, 1985.

46. Silverman interview.

47. Interview with James Bensfield, Washington, D.C., May 1, 1985.

48. Interview with David Austern, Washington, D.C., October 19, 1984.

49. Bensfield interview.

50. Schwartz interview.

51. McKay interview.

52. Schwartz interview.

53. Morrison interview; James McKay, Philip Heymann, and Robert Richter also discussed the problem of exposure in the early stages of the investigation.

54. Eisenstein, *Counsel for the United States*, chapter 7.

55. Silverman interview.

56. Interview with Judge Edward Lumbard, New York City, January 29, 1985; MacKinnon interview.

57. MacKinnon interview.

58. Christy interview; Silverman interview.

59. Leon Silverman interview.

60. Lumbard interview.

61. Interview with Richard Beizer, Washington, D.C., April 26, 1985; and "Inside: Justice Department; Coincidence?" *Washington Post*, April 11, 1984, p. A19.

62. Seymour interview.

63. McKay interview.

64. Morrison interview.

65. MacKinnon interview.

66. Christy interview.

67. Silverman interview.

68. Seymour interview.

69. Lumbard and MacKinnon interviews.

70. MacKinnon interview.

71. Glen Craney, "Split Trials Could Be Blow to Iran-Contra Case," *Congressional Quarterly Weekly Report* 46 (June 11, 1988): 1625-27; Craney, "Access to Secret Papers Snarls Iran-Contra Case," *Congressional Quarterly Weekly Report* 46 (April

30, 1988): 1157–58; "Two Iran-Contra Charges against North Dismissed," *Congressional Quarterly Weekly Report* 47 (January 14, 1989): 99; and Lawrence Walsh, *Independent Counsel's Report to the Subcommittee on Legislation of the Permanent Select Committee on Intelligence of the House of Representatives*, September 19, 1989 (photocopy obtained from Office of Independent Counsel.)

72. *United States v. North*, 910 F.2d 843 (D.C.Cir. 1990); *United States v. North*, 920 F.2d 940 (D.C.Cir. 1990).

73. Seymour interview.

74. Interview with Earl Dudley, Jr., Arlington, Va., July 13, 1989.

75. Eisenstein, *Counsel for the United States*, pp. 171–78.

76. *Martindale and Hubbel Lawyers Index*, 1982, 1983, 1984, 1985, 1986, 1987, 1988.

77. This is a description of special prosecutor appointees given by Judge Lumbard in interview.

78. Beizer interview.

79. Seymour interview.

80. Silverman interview.

81. Stein interview.

82. Seymour interview.

83. Morrison interview.

84. Stein interview.

85. Dudley interview.

86. Bensfield interview.

87. Seymour interview.

88. Aaron Freiwald, "Probe Tab $40 Million . . . and Rising," *Legal Times*, February 20, 1989, p. 10.

89. Nealon interview.

90. Gallinghouse interview.

91. Austern interview.

92. 28 U.S.C. 592(g) (1987).

93. Giuliani interview.

94. 28 U.S.C. 595 (1987).

95. Interview with Elise Bean, staff counsel, Subcommittee on Oversight of Government Management, Washington, D.C., July 14, 1989; interview with Mary Gerwin, minority staff counsel, Washington, D.C., July 17, 1989.

96. James Madison, "Federalist 51," in *The Federalist Papers*, edited by Isaac Kramnick (New York: Penguin Books, 1987), p. 319.

97. Lawrence Walsh, "The Independent Counsel and the Separation of Powers," *Houston Law Review* 25 (January 1988): 1–11.

98. Interview with John Nields, Chief Counsel for the House Select Committee to Investigate Covert Arms Transactions with Iran, Washington, D.C., October 16, 1989. Interview with Archibald Cox, Harvard Law School, Cambridge, Mass., February 5, 1985.

99. Nields interview; Joel M. Woldman, *Congress and the Iran-Contra Affair*, CRS Report 88-765F, November 1988, p. 15; and Samuel Dash, *Chief Counsel: Inside the Ervin Committee—The Untold Story of Watergate* (New York: Random House, 1976), pp. 124, 142–44.

100. Silverman interview; Joseph interview.

101. Silverman interview.

102. Beizer interview.

103. "Meese's Lawyers Protest Release of Travel Papers," *Washington Post*, April 7, 1984, p. A.8.

104. Beizer interview.

105. Morrison interview; Dudley interview.

106. McKay interview.

107. Walsh, "The Independent Counsel and the Separation of Powers"; Judge Gesell describes the procedures taken in the office in *United States v. Poindexter*, 698 F.Supp 300, 312-13 (D.D.C. 1988).

108. Steven Brill, "How a Legal Ploy Backfired: Cocaine Claim against Jordan Hurt Studio 54 Owners," *Washington Post*, November 4, 1979, p. C1.

109. *Report of the Congressional Committees Investigating the Iran-Contra Affair*, abridged ed. (New York: Random House, 1988), p. 7.

110. Heymann interview.

111. Lumbard interview.

112. Nealon interview.

113. Silverman interview.

114. Austern interview.

115. Bruce interview.

116. McKay interview.

117. Dudley interview.

118. Seymour interview.

119. Morrison interview.

120. Dudley interview.

121. Olson interview.

122. Cox interview.

CHAPTER 8. SYMBOLS AND POLITICS

1. For example, the Harris survey asks its respondents regularly, "How much confidence do you feel in the people who are running the Supreme Court? the Senate? the House? the Executive Branch?" The Center for Political Studies of the Institute for Social Research at the University of Michigan regularly asks, "How much of the time do you think you can trust the government in Washington to do what is right—just about always, most of the time, only some of the time, or none of the time?"

2. Walter Lippmann, *The Phantom Public* (New York: Macmillan, 1927), p. 64.

3. V. O. Key, Jr., *Public Opinion and American Democracy* (New York: Alfred A. Knopf, 1965), pp. 555-57.

4. Ibid., p. 557.

5. Ibid., p. 537.

6. W. Russell Neuman, *The Paradox of Mass Politics: Knowledge and Opinion in the American Electorate* (Cambridge, Mass.: Harvard University Press, 1986), pp. 170-71.

7. Ibid., p. 7.

8. Ibid., p. 186.

9. Murray Edelman, *The Symbolic Uses of Politics* (Urbana: University of Illinois Press, 1964), pp. 6-11.

10. Ibid., pp. 36-39.

11. Ibid., p. 10.

12. Ibid., p. 38.

13. Ibid., pp. 66–67.

14. Michael J. Robinson contends that through the 1960s, political scientists "seemed committed to the general theory of minimal effects . . . a theory which relegates television, and all mass media, to a position of relative impotence." "Public Affairs Television and the Growth of Political Malaise: The Case of 'The Selling of the Pentagon,'" *American Political Science Review* 70 (June 1976): 409–10.

15. Doris Graber, *Mass Media and American Politics*, 2d ed. (Washington, D.C.: Congressional Quarterly Press, 1984), p. 18.

16. Doris Graber, *Processing the News: How People Tame the Information Tide* (New York: Longman, 1984), p. 208.

17. Ibid., pp. 201–2. Similar results were obtained in a 1971 study conducted by Andrew Stern of Berkeley. In testing for aided and unaided recall of television news, Stern found that 51 percent of his respondents could remember none of the stories in that evening's newscast when asked "What do you recall from tonight's broadcast?" Of the 49 percent who remembered something, most recalled only one story in nineteen. Aided recall resulted in nine of nineteen stories being remembered by respondents. Stern also found that two-thirds of his respondents had either major or minor distractions while the news was on. Cited in Edwin Diamond, *The Tin Kazoo* (Cambridge, Mass.: MIT Press, 1975), pp. 65–68.

18. Graber, *Processing the News*, p. 202.

19. Diamond, *The Tin Kazoo*, p. 45. See also Diamond's article entitled, "The Folks in the Boondocks: Challenging the Journalistic Myth," *Columbia Journalism Review* (November–December 1973), pp. 58–59.

20. Austin Ranney, *Channels of Power: The Impact of Television on American Politics* (New York: Basic Books, 1983), pp. 69–70.

21. Neuman, *Paradox*, p. 136.

22. Edward Jay Epstein, *News from Nowhere* (New York: Random House, 1973), p. 215.

23. Ibid.

24. Ranney, *Channels of Power*, p. 61.

25. Robinson, "Public Affairs Television," p. 425.

26. Arthur Miller, Edie N. Goldenberg, and Lutz Ebring, "Type-Set Politics: Impact of Newspapers on Public Confidence," *American Political Science Review* 73 (March 1979): 81.

27. Gladys Engel Lang and Kurt Lang, *Politics and Television: Re-viewed* (Beverly Hills, Calif.: Sage Publications, 1984), p. 159. The Langs argue that televising the hearings helped legitimate the ousting of Nixon and thus television acted as a "unifying force."

28. Diamond, *The Tin Kazoo*, p. 53.

29. Graber, *Processing the News*, p. 208.

30. Ibid.

31. Gladys Engel Lang and Kurt Lang, *The Battle for Public Opinion: The President, the Press, and the Polls During Watergate* (New York: Columbia University Press, 1983), pp. 32–34.

32. Ibid., pp. 35–36.

33. Ibid., pp. 35–37.

34. Ibid., pp. 40–42.

35. Ibid., pp. 47–49.

36. Ibid., p. 49.

37. Ibid., p. 55.

38. Ibid., p. 49.

39. The *New York Times* was selected for this analysis because it is considered the American newspaper of record. It is therefore likely to have at least as extensive coverage of these events as other national newspapers and greater coverage than smaller local and regional papers. If saturation did not occur with *New York Times* coverage in these cases, then it is very unlikely to have occurred elsewhere. The *New York Times Index* (1979 to 1989) was used as the source for measuring coverage.

40. For example, two of the page one stories during the nine-day period (August 27–September 4, 1982) were on the front page of the second section, which focuses on New York City and regional news.

41. Scott Armstrong, "Iran-Contra: Was the Press Any Match for All the President's Men?" *Columbia Journalism Review* 29 (May–June 1990): 31-33.

42. The twenty-one months attributed to the Donovan case are misleading. The allegations surfaced in January 1981, during his confirmation hearings, and press coverage was high during those hearings. Once he was confirmed in February, there were no stories relating to the allegations until December of that year, a hiatus of nine months. The period of time between when the allegations resurfaced and when he was ultimately cleared was ten months. The thirty-three months of the Olson investigation is perhaps the most misleading. There were significant periods of down time in this investigation because of the extensive litigation that occurred over the special prosecutor's jurisdiction and, eventually, over the constitutionality of the arrangement itself. Actual investigation time was only about six months.

43. There was some effort by the Democrats to capitalize on the "sleaze factor" (the fact that so many Reagan appointees had been accused of wrongdoing) during the 1984 election campaign and the Meese investigation. However, there was no serious effort to imply that Reagan himself was involved in the alleged corruption.

44. The 1979 poll was conducted by ABC News on Tuesday, August 7. The sample size was 856 adults and the margin of error was 3.5 percent. In 1982 the Gallup Organization conducted a poll for *Newsweek* on June 2 and 3. The sample size was 519 adults and the margin of error plus or minus 5 percent. The results of this poll were published in "The Legacy of Watergate," *Newsweek*, June 14, 1982, pp. 36–45. In addition, an NBC News and Associated Press survey of opinion conducted June 14–15, 1982, among 1,597 adults, asked several questions regarding Watergate and its effects. The data set of the first poll was made available to me through the Roper Center at the University of Connecticut. *Newsweek* provided me with a computer printout with cross-tabulations of its data but the staff was unable to locate the tape of the data set. Information from the final poll is taken from a release from NBC News dated July 6, 1982. It is on file in the archives of the Roper Center.

45. The question read, "Thinking back to the 1970's, did you hear or read enough about Watergate to have an opinion about it? (If yes, ask) Do you think national politics is now less corrupt, more corrupt, or about the same as they were during the Watergate period?" 30 percent of the respondents answered no to the first part of the question.

46. The question read, "Some people believe that the disclosures of Watergate led to positive changes in many of our important democratic institutions; other people believe that some of these changes went too far or made things worse. For each of the following, please tell me if you think there have been changes for the better as a result of Watergate, or if you think changes have made things worse, or if you think there hasn't been any significant changes."

47. Epstein, *News from Nowhere*, pp. 215-20; Ranney, *Channels of Power*, pp.

58–62. For example, William Safire of the *New York Times* has been a vigorous proponent of the use of the special prosecutor. He also regularly labels political scandals with the appendage "-gate," suggesting their similarity to Watergate and thereby implying their seriousness and the possibility of a cover-up. Thus, the bungled Justice Department investigation into Billy Carter's connections with Libya was called "Billygate," and the failure to prosecute anyone for the pilfering of the 1980 Carter debate briefing book was labeled "Briefingate." Carter's former attorney general, Griffin Bell, suggests that Safire's motives may lie in his previous experience as a Nixon aide. "If Safire could demonstrate that other administrations played fast and loose with government, then the sins of the Nixon period would seem less sinful." Griffin B. Bell with Ronald J. Ostrow, *Taking Care of the Law* (New York: William Morrow, 1982), p. 207.

48. Critical articles were written by syndicated columnist Jack Anderson during the Jordan investigation and by William Safire during the Deaver investigation. One of Jordan's accusers told Anderson of his experiences of being interrogated by Arthur Christy, which led Anderson to suggest that the special prosecutor was working harder to disprove the accuser's story than he was to disprove Jordan's. See "Jordan's Nightlife under Scrutiny," *Washington Post*, March 17, 1980, p. C23; and "Jordan Investigators Battle Leaks," *Washington Post*, April 22, 1980, p. C8. The special prosecutor in the Deaver case described his relationship with Safire as antagonistic because he refused to give Safire an interview. Interview with Whitney North Seymour, November 30, 1989.

49. James C. McKay, *Report of Independent Counsel In Re Edwin Meese III*, Washington, D.C., July 5, 1988.

50. Special Committee to Study Federal Law Enforcement Agencies, *Removing Political Influence from the Federal Law Enforcement Agencies* (Washington, D.C.: The American Bar Association, 1975), pp. 12–13, 49–75; and *Preventing Improper Influence on Federal Law Enforcement Agencies* (Washington, D.C.: The American Bar Association, 1976), pp. 18–20, 81–110.

51. Quoted in Robert W. Meserve, *The American Bar Association: A Brief History and Appreciation* (New York: Newcome Society, 1973), p. 8.

52. American Bar Association, *Model Rules of Professional Conduct and Code of Judicial Conduct* (Washington, D.C.: American Bar Association, 1983), p. 9.

53. Ibid., pp. 9–10.

54. Ibid., p. 10.

55. Ibid.

56. Interview with Robert Evans, Washington, D.C., October 16, 1984.

57. Ibid.

58. Ibid.

59. Interview with Robert Evans, Washington, D.C., June 27, 1989.

60. John W. Gardner, *In Common Cause*, rev. ed. (New York: W. W. Norton, 1973). Gardner wrote on the need for the new lobby: "No serious observer can read the results of these surveys without uneasiness. The statistics are a prescription for social disaster. When citizens cease to have confidence in their own institutions, the nation is in trouble" (p. 25).

61. Andrew S. McFarland, *Common Cause: Lobbying in the Public Interest* (Chatham, N.J.: Chatham House Publishers, 1984), p. 8.

62. Gardner, *In Common Cause*, p. 31.

63. Ibid., p. 16.

64. McFarland, *Common Cause*, pp. 9–16. See also chapter 3 of this book.

65. Ibid., p. 19.

66. Ibid.

67. Interview with Marcy Frosh and Mike Mawby, Washington, D.C., October 17, 1989.

68. Interview with Jay Hedlund, Washington, D.C., October 17, 1984.

69. Ibid. See also Memorandum of Common Cause as *Amicus Curiae* in Support of the Constitutionality of the Special Prosecutor Law, *Kraft v. Gallinghouse*, CA No. 2952 (filed D.D.C., January 15, 1981).

70. Interview with Frosh and Mawby.

71. Hedlund interview.

72. Ibid.

73. *Testimony of Archibald Cox, Chairman of Common Cause, on the Independent Counsel Provisions of the Ethics in Government Act before the Subcommittee on Administrative Law and Governmental Relations of the House Judiciary Committee*, April 23, 1987 (copy obtained from Common Cause).

74. Interview with Frosh and Mawby.

75. Hedlund interview.

76. Ibid.

77. Ibid.; Evans interview; Frosh and Mawby interview; interview with Lloyd Cutler, Washington D.C., October 15, 1984.

78. Interviews with Mary Gerwin, Washington, D.C., October 16, 1984 and July 17, 1989; interview with Elise Bean, Washington, D.C., July 14, 1989.

79. 28 U.S.C. 595(e).

80. Interview with Rudolf Giuliani, New York City, January 24, 1985.

81. Those stating this position wished not to be identified.

82. Interview with Philip Heymann, Harvard Law School, Cambridge, Mass., March 26, 1985.

83. Ibid.

84. Interview with Marshall Jarret, Washington, D.C., June 27, 1985.

85. Interview with Gerald McDowell, Washington, D.C., June 28, 1989.

86. Interview with Richard Beizer, Washington, D.C., April 26, 1985.

87. Nadine Cohodas, "The Special Prosecutor as Special Protector," *Congressional Quarterly Weekly Report* 43 (March 2, 1985): 423. Interview with Archibald Cox, Cambridge, Mass., February 5, 1985.

88. Interview with David Zerhusen, Washington, D.C., June 28, 1989.

89. Lippmann, *Phantom Public*, pp. 68–69.

90. Lang and Lang, *Battle*, p. 100.

91. Ibid., p. 105.

92. Ibid., p. 133.

93. Lippmann, *Phantom Public*, p. 69.

94. Edelman, *Symbolic Uses of Politics*, p. 172.

95. Lang and Lang, *Battle*, p. 301.

96. Ibid., p. 300.

CHAPTER 9. ON "THE NECESSITY OF AUXILIARY PRECAUTIONS"

1. Benjamin R. Civiletti, "Post-Watergate Legislation in Retrospect," *Southwestern Law Journal* 34 (1981): 1061.

2. See, for example, Stephen L. Carter, "Comment: The Independent Counsel

Mess," *Harvard Law Review* 102 (1988): 105; and Terry Eastland, *Ethics, Politics, and the Independent Counsel* (Washington, D.C.: National Legal Center for the Public Interest, 1989), pp. 99-120.

3. Interview with Gerald McDowell, Public Integrity Section Chief, Washington, D.C., June 28, 1989.

4. Seymour M. Hersh, "The Iran-Contra Committees: Did They Protect Reagan?" *New York Times Magazine*, April 29, 1990, p. 64.

5. Interview with Mary Gerwin, Washington, D.C., July 17, 1989.

6. "Don't Wallow in the Iran Scandal," *The New York Times*, March 11, 1987, p. 26.

7. Ruth Marcus, "The World Series of White-Collar Crime," *Washington Post National Weekly Edition*, May 4, 1987, p. 13.

8. Ibid.

9. *United States v. North*, 910 F.2d 843 (D.C.Cir. 1990); Joan Biskupic, "Hill Reconsiders Immunity as North Case Is Set Back," *Congressional Quarterly Weekly Report*, 48 (August 18, 1990): 2668-72.

10. Harold Hongju Koh, *The National Security Constitution: Sharing Power after the Iran-Contra Affair* (New Haven, Conn.: Yale University Press, 1990), pp. 22-23.

11. Some opponents of the independent counsel arrangement tend to view all of the cases as resulting from Congress's desire to control the executive. See for example Gordon Crovitz, "The Criminalization of Politics," in *The Imperial Congress: Crisis in the Separation of Powers*, eds. Gordon S. Jones and John A. Marini, pp. 239-67 (New York: Pharos Books, 1988).

12. Interview with John Nields, Chief Counsel for the House Select Committee to Investigate Covert Arms Transactions with Iran, Washington, D.C., October 16, 1989; and William S. Cohen and George J. Mitchell, *Men of Zeal* (New York: Viking Press, 1988).

13. Lawrence Walsh, *Independent Counsel's Report to the Subcommittee on Legislation of the Permanent Select Committee on Intelligence of the U.S. House of Representatives*, September 19, 1989 (photocopy obtained from Office of Independent Counsel).

14. Dennis F. Thompson, *Political Ethics and Public Office* (Cambridge, Mass.: Harvard University Press, 1987), p. 40.

15. Ibid.

16. Glen Craney, "North Verdict Ends Chapter, But Story Continues On," *Congressional Quarterly Weekly Report* 47 (6 May 1989): 1055-56; "North Sentence: Maybe His Defense Worked," *The National Law Journal*, July 17, 1989, p. 6; "Excerpts from Remarks at Sentencing of North," *The New York Times*, July 6, 1989, p. 9.

17. Theodore Draper, "How Not to Deal with the Iran-Contra Crimes," *New York Review of Books*, June 14, 1990, p. 39.

18. Ibid., p. 44.

19. Ibid.

20. Eastland, *Ethics, Politics, and the Independent Counsel*, pp. 124-26.

21. Kenneth Mann discusses the ambiguity of many white-collar crime statutes in *Defending White Collar Crime* (New Haven, Conn.: Yale University Press, 1985), pp. 11-13.

22. John G. Peters and Susan Welch, "Political Corruption in America: A Search for Definitions and a Theory," *American Political Science Review* 72 (September 1978): 979.

23. Thompson, *Political Ethics*, p. 67.

24. Peters and Welsh, "Political Corruption," p. 979. This problem is becoming evident in efforts to enforce the lobbying restrictions of the Ethics in Government Act. The conviction of Lynn Nofziger under the act was overturned by an appeals court because of ambiguities in the language of the act as it applied to his case. *United States v. Nofziger*, 878 F.2d 442 (D.C.Cir. 1989).

25. Laura Shill Schrager and James F. Short, Jr., "How Serious a Crime? Perceptions of Organizational and Common Crimes," in *White Collar Crime*, eds. Gilbert Geis and Ezra Stotland, pp. 14–31 (Beverly Hills, Calif.: Sage Publications, 1980).

26. David R. Simon and D. Stanley Eitzen, *Elite Deviance*, 2d ed. (Boston: Allyn and Bacon, 1986).

27. Jeffrey Toobin, *Opening Arguments: A Young Lawyer's First Case, United States v. Oliver North* (New York: Viking, 1991), pp. 63–72.

28. James Madison, "Federalist 51," in *The Federalist Papers* (New York: Penguin Books, 1987).

BIBLIOGRAPHY

BOOKS

American Bar Association. *Model Rules of Professional Conduct and Code of Judicial Conduct*. Washington, D.C.: American Bar Association, 1983.
_____. Section on Criminal Justice. *Report to the House of Delegates*. Washington, D.C.: American Bar Association, 1987.
Association of the Bar of the City of New York. *Conflict of Interest and the Federal Service*. Cambridge, Mass.: Harvard University Press, 1960.
Bell, Griffin B. with Ronald J. Ostrow. *Taking Care of the Law*. New York: William Morrow, 1982.
Ben-Veniste, Richard, and George Frampton, Jr. *Stonewall: The Real Story of the Watergate Prosecution*. New York: Simon and Schuster, 1977.
Berg, Larry L., Harlan Hahn, and John R. Schmidhauser. *Corruption in the American Political System*. Morristown, N.J.: General Learning Press, 1976.
Bernstein, Carl, and Bob Woodward. *All the President's Men*. New York: Simon and Schuster, 1974.
Beyer, Barry. *Thomas E. Dewey, 1937–1947: A Study in Political Leadership*. New York: Garland, 1979.
Blumberg, Abraham S. *Criminal Justice*. Chicago: Quadrangle Books, 1967.
Bolles, Blair. *Men of Good Intentions: Crisis of the American Presidency*. Garden City, N.Y.: Doubleday, 1960.
Cater, Douglas. *Power in Washington*. New York: Random House, 1964.
Cohen, William S., and George J. Mitchell. *Men of Zeal*. New York: Viking Press, 1988.
Crovitz, L. Gordon, and Jeremy Radkin, eds. *The Fettered Presidency: Legal Constraints on the Executive Branch*. Washington, D.C.: American Enterprise Institute, 1989.
Cummings, Homer, and Carl McFarland. *Federal Justice*. New York: Macmillan, 1937.
Dash, Samuel. *Chief Counsel: Inside the Ervin Committee—The Untold Story of Watergate*. New York: Random House, 1976.
Davis, Kenneth Culp. *Discretionary Justice: A Preliminary Inquiry*. Baton Rouge: Louisiana State University Press, 1969.
Dean, John W. *Blind Ambition: The White House Years*. New York: Simon and Schuster, 1976.
Denhardt, Katherine G. *The Ethics of Public Service*. New York: Greenwood Press, 1988.
Diamond, Edwin. *The Tin Kazoo*. Cambridge, Mass.: MIT Press, 1975.
Donovan, Robert J. *Tumultuous Years: The Presidency of Harry S. Truman, 1949–1953*. New York: W. W. Norton, 1982.
Douglas, Jack D., and John M. Johnson, eds. *Official Deviance: Readings in Malfeasance, Misfeasance, and Other Forms of Corruption*. Philadelphia: J. B. Lippincott, 1977.

Doyle, James. *Not above the Law: The Battles of Watergate Prosecutors Cox and Jaworski*. New York: William Morrow, 1977.

Draper, Theodore. *A Very Thin Line: The Iran-Contra Affairs*. New York: Hill and Wang, 1991.

Eastland, Terry. *Ethics, Politics, and the Independent Counsel*. Washington, D.C.: National Legal Center for the Public Interest, 1989.

Edelman, Murray. *The Symbolic Uses of Politics*. Urbana: University of Illinois Press, 1964.

Eisenstadt, Abraham S., Ari Hoogenboom, and Hans L. Trefousse, eds. *Before Watergate: Problems of Corruption in American Society*. New York: Brooklyn College Press, 1978.

Eisenstein, James. *Counsel for the United States: U.S. Attorneys in the Political and Legal Systems*. Baltimore: John Hopkins University Press, 1978.

_____. *Politics and the Legal Process*. New York: Harper and Row, 1973.

Epstein, Edward Jay. *News from Nowhere*. New York: Random House, 1973.

Erlichman, John. *Witness to Power: The Nixon Years*. New York: Simon and Schuster, 1982.

Ervin, Samuel. *The Whole Truth: The Watergate Conspiracy*. New York: Random House, 1980.

Ferrell, Robert H. *Harry S. Truman and the Modern American Presidency*. Boston: Little, Brown, 1983.

Fisher, Louis. *Constitutional Conflicts between Congress and the President*. 3d ed., revised. Lawrence: University Press of Kansas, 1991.

_____. *Constitutional Dialogues*. Princeton, N.J.: Princeton University Press, 1988.

_____. *The Politics of Shared Power: Congress and the Executive*. 2d ed. Washington, D.C.: Congressional Quarterly, 1987.

Gardner, John W. *In Common Cause*. Revised edition. New York: W. W. Norton, 1973.

Goldwin, Robert, A., and Art Kaufman, eds. *Separation of Powers—Does It Still Work?* Washington, D.C.: American Enterprise Institute, 1986.

Graber, Doris. *Mass Media and American Politics*. 2d ed. Washington, D.C.: Congressional Quarterly Press, 1984.

_____. *Processing the News: How People Tame the Information Tide*. New York: Longman, 1984.

Haldeman, H. R. *The Ends of Power*. New York: Times Books, 1978.

Huston, Luther A. *The Department of Justice*. New York: Frederick A. Praeger, 1967.

Jones, Gordon S., and John A. Marini, eds. *The Imperial Congress: Crisis in the Separation of Powers*. New York: Pharos Books, 1988.

Key, V. O. *Public Opinion and American Democracy*. New York: Alfred A. Knopf, 1965.

Kingdon, John W. *Congressmen's Voting Decisions*. 2d ed. New York: Harper and Row, 1981.

Koh, Harold Hongju. *The National Security Constitution: Sharing Power after the Iran-Contra Affair*. New Haven, Conn.: Yale University Press, 1990.

Kurland, Phillip. *Watergate and the Constitution*. Chicago: University of Chicago Press, 1978.

Kutler, Stanley I. *The Wars of Watergate*. New York: Alfred A. Knopf, 1990.

Lang, Gladys Engel, and Kurt Lang. *Politics and Television: Re-Viewed*. Beverly Hills, Calif.: Sage Publications, 1984.

_____. *The Battle for Public Opinion: The President, the Press, and the Polls during Watergate.* New York: Columbia University Press, 1983.

Lippmann, Walter. *The Phantom Public.* New York: Macmillan, 1927.

McDonald, William F., ed. *The Prosecutor.* Beverly Hills, Calif.: Sage Publications, 1979.

McFarland, Andrew S. *Common Cause: Lobbying in the Public Interest.* Chatham, N.J.: Chatham House Publishers, 1984.

Manheim, Jarol B. *Déjà Vu: American Political Problems in Historical Perspective.* New York: St. Martin's Press, 1976.

Mann, Kenneth. *Defending White Collar Crime.* New Haven, Conn.: Yale University Press, 1985.

Manning, Bayless. *Federal Conflict of Interest Law.* Cambridge, Mass.: Harvard University Press, 1964.

Marshall, Burke, ed. *A Workable Government? The Constitution after 200 Years.* New York: W. W. Norton, 1987.

Mayhew, David. *Congress: The Electoral Connection.* New Haven, Conn.: Yale University Press, 1974.

Merry, Henry J. *Five Branch Government: The Full Measure of Constitutional Checks and Balances.* Urbana: University of Illinois Press, 1980.

Meserve, Robert W. *The American Bar Association: A Brief History and Appreciation.* New York: Necome Society, 1973.

Morris, Newbold. *Let the Chips Fall: My Battles with Corruption.* New York: Appleton-Century-Crofts, 1955.

Mosher, Frederick C. *Watergate: Implications for Responsible Government.* New York: Basic Books, 1974.

Navasky, Victor. *Kennedy Justice.* New York: Atheneum, 1971.

Neuman, W. Russell. *The Paradox of Mass Politics: Knowledge and Opinion in the American Electorate.* Cambridge, Mass.: Harvard University Press, 1986.

Nixon, Richard M. *RN: Memoirs of Richard Nixon.* New York: Grosset and Dunlap, 1978.

Noggle, Burt. *Teapot Dome: Oil and Politics in the 1920's.* Baton Rouge: Louisiana State University Press, 1962.

Ogul, Morris. *Congress Oversees the Bureaucracy.* Pittsburgh: University of Pittsburgh Press, 1976.

Polsby, Nelson. *Congress and the Presidency.* 4th ed. Englewood Cliffs, N.J.: Prentice-Hall, 1986.

Pomper, Gerald, et al. *The Election of 1976: Reports and Interpretations.* New York: David McKay, 1977.

Principles of Federal Prosecution. Washington, D.C.: Department of Justice, 1980.

Ranney, Austin. *Channels of Power: The Impact of Television on American Politics.* New York: Basic Books, 1983.

Report of the Congressional Committees Investigating the Iran-Contra Affair. Abridged ed. New York: Times Books, 1988.

Richardson, Elliot. *The Creative Balance.* New York: Holt, Rinehart, and Winston, 1976.

Ripley, Randall B. *Congress: Process and Policy.* 4th ed. New York: W. W. Norton, 1988.

Ripley, Randall B., and Grace A. Franklin. *Congress, the Bureaucracy, and Public Policy.* 3d ed. Homewood, Ill.: Dorsey Press, 1984.

Rossiter, Clinton, ed. *The Federalist Papers.* New York: New American Library, 1961.

Schlozman, Kay L., and John T. Tierney. *Organized Interests and American Democracy.* New York: Harper and Row, 1986.

Seidman, Harold. *Politics, Position and Power: The Dynamics of Federal Organization.* 3d ed. New York: Oxford University Press, 1980.

Sirica, John. *To Set the Record Straight: The Break-in, the Tapes, and the Pardon.* New York: W. W. Norton, 1979.

Smith, Richard Norton. *Thomas E. Dewey and His Times.* New York: Simon and Schuster, 1982.

Sorenson, Theodore. *Watchmen in the Night: Presidential Accountability after Watergate.* Cambridge, Mass.: MIT Press, 1975.

Special Committee to Study Federal Law Enforcement Agencies. *Preventing Improper Influence on Federal Law Enforcement Agencies.* Washington, D.C.: American Bar Association, 1976.

————. *Removing Political Influence from Federal Law Enforcement Agencies.* Washington, D.C.: American Bar Association, 1975.

Sundquist, James. *The Decline and Resurgence of Congress.* Washington, D.C.: Brookings Institution, 1981.

Thompson, Denise F. *Political Ethics and Public Office.* Cambridge, Mass.: Harvard University Press, 1987.

Thompson, Fred. *At That Point in Time: The Inside Story of the Watergate Committee.* New York: Quadrangle/New York Times Books, 1975.

Toobin, Jeffrey. *Opening Arguments: A Young Lawyer's First Case, United States v. Oliver North.* New York: Viking, 1991.

Vaughn, Robert G. *Conflict of Interest Regulation in the Federal Executive Branch.* Lexington, Mass.: D. C. Heath, 1979.

Vile, M. J. C. *Constitutionalism and the Separation of Powers.* Oxford: Clarendon Press, 1967.

Watergate and the White House: June 1972–July 1973. Vol. 1. New York: Facts on File, 1973.

Watergate and the White House: July–December 1973. Vol. 2. New York: Facts on File, 1974.

Watergate and the White House: January–September 1974. Vol. 3. New York: Facts on File, 1974.

Winter, Ralph K. *Watergate and the Law: Political Campaigns and Presidential Power.* Washington, D.C.: American Enterprise Institute, 1974.

Woodward, C. Vann, ed. *Responses of the Presidents to Charges of Misconduct.* New York: Delacorte Press, 1974.

ARTICLES

Albert, Lee A., and Larry G. Simon. "Enforcing Subpoenas against the President: The Question of Mr. Jaworski's Authority." *Columbia Law Review* 24 (1974): 545–60.

Alschuler, Albert. "The Defense Attorney's Role in Plea Bargaining." *Yale Law Journal* 84 (1975): 1179–1314.

————. "The Prosecutor's Role in Plea Bargaining." *University of Chicago Law Review* 36 (1968): 50–112.

Armstrong, Scott. "Iran-Contra: Was the Press Any Match for All the President's Men?" *Columbia Journalism Review* 29 (May/June 1990): 27–35.

Baker, Howard H., Jr. "The Proposed Judicially Appointed Independent Office of Public Attorney: Some Constitutional Objectives and an Alternative." *Southwestern Law Journal* 29 (1975): 671–83.

Bertozzi, Mark. "The Federal Special Prosecutor: Too Special?" *Federal Bar News and Journal* 29 (1982): 222–30.

_____. "Separating Politics from the Administration of Justice: The Role of the Federal Special Prosecutor." *Judicature* 67 (May 1984): 486–98.

Carter, Stephen L. "Comment: The Independent Counsel Mess." *Harvard Law Review* 102 (1988): 105–41.

Christman, Kenneth W. "The Limits of Presidential Removal Power." *Ohio State Law Journal* 35 (1974): 513–31.

Cohadas, Nadine. "Meese Is Confirmed by Senate in Unusual Saturday Session." *Congressional Quarterly Weekly Report* 43 (March 2, 1985): 385.

_____. "The Special Prosecutor as Special Protector." *Congressional Quarterly Weekly Report* 43 (March 2, 1985): 423.

Cole, George F. "The Decision to Prosecute." *Law and Society Review* 4 (February 1970): 313–43.

"Congress's Popularity Lower than Ford's." *Current Opinion* 3 (April 1975): 34.

Cooper, Ann. "Watergate-Inspired Bill May Force House to Vote on Korea Probe Issue." *Congressional Quarterly Weekly Report* 36 (March 18, 1978): 683.

Cutler, Lloyd N. "Conflicts of Interest." *Emory Law Journal* 30 (1981): 1015–17.

_____. "A Proposal for a Continuing Public Prosecutor." *Hastings Constitutional Law Quarterly* 2 (1975): 21–25.

Dam, Kenneth W. "The Special Responsibility of Lawyers in the Executive Branch." *Chicago Bar Record* 55 (1974): 4–12.

Diamond, Edwin. "The Folks in the Boondocks: Challenging the Journalistic Myth." *Columbia Journalism Review* (November–December 1973): 58–59.

Draper, Theodore. "Rewriting the Iran-Contra Story." *New York Review of Books* (January 19, 1989): 38–45.

Dudley, Earl, Jr. "Morrison v. Olson: A Modest Assessment. *American University Law Review* 38 (Winter 1989): 255–74.

Elving, Ronald D., and Janet Hook. "The Reagan Presidency Fades into the Twilight." *Congressional Quarterly Weekly Report* 45 (October 17, 1987): 2499–2503.

Goodpaster, Gary. "Rules of the Game: Comments on Three Views of the Independent Counsel Case." *American University Law Review* 38 (Winter 1989): 383–93.

"Increase in Approval of Congress." *Current Opinion* 2 (October 1974): 119.

Johnson, James N. "The Influence of Politics upon the Office of the American Prosecutor." *American Journal of Criminal Law* 2 (1973): 187–215.

Johnstone, John W. C., Edward J. Slawski, and William W. Bowman. "The Professional Values of American Newsmen." *Public Opinion Quarterly* 36 (Winter 1972-1973): 522–40.

Kaiser, Frederick M. "Federal Law Enforcement: Structure and Reorganization." *Criminal Justice Review* 5 (Fall 1980): 101–18.

Kramer, Victor, and Louis P. Smith. "The Special Prosecutor Act: Proposals for 1983." *Minnesota Law Review* 66 (1982): 963–96.

Krent, Harold. "Separating the Strands in Separation of Powers Controversies." *Virginia Law Review* 74 (1988): 1253–84.

Kutner, Luis. "Nixon v. Cox: Due Process of Executive Authority." *St. John's Law Review* 48 (March 1974): 441–60.

Lang, Gladys Engel, and Kurt Lang. "Televised Hearings: The Impact Out There." *Columbia Journalism Review* 12 (November–December 1973): 52–57.

Link, Mary. "Senate Prepares to Debate Watergate Reform Measure." *Congressional Quarterly Weekly Report* 34 (July 17, 1976): 1903–4.

_____. "Senate Passes Watergate Reform Measure with Administration Changes." *Congressional Quarterly Weekly Report* 34 (July 24, 1976): 1953–54.

Logan, David. "Historical Uses of a Special Prosecutor." Congressional Research Service, 1973.

Malbin, Michael. "Legislative-Executive Lessons from the Iran-Contra Affair." In *Congress Reconsidered*, 4th ed., edited by Lawrance C. Dodd and Bruce I. Oppenheimer, 375–392. Washington, D.C.: Congressional Quarterly Press, 1989.

Maskell, Jack. "Independent Investigations of Allegations of Wrongdoing by Members of Congress." Congressional Research Service, July 6, 1988.

Miller, Arthur S. "The Attorney General as the President's Lawyer." In *Roles of the Attorney General of the United States*, pp. 41–70. Washington, D.C.: American Enterprise Institute, 1968.

Miller, Arthur, Edie N. Goldenberg, and Lutz Ebring. "Type-Set Politics: Impact of Newspapers on Public Confidence." *American Political Science Review* 73 (March 1979): 67–84.

Mixter, Stephen C. "The Ethics in Government Act of 1978: Problems with the Attorney General's Discretion and Proposals for Reform." *Duke Law Journal* 1985: 497–522.

"More Confidence in Leadership." *Current Opinion* 5 (1977): 3.

Nadjari, Maurice H. "New York State's Office of Special Prosecutor: A Creation Born of Necessity." *Hofstra Law Review* 2 (1974): 97–124.

"New Senate Bill Allows Special Prosecutor, Sets Financial Disclosure." *Congressional Quarterly Weekly Report* 35 (June 18, 1977): 1235–6.

O'Keefe, Constance, and Peter Safirstein. "Fallen Angels, Separation of Powers, and the Saturday Night Massacre: An Examination of the Practical, Constitutional, and Political Tensions in the Special Prosecutor Provisions of the Ethics in Government Act." *Brooklyn Law Review* 49 (Fall 1982): 113–47.

Palmer, Robert. "The Confrontation of the Legislative and Executive Branches: An Examination of the Constitutional Balance of Power and the Role of the Attorney General." *Pepperdine Law Review* 11 (1984): 331–53.

"Priorities for New Congress." *Current Opinion* 4 (December 1976): 128.

"Removing Politics from the Justice Department: Constitutional Problems with Institutional Reform." *New York University Law Review* 50 (1975): 366–435.

Robinson, Michael J. "The Impact of the Televised Watergate Hearings." *Journal of Communication* 24 (Spring 1974): 17–30.

_____. "Public Affairs Television and the Growth of Political Malaise: The Case of 'The Selling of the Pentagon.'" *American Political Science Review* 70 (June 1976): 409–10.

Rosenberg, Morton. "Congressional Control of Agency Decisions and Decisionmakers: The Unitary Executive Theory and Separation of Powers." Congressional Research Service, 1987.

Simon, Donald J. "The Constitutionality of the Special Prosecutor Law." *University of Michigan Journal of Law Reform* 16 (1982): 45–73.

"The Special Prosecutor in the Federal System: A Proposal." *American Criminal Law Review* 11 (Spring 1977): 577–638.

"Symposium on Special Prosecutors and the Role of Independent Counsel." *Hofstra Law Review* 16 (Fall 1987).

Tiefer, Charles. "The Constitutionality of Independent Officers as Checks on Abuses of Executive Power." *Boston University Law Review* 63 (January 1983): 59–103.

Timbers, Edwin. "Legal and Institutional Aspects of the Iran-Contra Affair." *Presidential Studies Quarterly* 20 (Winter 1990): 31–41.

Turkheimer, Frank M. "The Executive Investigates Itself." *California Law Review* 65 (1977): 597–635.

Walsh, Lawrence E. "The Independent Counsel and the Separation of Powers." *Houston Law Review* 25 (January 1988): 1–11.

"Watergate Chronology of 1973." In *Congressional Quarterly Almanac 1973*. Washington, D.C.: Congressional Quarterly, 1974.

Woldman, Joel. "Congress and the Iran-Contra Affair." Congressional Research Service, November 1988.

Weaver, Paul. "Is Television News Biased?" *Public Interest* No. 26 (Winter 1972): 57–74.

PUBLIC DOCUMENTS

Brief Amicus Curiae of the American Civil Liberties Union in Support of Brief of Appellant. *United States v. North*, No. 89-3118. Filed D.C.Cir. December 20, 1989.

Brief of Appellant. *United States v. North*, No. 89-3118. Filed D.C.Cir. November 22, 1989.

Brief of Appellant. *United States v. Poindexter*, No. 90-3125. Filed D.C.Cir. December 14, 1990.

Brief of Appellee. *United States v. North*, No. 89-3118. Filed D.C.Cir. December 22, 1989.

Brief of Appellee. *United States v. Poindexter*, No. 90-3125. Filed D.C.Cir. January 18, 1991.

Christy, Arthur. *Report of the Special Prosecutor on Alleged Possession of Cocaine by Hamilton Jordan in Violation of 21 U.S.C. Sec. 844(a)*, New York. Washington, D.C., May 28, 1980.

Curran, Paul. *Investigation of Carter's Warehouse and the National Bank of Georgia. Report to the Congress of the United States*. October 1979.

Executive Branch Lobbying: Report to Congress by Independent Counsel in the Michael Deaver Case. Washington, D.C.: Government Printing Office, 1989.

Gallinghouse, Gerald. *In Re Investigation of Allegations Concerning Timothy E. Kraft: Report of Special Prosecutor in Compliance with 28 U.S.C. 595(b)*, New Orleans. Washington, D.C., January 15, 1982.

McKay, James. *Report of Independent Counsel in Re Edwin Meese III*. Washington, D.C., July 5, 1988.

Morrison, Alexia. *In Re Theodore B. Olson and Robert M. Perry: Report of the Independent Counsel*. Washington, D.C.: December 27, 1988.

Office of Independent Counsel. *Independent Counsel's Report to the Subcommittee on Legislation of the Permanent Select Committee on Intelligence of the United States House of Representatives*. September 19, 1989. (Photocopy obtained from the Office of Independent Counsel.)

Silverman, Leon. *Report of the Special Prosecutor*. Washington, D.C. June 25, 1982.

Stein, Jacob. *Report of the Independent Counsel Concerning Edwin Meese III.* Washington, D.C. September 20, 1984.

U.S., Congress. House. Committee on the Judiciary. *Investigation of the Department of Justice. Hearings before the Special Subcommittee to Investigate the Justice Department,* 82d Cong., 2d sess., 1952.

———. Ways and Means Committee. *Final Report of the Subcommittee on Administration of Revenue Laws,* 82d Cong., 2d sess., 1952.

———. Committee on the Judiciary. *Special Prosecutor and Watergate Grand Jury Legislation. Hearings before the Subcommittee on Criminal Justice,* 93d Cong., 1st sess., 1973.

———. Committee on the Judiciary. *Provision for Special Prosecutor. Hearings before the Subcommittee on Criminal Justice,* 94th Cong., 2d sess., 1976.

———. Committee on the Judiciary. *Amendment of the Special Prosecutor Provisions of Title 28. Hearings before the Subcommittee on Administrative Law and Governmental Relations,* 97th Cong., 2d sess., 1982.

———. Committee on the Judiciary. *Report on the Investigation of the Role of the Department of Justice in the Withholding of Environmental Protection Agency Documents from Congress in 1982-1983.* 98th Cong., 1st sess., 1985.

———. *Independent Counsel Reauthorization Act of 1987.* Conference Report. H.R. 100-452, 100th Cong., 1st sess., 1987.

U.S. Congress. Senate. Committee on Public Lands and Surveys. *Leases upon Naval Oil Reserves,* 68th Cong., 1st sess., 1923.

———. Committee on the Judiciary. *Nomination of Elliot Richardson to Be Attorney General,* 93d Cong., 1st sess., 1973.

———. Committee on the Judiciary. *Special Prosecutor,* 93d Cong., 1st sess., 1973.

———. Committee on the Judiciary. *Removing Politics from the Administration of Justice. Hearings before the Subcommittee on the Separation of Powers,* 93d Cong., 2d sess., 1974.

———. Select Committee on Presidential Campaign Activities. *Final Report,* S. Rept. 93-981, 93d Cong., 2d sess., 1974.

———. Committee on Government Operations. *Watergate Reorganization and Reform Act of 1975. Part I,* 94th Cong., 1st sess., 1975.

———. Committee on Government Operations. *Watergate Reorganization and Reform Act of 1975. Part II,* 94th Cong., 2d sess., 1976.

———. Committee on Governmental Affairs. *Public Officials Integrity Act of 1977, Blind Trusts, and Other Conflict of Interest Matters,* 95th Cong., 1st sess., 1977.

———. Committee on Governmental Affairs. *The Ethics in Government Act of 1978.* S. Rept. March 16, 1977. Reprinted in *U.S. Code Congressional and Administrative News* 95-170, 95th Cong., 2d sess., 1978. (Saint Paul, Minn.: West Publishing, 1979.

———. Committee on Governmental Affairs. *Special Prosecutor Provisions of the Ethics in Government Act of 1978. Hearings before the Subcommittee on Oversight of Government Management,* 97th Cong., 1st sess., 1981.

———. Committee on Governmental Affairs. *Ethics in Government Act Amendments of 1982. Hearings before the Subcommittee on Oversight of Government Management,* 97th Cong., 2d sess., 1982.

———. Committee on Governmental Affairs. *Independent Counsel Reauthorization Act of 1987.* S. Rept. 100-123, 100th Cong., 1st sess., 1987.

U.S. Congress. House Select Committee to Investigate Covert Arms Transactions with Iran and Senate Select Committee on Secret Military Assistance to Iran and the Nicaraguan Opposition. *Report of the Congressional Committees Investigating the Iran-Contra Affair.* H. R. 100-433, Senate Report No. 216, 100th Cong., 1st sess., 1987.

U.S. Department of Justice. Attorney General. *Report of the Department of Justice Regarding Richard V. Allen's Ethics in Government Act Disclosure Report.* Washington, D.C. December 22, 1981.

———. Attorney General. *Report of the Attorney General Pursuant to 28 U.S.C. sec. 592(b).* Filed with the United States Court of Appeals for the District of Columbia Circuit, Special Prosecutor Division. February 1, 1979.

———. Attorney General. *Report of the Attorney General Pursuant to 28 U.S.C. 592(b). Subject: Assistant to the President for National Security Affairs Richard Allen.* Filed with the United States Court of Appeals for the District of Columbia Circuit, Special Prosecutor Division. December 22, 1981.

Watergate Special Prosecution Force. *Report.* Washington, D.C., 1975.

CASES CITED

Banzhaf v. Smith, 588 F.Supp. 1498 (D.D.C. 1984), *vacated* 737 F.2d 1167 (D.C. Cir. 1984).

Bowsher v. Synar, 478 U.S. 714 (1986).

Boyd v. United States, 345 F.Supp. 790 (E.D.N.Y. 1972).

Deaver v. Seymour, 656 F.Supp. 900 (D.D.C. 1987).

Dellums v. Smith, 573 F.Supp. 1489 (N.D.Cal. 1983).

Dellums v. Smith, 577 F.Supp. 1449 (N.D.Cal. 1984).

Dellums v. Smith, 797 F.2d 817 (9th Cir. 1986).

Ex Parte Siebold, 100 U.S. 371 (1897).

Hobsen v. Hansen, 265 F.Supp. 902 (D.D.C. 1967).

Humphrey's Executor v. United States, 295 U.S. 602 (1935).

In Re Theodore Olson, 818 F.2d 34 (D.C. Cir. 1987).

In Re Sealed Case, 665 F.Supp 56 (D.D.C. 1987).

In Re Sealed Case, 666 F.Supp 231 (D.D.C. 1987), *affd.,* 829 F.2d 50 (D.C.Cir. 1987).

In Re Sealed Case, 827 F.2d. 776 (D.C. Cir. 1987).

In Re Sealed Case, 838 F.2d 476 (D.C. Cir. 1988).

INS v. Chadha, 462 U.S. 919 (1983).

In the Matter of Hennan, 83 U.S. 230 (1834).

Milliken v. Stone, 7 F.2d 397 (S.D.N.Y. 1925).

Mistretta v. United States, 488 U.S. 361 (1989).

Morrison v. Olson, 487 U.S. 654 (1988).

Moses v. Kennedy, 219 F.Supp. 762 (D.D.C. 1963).

Nader v. Bork, 366 F.Supp. 104 (D.D.C. 1973).

Nathan v. Attorney General, 563 F.Supp. 815 (D.D.C. 1983), *reversed,* 737 F.2d 1069 (D.C. Cir. 1984).

Newman v. United States, 382 F.2d 479 (D.C. Cir. 1967).

Nixon v. Sirica, 487 F.2d 700 (D.C. Cir. 1973).

North v. Walsh, 656 F.Supp. 414 (D.D.C. 1987).

Ponzi v. Fessenden, 258 U.S. 244 (1922).

Powell v. Katzenbach, 359 F.2d 234 (D.C. Cir. 1965).

Pugach v. Klein, 193 F.Supp. 634 (S.D.N.Y. 1961).
Springer v. Philippines, 277 U.S. 189 (1928).
The Confiscation Cases, 74 U.S. (7 Wall.) 458 (1868).
United States v. Cox, 342 F.2d 167 (5th Cir. 1965), *cert. den.* 381 U.S. 935 (1965).
United States v. Fernandez, 887 F.2d 465 (4th Cir. 1989).
United States v. House of Representatives, 556 F.Supp 150 (D.D.C. 1983).
United States v. Marzano, 149 F.2d 923 (2d Cir. 1945).
United States v. Nixon, 418 U.S. 683 (1974).
United States v. Nofziger, 878 F.2d 442 (D.C. Cir. 1989).
United States v. North, 910 F.2d 843 (D.C. Cir. 1990).
United States v. North, 920 F.2d 940 (D.C. Cir. 1990).
United States v. Poindexter, 698 F.Supp. 300 (D.D.C. 1988).
United States v. Poindexter, 859 F.2d 216 (D.C. Cir. 1988).
United States v. San Jacinto Tin Co., 125 U.S. 279 (1887).
United States v. Solomon, 216 F.Supp. 835 (S.D.N.Y. 1963).
Weiner v. U.S., 357 U.S. 349 (1958).
Youngstown Sheet and Tube v. Sawyer, 343 U.S. 579 (1952).

ARCHIVAL MATERIALS

Jaworski, Leon. Papers. Texas Collection. Baylor University. Waco, Texas.
Pomerene, Atlee. Papers. Teapot Dome files. National Archives, Washington, D.C.
Roberts, Owen. Papers. Teapot Dome files. National Archives, Washington, D.C.
Seidman, Harold. Papers. "Oral History Interview with Dr. Harold Seidman," transcript of interview conducted by Jerry Hess, 1970. University of Connecticut, Storrs. Original in Truman Library, Independence, Mo.

PERSONAL INTERVIEWS

Austern, David, deputy independent counsel in first Meese investigation. Washington, D.C., October 19, 1984.
Barcella, E. Lawrence, defense attorney for Lynn Nofziger. Washington, D.C., June 30, 1989. (Joint interview with Robert Plotkin)
Bean, Elise, staff counsel, Subcommittee on Oversight of Government Management. Washington, D.C., July 14, 1989.
Beizer, Richard, deputy independent counsel in first Meese investigation. Washington, D.C., April 26, 1985.
Bensfield, James, deputy independent counsel in first Meese investigation. Washington, D.C., May 1, 1985.
Bruce, Carol, deputy independent counsel in second Meese investigation. Washington, D.C., July 13, 1989. (Joint interview with James McKay)
Christy, Arthur, special prosecutor in Jordan investigation. New York, N.Y., September 17, 1984.
Civiletti, Benjamin, attorney general in Carter administration. Washington, D.C., October 19, 1984.
Cox, Archibald, Watergate special prosecutor and Harvard law professor. Cambridge, Mass., February 5, 1985.

Curran, Paul, special counsel in Carter warehouse investigation. New York, N.Y., January 25, 1985.

Cutler, Lloyd, White House counsel in Carter administration. Washington, D.C., October 15, 1984.

Davis, Gary, Office of Government Ethics. Telephone interview. July 11, 1989.

Dennis, Edward, Department of Justice in Reagan and Bush administrations. Washington, D.C., June 29, 1989.

Dudley, Earl, Jr., deputy independent counsel in Olson investigation. Arlington, Va., July 13, 1989.

Evans, Robert, American Bar Association. Washington, D.C., October 16, 1984, and June 27, 1989.

Fielding, Fred, White House counsel in Reagan administration. Washington, D.C., July 19, 1989.

Frampton, George, Watergate Special Prosecution Force and deputy independent counsel in first Meese investigation. Washington, D.C., October 19, 1984.

Frosh, Marcy, Common Cause. Washington, D.C., October 17, 1989. (Joint interview with Mike Mawby)

Gallinghouse, Gerald, special prosecutor in Kraft investigation. Telephone interview. October 28, 1985.

Gerwin, Mary, minority staff counsel on Subcommittee on Oversight of Government Management. Washington, D.C., October 16, 1984, and July 17, 1989.

Giuliani, Rudolf, Department of Justice and U.S. attorney for Southern District of New York. New York, N.Y., January 24, 1985.

Green, Thomas, defense attorney for Kraft. Washington, D.C., May 5, 1985.

Greiner, Stephen, assistant special prosecutor in Jordan case. New York, N.Y., September 25, 1984.

Hedlund, Jay, Common Cause. Washington, D.C., October 17, 1984.

Heymann, Philip, Watergate Special Prosecution Force, Department of Justice in Carter administration, Harvard law professor. Cambridge, Mass., March 26, 1985.

Jarret, Marshall, Public Integrity Section of Department of Justice. Washington, D.C., June 27, 1985.

Joseph, Gregory P., assistant special prosecutor in Donovan case. New York, N.Y., September 25, 1984.

Lumbard, Edward, member of special division of court. New York, N.Y., January 29, 1985.

McDowell, Gerald, Public Integrity Section of Department of Justice. Washington, D.C., June 28, 1989.

McKay, James, independent counsel for Nofziger investigation and second Meese investigation. Washington, D.C., July 13, 1989. (Joint interview with Carol Bruce)

MacKinnon, George E., member of special division of court. Washington, D.C., July 17, 1989.

Martin, Thomas, defense attorney for Olson. Washington, D.C., June 28, 1989. (Joint interview with David Zerhusen)

Mawby, Mike, Common Cause. Washington, D.C., October 17, 1989. (Joint interview with Marcy Frosh)

Miller, Jack, defense attorney for Deaver. Washington, D.C., July 18, 1989. (Joint interview with Randall Turk)

Morgan, Peter, defense attorney for Meese. Washington, D.C., May 8, 1985. (Joint interview with Paul Stevens)

Morrison, Alexia, independent counsel in Olson investigation. Washington, D.C., July 21, 1989.

Nealon, Arthur, assistant special prosecutor in Jordan case. New York, N.Y., September 24, 1984.

Nields, John, chief counsel for House Select Committee to Investigate Covert Arms Transactions with Iran. Washington, D.C., October 16, 1989.

Olson, Theodore, Department of Justice in Reagan administration and target of independent counsel investigation. Washington, D.C., October 15, 1990.

Plotkin, Robert, defense attorney for Lynn Nofziger. Washington, D.C., June 30, 1989. (Joint interview with E. Lawrence Bercella)

Richter, Robert, formerly with Public Integrity Section of Department of Justice. Washington, D.C., July 1, 1985.

Schwartz, Bart, assistant special prosecutor in Donovan investigation. New York, N.Y., January 24, 1985.

Seymour, Whitney North, independent counsel in Deaver investigation. Telephone interview. November 30, 1989.

Shattuck, William, counsel for House Subcommittee on Administrative Law and Governmental Relations. Washington, D.C., July 1, 1985.

Silverman, Leon, special prosecutor in Donovan case. New York, N.Y., September 25, 1984.

Stein, Jacob, independent counsel for first Meese investigation. Telephone interview. May 2, 1985.

Stevens, Paul, defense attorney for Meese. Washington, D.C., May 8, 1985. (Joint interview with Peter Morgan)

Turk, Randall, defense attorney for Deaver. Washington, D.C., July 18, 1989. (Joint interview with Jack Miller)

Zerhusen, David, defense attorney for Olson. Washington, D.C., June 28, 1989. (Joint interview with Thomas Martin)

INDEX

CLASSIC

Date 6/2005

Initials CJW-BRfAL

Initials _____